citizen
brand

citizen brand

10 Commandments for Transforming Brands in a Consumer Democracy

marc gobé

ALLWORTH PRESS
NEW YORK

© 2002 Marc Gobé

07   06   05   04   03   02   5   4   3   2   1

Published by Allworth Press
An imprint of Allworth Communications
10 East 23rd Street, New York, NY 10010

Cover design by Joan O'Connor
Page design by Phyllis Aragaki
Page composition/typography by Sharp Des!gns, Lansing, MI

LIBRARY OF CONGRESS CATALOGING-IN-PUBLICATION DATA
Gobé, Marc.
Citizen brand : 10 commandments for transforming brand culture in a consumer democracy / Marc Gobé.
   p.   cm.
Includes bibliographical references and index.
ISBN 1-58115-240-X
1. Brand name products. 2. Brand name products—Marketing. 3. Consumers' preferences. 4. Motivation research (Marketing) I. Title: 10 commandments for transforming brand culture in a consumer democracy. II. Title: Ten commandments for transforming brand culture in a consumer democracy. III. Title.
HD69.B7 G6 2002
658.8'27—dc21
                                         2002009119

Printed in Canada

"We need discussions about whether the rich world is giving back what it should in the developing world."

–Kofi Annan, Secretary General of the United Nations

table of contents

foreword

Not so long ago, when marketing folks talked about brands, they were really only talking about the product, its qualities, price, and function. Later, marketers developed perceived benefits, those additional and sometimes questionable qualities that were ascribed to the products they were promoting. More recently, we have witnessed the emergence of lifestyle associations with brands; communication aimed at engaging consumers with the product, not so much for what it does but for what it says about the person who buys, wears, eats, or uses it. The fact is that great brands have personalities; they have attitude and they give greater depth and meaning to the product. Just think of Timberland, Coca-Cola, Disney, or Starbucks. In highly competitive markets, the brand creates choices and helps consumers make decisions about what they want to buy.

The evolutionary process continues apace with what Marc Gobé describes as the emergence of the "Citizen Brand." The Citizen Brand is built around the increasing significance of the emotional content and the actual relevance to the consumer of, not just the brand, but also the company behind it. That's something I can relate to both as a consumer and as a businessman.

The fact is that a great brand is more than simply a great marketing campaign or product. Increasingly, brands will reflect the deeper personalities, culture, and behaviors of the organization that gives birth to them rather than simply offering consumers a hollow creative form generated by a marketing agency. It's this deeper relationship that The Body Shop typifies in its commitment to strong ethical practices and campaigns to protect the environment and promote human rights. These are strong and distinct attributes of the company and they're reflected, not just in the way the products are made, but also in how the company talks to its consumers. The same is becoming increasingly true for business in general. The rising tide of anti-globalization protests and the targeting of companies is just one of the factors moving businesses toward a more meaningful relationship with their consumers, the communities in which they operate, and wide stakeholder groups.

There are a number of reasons why *a citizen approach is becoming more mainstream and complementary, if not essential, to operating as a successful business.*

First, the use of cause-related marketing to promote brands and put the feel-good factor into business is a popular strategy for many companies. Recent research by the organization Business in the Community found that 81 percent of U.K. consumers agreed that, when price and quality are equal, they would switch brands or change retail outlets to a company that is trying to benefit society. Consumers will more often than not engage with the ethics of a business through its cause-related marketing activities. *However, simply using good causes to promote the company or its product will not be good enough in itself.* The consumer is increasingly wary and cynical of business and wants to see evidence that the company lives up to the values that it promotes.

Secondly, there are those companies that are trying to deal with reputational issues, those such as Monsanto, Rio Tinto, or Nike. There's another side to the increasing influence and profile of business and brands—the scrutiny of media and interest groups. It's one of the reasons why in recent years we have seen an upsurge in companies around the globe, spanning a broad range of sectors, beginning to embrace this new philosophy of "corporate citizenship." These companies are seeking to gain broader trust and legitimacy through active engagement with their stakeholders and public disclosure of their social and environmental performance.

The companies leading the way include some of those most noted in the past for their place at the top of interest groups' "hit" lists such as Shell–with many others from the oil, mining, tobacco, nuclear, and drug industries following suit. These are companies that have realized the importance, not just of reputation management, but also of the need to build long-term trust and engagement with their consumers. The question increasingly being asked by commentators such as Naomi Klein in her book *No Logo* and others in the forefront of the anti-globalization debate is, what is the reality behind the brands that are increasingly designed to reflect our lifestyles, to reflect the sort of persons we are or aspire to be, the values with which we wish to be associated?

Finally, there are those companies that take an ethical approach in the way they operate; Patagonia and Ben and Jerry's, along with The Body Shop, are examples. For these companies there is no other way of doing business–ethics are fundamental to their way of thinking and of operating. What's interesting is that such an approach, which a decade or so ago would have been considered not only unconventional, but also unworkable, is today the magnetic north toward which other businesses are increasingly pointing.

One very tangible example of what this sort of approach looks like is The Body Shop Community Trade program. This involves the company in sourcing raw materials for inclusion in some of their best-selling products, from cocoa butter to babassu oil, as well as accessory items including massagers from India and baskets from the Philippines. The Community Trade Program is aimed at small producer communities around the world who supply The Body Shop with accessories and natural ingredients. Fair prices help producers to feed, clothe, and educate their families and allow money to go back into the community to supply basic needs such as water, health, and education. But what's more important than the financial value is the day-to-day impact of this program on people's lives.

The Body Shop Community Trade program is unusual but not unique; others, such as Starbucks, have set up their own relationships resulting in support for hundreds of people in building livelihoods for themselves and their families. The Body Shop program has also brought educational and health benefits to many of its suppliers. Two of the longest standing suppliers, Teddy Exports in India and Get

Paper Industries in Nepal, have, with support from The Body Shop, set up AIDS-awareness projects that now attract international funding.

So this is one example of great business practices combining with the responsible sourcing of ingredients and products. It also provides a source of engaging and very real stories about the way a company's trade positively touches the lives of people.

I don't just recount this story because of my previous role as chief executive of the noted "green" retailer. I say this as a businessman who came from a more traditional commercial background with companies such as Groupe Danone. The drive toward greater transparency, more honesty, respect, and thoughtfulness in the how and why you do business are essential ingredients in the molding of the businesses and brands of the future.

The evidence suggests that business, the consumer, and wider stakeholder groups all benefit from a more ethical approach to doing business. Consumers, particularly in markets such as the United Kingdom, increasingly expect business to be socially responsible, and it makes a profound difference to their perception of a company, loyalty to its products, and purchasing preferences. Welcome to the shape of the future, the Citizen Brand.

–Patrick Gournay, former CEO, The Body Shop International

acknowledgments

In preparing for *Citizen Brand*, I have had the honor and pleasure of meeting with and interviewing CEOs and marketing visionaries of major corporations from the world of art, fashion, beauty, home improvement, pharmaceuticals, car manufacturing, and mass transportation. Their insights have influenced my thinking about Citizen Brand, but, most importantly, they inspired and motivated me as I wrote this book. Patrick Gournay, then CEO of The Body Shop International; Sidney Taurel, chairman, president, and CEO of Eli Lilly; Patrick Spainhour, chairman and CEO of Ann Taylor; Steve McCraken, president of DuPont Apparel and Textile Sciences; Matthew Rubel, chairman and CEO of Cole Haan; Brian Kennedy, executive vice president of sales and marketing of the Hertz Corporation; Mike Wells, vice president of marketing for Lexus; Tom Kowaleski, vice president of global products for General Motors; Dick Sullivan, former senior vice president of marketing for Home Depot; Ira Livingston, senior vice president of marketing information at Cotton Incorporated; Ben Hartley of Ben Hartley Consulting, formerly of the Guggenheim Museum; Jeffrey Levine and Eric Olson, respectively, vice president for marketing and communication, and director of design at BAM; and Steve McIvor, head of communications for The Body Shop International, all gave me precious time out of their busy schedules. I want to thank them for sharing their vision with me.

I also want to thank all the numerous friends, whose unprompted contribution through casual conversations or examples led me to explore new ideas and sometimes redirect some of my thinking; among them, H. Kaneda, Grégoire Sentilhes, Raymond Debbanne, Jean Chabre, Geneviève Rosenvallon, Robin Lewis, Michael Bierut for loaning me his new version of the Enron logo, my two daughters, Emilie and Gwenaelle, and, most important of all, my father.

I have to acknowledge, again in this book, the extraordinary effort of Alisa Clark, who took on this book as project manager, writing consultant, and research activist. Her contribution was fundamental in bringing this book to completion; her intuitive and conceptual skills as well as her understanding of branding were essential in supporting this project and keeping it moving forward, given my otherwise very active life as a branding professional. Tabby McDaniel's input on African-American and diversity issues was insightful and relevant; as a professional photographer, she has an eye for trends and changes in our society. My assistant Valérie Le Deroff brought her organizational skills to help complete this project smoothly. I also want to thank my partners in the company, Peter Levine, Phyllis Aragaki, and David Ashen for their input and vision. Thanks to the talented and dedicated staff at Allworth Press for their belief in and commitment to my writing projects.

Citizen Brands in a Consumer Democracy

This book updates and further develops the concept of Emotional Branding explored in my first book, *Emotional Branding: The New Paradigm for Connecting Brands to People* (Allworth Press, 2001). Emotional Branding–the idea that, beyond a product's offering its functional benefits, people today are keenly interested in buying an *emotional experience*–has had terrific appeal, because it represents not only a new branding process, but an entire *philosophy* and a *motivational* tool that reaches beyond mere observations to inspire *creative solutions.* As I said at the conclusion of my last book, the lofty goal of connecting brands with people on the level of their deepest desires is a complex one. The Emotional Branding strategy was the result of an ongoing exploration of ways of thinking outside the box about what really makes people love a particular brand. I predicted that there would be many more evolutions to the focus and scope around the Emotional Branding concept, and here I will introduce you to the most recent expansion in my thinking about Emotional Branding. This book will explore a new concept called "Citizen Brand," which I believe encapsulates the essence of the Emotional Branding strategy and responds to the most recent crucial evolutions of the way people view corporations and branding in a changing global world.

At the conclusion of my last book I emphasized the concept that, in a society where change is the norm, a book is more potent if treated as a work in progress than it is as the "be-all, end-all," of a particular idea. *A posteriori*, the premise of Emotional Branding has revealed itself to be a much bigger idea than I originally thought. Work by internationally recognized academics, neurologists, and philosophers, some of which I will discuss throughout the book, confirms that there is a collective uncovering and recognition of the "emotion factor" today, which reflects a profound change in our society.

Subsequent to the successful launch of *Emotional Branding*, and in the process of preparing for the numerous conferences where I was privileged to be invited to speak, I have continued to be very motivated in an ongoing process of discovery in this amazing new field. And now I want to share with you these new thoughts and observations as they apply to the concept of Citizen Brand. Once again, as in my last book, I will often be looking through the lens of my experience as a designer and relying a lot on "guts and intuition."

One thing I have consistently observed is that not all brands are created equal. Brands that have achieved an emotional relevancy in people's lives are, quite simply, responding to one

People need to believe in and trust their brands.

fundamental, new, consumer expectation: People need to believe in and trust their brands. I am intrigued by the factors inherent in our positive perception of an "emotional brand," and in trying to elucidate these factors, I have realized that emotional brands seem to share a common set of values that elevate them to this sought-after status. In fact, most emotional brands seem to share the three following traits:

1. *A great corporate culture focused above all on people*, both in the office and in the public community
2. *A communication style and philosophy that stands out from the crowd*, as in the case of Apple or Target, where the look of the products and the feel of the advertising are consistent
3. *An emotional hook that draws us to their promise*, or, in other words, a value proposition that reinforces a brand commitment to their audience

In this new book, *Citizen Brand* (which, by the way, has no connection with *Citizen Kane*, except perhaps as an antithesis to the detachment from humanity that this character embodied), I will explore these ideas, showing you how these three elements combine to build a brand culture that can motivate people–both employees and con-sumers–to become passionate about a brand. And I will show you strong evidence as to why corporations today must be built on trust and ethics with a real dedication to being part of human solutions around the world. I believe quite simply that these are the corpora-tions that will survive. Most importantly, I want to share with you a prevailing and converging idea that *in a global world influenced more and more by local politics, religious upheaval, and social aware-ness, the role of businesses will change in a dramatic way. The need to reassess one's corporate responsibility is critical in a changed world.*

The focus here is not neces-sarily to provide any cut-and-dry solutions or draw a dramatic conclusion, but to challenge the present in order to better understand the future. I will rely on what a designer is best at: cross-societal observations, assessing technological changes and the role culture, art, and communications have and will play as prophets and ambassadors of a changed universe.

The focus here is not necessarily to provide any cut-and-dry solutions or draw a dramatic conclusion, but to challenge the present in order to better understand the future.

As a constant backdrop to the Citizen Brand concept, I will focus on the two most powerful emotions known to man–love and fear–and the importance of their roles in clarifying a branding paradigm and changing a brand's perception from negative to positive.

Like pop-culture hero Harry Potter–a seemingly normal boy who suddenly discovers he is a wizard and is thrust into finding solutions to totally unexpected, otherworldly challenges "on the fly"–we are no longer able to rely in the least bit on past experiences to solve today's problems. The perspective embodied in this book is meant to serve as a tool for the transformation of attitude necessary for facing this uncertain future. The narrative is meant to be a real emotional adventure. You might feel at times engaged, surprised, or even sus-picious, but I sincerely doubt that these observations will leave you cold. It is my profound wish to engage you in a real reevaluation about what might help corporations become more relevant in a new global world.

The Meaning of Brands Will Never Be the Same

The concept behind my first book needed to be updated based on recent and defining events that happened before, on, and since September 11 (as a New Yorker I have lived the tragedy in a personal way, and I am still spiritually and emotionally struck by it). The world we have known will never be the same. In the two years since my first book came out, we have seen an economy go from glorious to bust and have witnessed the end of the dot.com bubble. We have also seen the first serious activist movement by youth against globalization and against the role the World Bank has played in poorer nations. Major books and publications on the negative impact of branding as a predatory and manipulative marketing approach have become best sellers. And, of course, we have witnessed the crash of Enron, one of the most successful New Age businesses in this country that turned out to be the most crooked and greedy–a disgrace to our free economy and an example that will create more scrutiny by people on business in general. Most important of all, though, the first major attack against U.S. civilians on their own soil by a group of determined terrorists under the guise of religion has changed the way our world will see itself.

What all of this will mean for U.S. national and global corporations in managing their brands is clearly a topic to be discussed. A new debate needs to be held on the future of branding as a marketing tool. How corporations will conduct business in the future will need to be completely rethought to reflect the huge change in the world. U.S.

corporations, for instance, will receive a new focus of attention from dissidents at home and activists abroad who might find a great opportunity to make their complaints heard by burning a McDonald's or boycotting a particular U.S. product. Brands will be negatively manipulated by some political groups as a means to show their resentment of the power of the United States as a dominant military, political, cultural, and business entity. The rest of the Western world will not escape this resistance and will need to be prepared to react to a new world.

The entire notion of a "consumer society and free markets" will be challenged and sometimes vilified. What has come through in a major way for many following the tragedy of September 11 is that the vast discrepancy that exists between poor and rich nations can no longer be ignored or denied. What good is our progress if half of the world is barely surviving at our doorstep? Branding as a conduit to an intimate emotional connection can become a unique way to close the gap between cultures, people, and societies in a decent way. This is the way corporations' roles will have to evolve in the future if they want their brands to be loved by people.

I am pleased to report that a lot of corporations have already begun to move in the direction of building a corporate culture based on social responsibility and that some have created initiatives well worth considering as examples. Actually, I was surprised by the monumental efforts undertaken by some businesses in terms of practicing this concept of brand citizenship. *In this book, through the lens of my now somewhat famous "Ten Commandments of Emotional Branding," I will review the dos and don'ts for creating emotionally relevant brands and show the clear path for corporations to succeed through using "citizenship" to connect with people on a global level in an emotionally positive way.*

People Love "Good" Brands

Before introducing you to this new world of the Citizen Brand, I want to address a key consumer issue of our time that has served as a launching pad for the Citizen Brand concept. This is the idea, which has been growing in popularity, that consumerism and brands are "bad" because large corporations are controlling the world through globalization, the perception that people are powerless against omnipotent, soulless corporations who routinely abuse both the environment and the rights of the people. This *anti-consumerism philosophy* of resentment set forth in a handful of best-selling anti-branding books over the past year, has clearly touched a nerve with the public. We have witnessed a corresponding trend of consumer backlash propagated by a new generation of activists attacking specific corporations and brands instead of (or in addition to) policies and governments. However, I believe that the real importance of this trend lies in its existence as an indicator that *the all-powerful consumer today expects a deepening level of emotional commitment, sincerity, and social responsibility from brands and corporations*–and not as a movement toward anti-consumerism per se.

I would argue that contrary to feeling that brands are bad, most consumers today feel that brands are an essential element of their lives, creating jobs and serving as guarantors of a level of quality of product and experience. Brands simplify the lives of busy, time-starved consumers, helping them to make choices in an overcrowded market. But even more important is the fact that people love "good" brands. "Good" brands can make us feel secure and they can make us dream. They can bring fun, hope, sensory experience, comfort, and an overall added dimension of personality into what can be perceived as a cold, high-tech world. A truly "good" brand can even represent the qualities we seek most in friends and family–qualities like warmth, familiarity, and trust.

Of course it does happen that corporations commit evil deeds, but when it does, people everywhere find out about it–and fast. People today have an unsurpassed access to information through technology and a strong desire to know the truth about the brands they are supporting. They understand their own power in the market. They are extremely marketing savvy and very aware of the fact that they have thousands of products or services to choose from every time they make a purchase. Corporations and brands, not unlike politicians, are elected every day by people. Consumers vote with their wallets. As Rita Clifton, Chief Executive of Interbrand, puts it, "Brands are the ultimate accountable institution. If people fall out of love with your brand, you go out of business."[1]

It is time that businesses everywhere understood that *brands do not belong to corporations but to people–and this is even more the case with brands that have managed to capture people's hearts and become truly "emotional" brands, because the strong bond they have built with people create a true sense of "ownership."*

Forgetting that human emotion is the key to success in this marketplace is like forgetting that oxygen is the most important element for our survival. But still today I find that few realize the emotional power and support that can be gained by practicing a new kind of people-driven marketing.

In my first book, *Emotional Branding*, I examined why and how some brands are better able to establish an emotional identity than others–why some brands are perceived differently in the marketplace. Some brands are well known and enjoy a very high score of "awareness," but they are not necessarily preferred or loved. Many corporations still confuse awareness with emotional connection–but the truth is very different. The challenge is to evolve the existing concept of corporate identity (C.I.), which is "corporate-driven," toward an emotional identity (E.I.), a people-driven approach. Brands with a strong E.I. component resonate emotionally in our lives. This is because emotions are quite simply the conduit that best connects brands with people, elevating our perception of a product or service to the level of aspiration. *Corporate-driven messages need to be replaced by people-centric dialogues.* Consumers today not only want to be *romanced* by the brands they choose to bring into their lives– they absolutely want to establish a multifaceted, holistic *relationship* with that brand, and this means that they expect the brand to play a positive, pro-active role in their lives, which goes far beyond a mere business transaction and into the realm of the emotional. How to become a brand with E.I.? This book will investigate the very important connection between the internal culture of a company and the external expression of the brand. *Corporations with E.I. have an imaginative and innovative culture turned toward people (a "citizen culture"), exemplified by the extra steps they take in knowing and serving well the communities in which they operate.*

Brands with E.I. own a unique visual and verbal vocabulary, one that stands out from the crowd. Apple, Target, Starbucks, and Coca-Cola have responded to this challenge, but many haven't. Like people, most brands have definite character and personality. You remember people because of their look, style, intellect, charisma, and involve-

Takara's lemon taste with a Braille message on the can's lid.

ment in their community. When meeting with someone, if asked the question, "Who are you?" answering, "I don't know; whatever you want me to be," would not help you make a huge impact or prompt respect from the person asking! *Successful brands articulate a strong vision through verbal and visual traits consistent with their image and relevant to their audience.* Sony is about innovation, Target is about the joy of shopping, and Apple is about accessibility and design for people. Remember this when your brand has to answer the question, "Who are you?"

It is my very strong belief that design is one of the best conduits to help corporations answer this question and show their true colors and thinking. The Emotional Identity approach is at the core of a Citizen Brand culture. It is about creating products whose beauty and functionality help us live our lives better. This is good business–that extra touch that demonstrates that people come first in a corporation. All brand communications–from environmental to products to marketing messages and the look of corporate offices–send strong messages about a corporation's E.I. (or a lack thereof) that could make a lasting impression on people. *It could mean something as simple (and brilliant!) as having Braille messages on a can lid,* as one Japanese sake product does. This is not only a great statement for visually impaired people but also sends a strong emotional message to the rest of us.

Market insights based on people's aspirations and supported by innovation, is what makes Emotional Branding the new marketing paradigm and the force that will change corporate culture. It's not just a new marketing technique but a fundamental value-driven solution to connect brands to people in a powerful, relevant, and meaningful way. It's about "ideas you can see."

It is clear that consumers today are open as never before to a real emotional connection with brands.

It is clear that *consumers today are open as never before to a real emotional connection with brands,* and I will show you here the ways in which this openness is manifesting itself with people today and how brands can respond by building and refining a powerful E.I.

The New Emotional Landscape

There have been times in history, such as at the end of the eighteenth century during the Romantic movement, when emotion has been in great favor and has permeated people's lives. And today, again, this philosophy has appeared, in contrast to the psychology of last century's industrial age that largely saw emotions as a flaw in comportment and a handicap. This new emotions-driven philosophy declares that, in the words of Michel Lacroix, author of *The Cult of Emotion,*[2] "We are as much 'homo-sentiens' as 'homo-sapiens.'"

Emotions are in fact serving to fill the vacuum caused by the disappearance of what Ernst Bloch called the "hope principle." This vacuum is a result of a major weakening of religious and political ideologies, the end of the utopian "class struggle," and the dehumanization brought on by new technologies, which is in some ways perceived by people as a loss of control over their future.

So, as passive spectators of this new world, since we often cannot act, we emotionalize. The desire for change that may now seem impossible on the outside is redirected toward our internal lives. People are thirsty for strong sensory emotions. *We have become sensation seekers.* But today, not only do we "emotionalize" as individuals, we also want to emotionally vibrate *together.* We have the need to seek and embrace groups that will share and enhance our emotional experience. There is a recognition of the tremendous influence and power in collective emotion. In Salt Lake City, the uproar caused by the audience and reflected by the media during the Winter Olympics regarding the unfair treatment of the Canadian skating team led to the discovery of a judge-fixing scandal! In an unusual decision, the I.O.C. and I.S.U. presidents Jacques Rogge and Ottavio Cinquanta decided to award a second set of gold medals to the Canadian team in pair skating.

We are seeing major trends toward a "tribalization" and ethnic regrouping, which are a direct result of people's need to magnify their personal experiences in the context of a group. In a recent *New York Times Magazine* article entitled, "In My Tribe,"[3] the author states, "It may be true that 'never-marrieds' are saving themselves for something better." That something better is a tribe of close-knit friends, and he explains that he is using the concept of "tribe" quite literally. It is "a tight group, with unspoken roles and hierarchies, whose members think of each other as 'us' and the rest of the world as 'them.' This bond is clearest in times of trouble, when our instinct to protect the group is no different from what I'd feel for my family."

"Cities," he continues, ". . . are not emotional wastelands where fragile individuals with arrested development mope around self-indulgently searching for true love. There are rich landscapes filled with urban tribes. *Tribal behavior does not prove a loss of family values . . . it is a fresh expression of them.*" *Seinfeld* and *Friends* indeed are great mirror images of this concept. Does this mean that the cult of the individual is dead? Yes, if it is about self-interest. But if it is individuality expressed as part of a group or tribe, then it is very relevant. The comfort and safety of the group is the perfect environment for legitimate, heartfelt individual expression. CK1 and Abercrombie & Fitch were among the first brands to show an understanding of the importance of this new cultural switch with advertising images portraying groups of young people from a vast array of ethnic and cultural backgrounds, clearly individuals but bound together as a tribe of friends.

From a branding perspective, these fundamental social changes are at the core of a new marketing paradigm. Emotional Branding represents a profound social evolution and change in consumer expectations that needs to be recognized. How does that translate?

Technology has reduced our need to exert ourselves in physical labor, and instead we put ourselves into activities that bring jubilation and ecstasy. We are no longer satisfied with pure athleticism in sports, but prefer activities that deliver a "sensorial high," such as skateboarding, surfing, and rafting. For this reason, emotionally charged

Emotional Branding represents a profound social evolution and change in consumer expectations that needs to be recognized.

programs such as *Survivor*, which balance danger, physical prowess, and euphoria, are major hits. The immense appeal of snowboarding during the 2002 Salt Lake City Winter Olympics is a huge tribute to this theory. Free from the need for intense physical, muscular efforts, the body is also free to enjoy the pleasure of the senses.

Instead of watching or experiencing tragedies or victories in our own homes, we share our pleasure and grief together in the street. We demand from our politicians that they share their own emotions, and at our work, training programs on how to be a team player and being open to share affective thoughts are encouraged. *To manage and exploit the power of emotions as a group has become a most-encouraged skill.*

On the branding front, according to Michel Lacroix, Coca-Cola offered in 2000 a prize promotion based on the senses. Winners visited a "destination for all the senses": a visit to the Grand Canyon in a helicopter ("sight"); a snowboarding trek in the snowy mountains of Chile ("touch"); participation in the Carnival of Brazil ("hearing"); a "hot flavored" adventure through Sri Lanka on the back of an elephant ("taste"); a jet-ski ride in Tahiti in the fragrant winds of the Pacific ("smell"). The great success of food and beverage products with energizing properties such as Red Bull, Gatorade, the Power Bar; the rise of aromatherapy; and the popularity of extreme sports all bear testament to our need to optimize feelings and energy, to balance our emotional strength (the mind) with physical pleasure (the body) through increased sensations. We'll also increasingly see enhanced sensory experiences in places of work, and sensory propositions where products are sold. Advertising images will not show individuals as perfect, monolithic icons, but as participants in enhanced emotional experiences. In fact, *this search by contemporary human beings for emotional and sensorial experiences is more than an escape–it is a desire to find one's true self.* This contemporary quest for individual fulfillment leads to a rich life that is authentic, human, and the key to human development. You are "it"! You are a tribe, you are a cult, you are complex!

Who Are the True Citizens?

This new cult of emotions and tribal experience is even more potent now after the tragic events of terrorism and worldwide economic challenges, both of which will have an effect on everybody's life for some time.

The World Trade Center disaster was a great lesson in the power of emotions and the way that corporations can respond with sensitivity to people in a time of tragedy. As we all witnessed, even before their governments could react, the free world was bonding spontaneously and powerfully together in support of the American people. People from all nations offered their services. People from all over joined in the biggest worldwide peace rally ever put together, carrying candles in the street, showing their grief and disgust. People cared! Even the French leftist newspaper *Le Monde* titled their September 13 issue, "We are all Americans."

One might ask why there was such renewed global and unconditional support for the United States? America, like other countries, is

Le Monde's headline, September 13, 2001, issue: "We are all Americans."

of course a branded entity; with its flag, "the stars and stripes," and its national anthem, it is a country like any other. It has to compete with other nations on a global level to bring security and prosperity to its citizens–even more so today. *America* as a concept, on the other hand, is not really a physical place. America is an aspiration. It is about hope, freedom, equality, and opportunity. It is about being a destination and safe haven for people, offering liberty and justice for all! *The attack on the World Trade Center was an attack not only on the United States but on values shared by the rest of the free world.* America indeed has transcended its political meaning to become the powerful emotional attribute of the United Stated brand, and the very concept of "America" was attacked.

The connection to branding is interesting. Again, it reinforces the notion that Emotional brands–whether political or commercial–do not belong to corporations or countries but to people! Is there a lesson for corporations to learn from how people supported the brand America in such a trying time?

Some businesses recognized that a unique and historic time existed for them to show their true "citizen colors." Observing how corporations reacted to the awful drama of the World Trade Center disaster shows us that some brands care, and they have proven to us all that we do not exist in a world where **Some businesses recognized that a unique and historic time existed for them to show their true "citizen colors."** people and corporations are two different entities, constantly at odds with each other. They showed that *people as employers, people as employees, people as buyers, and people as sellers can all share the same values* and all be a part of a solution. In the support category, marketers from all over the world responded with donations, either monetary or in-kind, that were previously unheard of. More than $100 million for the families of the victims, for the United Way and the Red Cross, for the rescue and clean-up operations. Brands like Coca-Cola, Gatorade, Crystal Geyser, and Home Depot donated free supplies, logistics, and help of all kinds for the volunteers. Coke pledged $12 million for disaster relief, half of it for the Red Cross. General Electric, Cisco Systems, Dassault Falcon, Microsoft, Daimler Chrysler, Kellogg's, McDonald's, Burger King, Wal-Mart, and Michelin were among the first to contribute. Insurance companies like Allstate spent a huge amount on advertising to reassure its clients that their claims would be addressed quickly, asking people to contact them without hesitation and setting up special information desks. Allstate lived up to its slogan of "you're in good hands" by alleviating people's fears and building trust with them in their weakest states. Corporations accepted a new role during this crisis, and participated along with people in their sorrow–the right way to do it.

The weekend after the attack, almost every ad in the *New York Times* expressed support and sympathy for the American people. The entire weekend edition of the *Times*, which of course is huge, was filled with patriotic messages like this one from Kenneth Cole: "What we stand for is more important than what we stand in." Ensuing branding efforts over the next several weeks–such as GM's very successful "Keep America Rolling" campaign, which displayed moving, people-oriented imagery imbued with a subtle patriotism and announced a 0-percent financing promotion for cars in light of the difficulties America faced–showed exactly who understood the mood of the country and rallied to convey sympathy. On the other hand, the airlines largely missed their own opportunity to "keep American flying" by not reassuring people that it was safe to fly, and by not acknowledging the tragedy and people's emotional state quickly and with enough sensitivity. There were many other lessons to learn and questions raised from corporate responses to this unprecedented tragedy–in some cases it seemed that brands were capitalizing on the unfortunate situation by "pat on the back" ads touting how much they had donated, while other companies floundered by playing on people's fears instead of inspiring hope. Emotions are incredibly potent, as we all know, and there are no exact formulas. If the wrong note is sounded, it could be devastating to a brand's future. This event is indeed very fertile ground for illustration of the Citizen Brand concept and because of that, it is a topic I will touch on at various points in this book.

Branding, with its unique ability to motivate and convince, suddenly takes on the added role of being part of an economic solution.

One of the results of all of this is that branding, with its unique ability to motivate and convince, suddenly takes on the added role of being part of an economic solution. But to be successful and gain consumer trust and support today, corporations must demonstrate that they will operate in a completely different manner and connect in a more profound way with consumers, developing their own

"America"–a value-driven rallying point for people to meet behind and buy not only products, but also, and most importantly, a corporate ethic.

"Patriotic Shoppers" in a New Market Economy

Unfortunately, branding is a concept that is most often abandoned by many companies in challenging times. But the fact is, the old corporate mantra–to focus on the bottom line instead of on people's needs–only creates short-term solutions and long-term, irreparable damage. This is truly sad in light of the fact that people still want very much to be convinced of a brand's aspirational value and are very willing to fall in love with brands. Take for example the phenomenon of the "patriotic shopper," which appeared shortly after the September 11 terrorist attacks. *Days later people actually went out to shop to show their support for businesses and the economy*–not because they really needed to be shopping for anything. This shows that consumers do indeed understand that they are in a partnership with brands that

USA Today, October 2001 article about patriotic shopping.

cannot exist without their support. But brands themselves need to realize this elemental fact and find a way to connect to this kind of fierce emotions-based loyalty!

Clearly, in a changed world we must reevaluate our entire approach to branding and advertising communications. Remi Babinet, a leading creative at Euro RSCG, was quoted in the French magazine *Liberation*: "We need to speak with less arrogance and more sensitivity. Insouciance is not compatible anymore with a new reality." The stereotypical Hollywood, occidental white male success symbol, with the perfect job and athletic record, needs to be revised toward a more multicultural and diverse personality. As Maureen Dowd of the *New York Times* explained in one of her articles, "The children of Baby Boomers thought that they would live in a sure and aseptic world, where old age and death will be postponed, and microbes will be fought by antimicrobian tooth paste, where exercise and weight loss programs will take care of obesity and wrinkles solved by collagen. Where impotence will be solved by Viagra and sickness by 'new scientific discovery.' *The eruption of the tragedy in New York*, as well as very tough economic times, *has blown away the utopia perfect image we have come to believe!*"

In their now prophetic 1997 book, *The Fourth Turning*,[4] William Strauss and Neil Howe laid out a vision of our society that reveals with startling clarity the cycles of American history. According to their theory, based on a historical analysis of the past five hundred years, we can observe four ongoing cycles as a natural, repetitive evolution: growth, maturation, entropy, and rebirth—each following one another in succession and lasting about twenty years apiece. When the book was written, we were in the middle of the third cycle moving into the last one defined as "Rebirth." This is a trying time, defined by the authors as "crisis," which they said could begin through the dramatic catalyst of a tragic emergency.

If the authors of *The Fourth Turning* are the prophets they claim, and seem to be, it is very critical to understand what this will mean from a business standpoint as well as for our society's future in general. This fascinating material is far too complex to address in depth in the context of this book, but the most salient point would seem to be that we have officially left the cycle the authors call the "Unraveling" (or maturation) phase in which individualism triumphs over crumbling institutions, and have entered the rebirth phase, which the authors describe as a time when society's energies will be sharply focused on passing through a "great and perilous gate in history, to be 'reborn' as a new and very different (for better or worse) society." The book explains that in the trying times of a "Crisis" phase (such as World War II) we will emphasize collective duties over personal concerns and the economy will vacillate according to extreme shocks. It is a "rite of passage" period for people, which will be experienced differently by different generations who will each have a particular role to play in the unfolding drama. *Overall, however, according to the authors, an entire value system will be altered to reflect less cynicism and a deep desire to rebuild trust and hope for the collective good. In the business world, distinctions will be drawn between people who can be counted on and those who cannot, with great emphasis on the values of honor, integrity, family commitments, cultural decency, and trust—anything that has to do with being a good citizen.* Businesses perceived as predatory, as parasitical, or as corrupting influences will be at risk. The loyalty to national community will be integrated in context of the loyalty to your own group, or tribe. This brings a new layer to the theory of the individual in society, and it is a definite shifting from the theory of the ultimate powerful individual presented in my last book. The powerful individual does not completely disappear in this new scenario, but in time becomes changed to include a collective spirit. Above all, this period will be marked by the fall of the hedonistic, self-absorbed, self-indulgent role model of the past and the celebration of individuality in the context of a particular group.

I don't know if *Sex and the City* will survive this—it may do so by focusing less on the obsessive indulgences of the heroines (and the trendy shoes they purchase for thousands of dollars) and more on the real aspects of the very close, tribal-like friendship of a group of urban women it portrays. What is certain, however, is that the shallow, superficial reality of supermodels, or the hedonistic unrealistic expression of the "gym-perfect body," will suddenly seem incredibly hollow, as people will look for brands that understand their need to meet, hug, and bring "optimism" in a real way! It will be critical now more than ever to find an honest, fundamental link to a brand and develop it. *To be a confidante will be more important than being a guru, to be a friend will be more credible than being inaccessible.* Role models and poetry might gain new life again. Brands with real heritage, a sense of nostalgia, and human sensitivity will be preferred.

Citizen Brand Is the Future!

A very important part of people's emotional bond with the brand is knowing that their brands not only behave well, but are actively involved in making the world a better place. The absolute truth is that corporations, like governments, can't survive without a *true partnership* with their constituency, particularly at a time when brands are struggling to survive. Corporations need to embrace their roles as corporate *citizens* by starting a new and rich dialogue between themselves and the marketplace, by sharing the concerns of their audiences. *The shift in thinking is from asking how we can motivate consumers to buy our product to asking instead how we can touch our consumers' lives.* And I mean asking that question with absolute sincerity and passion. Because the power balance between businesses and people is evolving toward a partnership-oriented relationship of *equality*, brands must approach buyers entirely differently. The paternalistic corporate philanthropy of the past will evolve into the concept of a brand helping as a compassionate friend or neighbor. The new attitude must be one of sensitivity to people's emotional states and needs, and the key phrase for our times—one that will touch the deepest chords in people—is *generosity.*

The search for humanity in this time will be huge. Our conceptions of "rich versus poor," along with a new, strong, collective realization that we can't have a world with a few very rich and many very poor has forever changed people's global social conscience and brands will again need to respond by embodying the generosity of spirit people today are seeking. Most importantly, brands today have an opportunity to own the future and be a part of the solution—instead of being part of the problem.

Although we certainly continue to live in a far less than perfect society, and class struggles continue to exist, albeit more hidden, the Western world has moved to a "cleaner economy" than existed in the beginning of the twentieth century. We are supported by a robotized infrastructure and computerized tools, and there are fewer jobs that are truly physically unbearable. Labor laws that did not exist in the past guarantee a minimum income for working people, protection through labor representation, and health support for most workers. Stock options at all levels have helped many build a nest egg and social security brings a blanket security for those who can no longer participate in the work force. *Our free Western society has fought, evolved, and improved to have access to basic human rights and social protection.* Furthermore, the concept of freedom and the right to choose has permeated our society and motivated individuals to continue an ongoing process of building a better world for everyone. Our shared economic success has been responsible for more jobs and opportunities and has helped sustain great artistic movements based on the importance of individuals' need to express themselves. A society that strives to provide access to a system of education that creates opportunity for most has been the backbone for helping people reach out toward their dreams.

One of the most profound results of this evolution toward popular empowerment is that as people have become more and more empowered, commerce, in order to succeed, has had to begin to strive to be more relevant to people's needs and desires. A unique partnership started to evolve where corporations realized that, unless they had people as allies, their road to success would be impossible to travel. And this is, of course, why branding was born: to help people recognize the identity of a particular product and its values compared to its competitors. My concept, Emotional Branding, went several steps further in terms of developing a sensitivity toward people's emotional needs. And now I believe we are at a different stage altogether in this natural evolution toward buyers' empowerment and "brand partnership."

Citizen Brand takes the concept of Emotional Branding into the *modus operandi* of a corporation. It will, among other things, explore the huge potential that exists for changing the internal mentality **"Cause marketing" programs abound in almost every company, and corporations are realizing more and more just how effective and necessary these programs are today.** within a company so that corporate policy is in sync with the private aspirations of desired shoppers. By making a better connection with their audiences, corporations can achieve meaningful dialogue with people and access limitless information resources. The key here is to be able to ask the right questions, to be able to speak the right language, and, above all, to be able to listen more! In my last book I talked a lot about communications programs of certain brands, how these programs show a true sensitivity to the new role of women in our society, racial diversity, gender issues, and sexual preferences. In the section on cause marketing I spoke about the importance of corporate involvement in the community and the investment some companies are making in various causes or through philanthropy. This book goes further in exploring the true corporate responsibility expected today by people at large. There is certainly nothing new about the trend toward increasing this responsibility–"cause marketing" programs abound in almost every company, and corporations are realizing more and more just how effective and necessary these programs are today. In fact, the *New York Times* recently cited a poll where three-quarters of the one thousand people surveyed agreed that companies have a responsibility to support worthy causes–up from two-thirds who felt that way in a similar poll taken eight months prior.[5]

However, I do not sense that there exists a true understanding of why these programs are so successful, and exactly how to harness the emotional power of this approach. Despite the existence and growing popularity of programs such as Boston College's fifteen-year-old Center for Corporate Citizenship, which has excellent training programs, research and consulting services, most corporations have no real coherent strategy or programs in place for improving their corporate citizenship. My aim here has been to give a new perspective on corporate responsibility.

By understanding corporate responsibility, or "Citizen Brandship," within the framework of the Emotional Branding strategy, you will gain the tools necessary for leveraging this emotional power. I strongly believe, for example, that *design as a part of a Citizen Branding strategy can become the real conduit and vehicle to bring this new, humanistic message to society.*

One could argue that businesses don't have such missions and should not necessarily be involved in those issues, but the reality is quite different and is unavoidable. *I would argue that because brands are bringing deeper emotional benefits to people today–almost on the level of the role of politics and religion in the past, they now must become Citizen Brands.* It is the expectation. And, furthermore, if that expectation is not met, expect havoc.

Managing a business today requires another dimension that takes into consideration the local market's sensitivities as well as people's global opinions. Globalization has been hugely successful for a lot of corporations. It has generated more profits and opened new markets. It has allowed access for cheaper labor and new manufacturing resources. But *we can't recreate outside of our borders the same insensitivity we have been fighting to eradicate in our own countries without paying a price.* We are living today in a very close-together world where highly educated audiences and buyers are watching carefully how we behave outside of our own country. Globalization is indeed a marvelous opportunity; handled rightly it can encourage a true multiculturalism and enrich everyone's lives.

Globalization is indeed a marvelous opportunity; handled rightly it can encourage a true multiculturalism and enrich everyone's lives.

Handled wrongly it can lead to corporations becoming hostages to local politics or to situations such as the poor image the pharmaceutical industry is experiencing globally.

As people increasingly seek both spiritual and physical stimulation from the world around them and become more open to building strong emotional attachments to brands that view them in this holistic manner, the expectations are all the higher–and the possibility for a sense of disdain or betrayal is all the more present as well. *It's as if people are saying: "We have loved your brands and appreciated how you have helped us, you have built our trust in your offering–you have understood our needs and even supported our causes. You have us now, but we want you to be responsible!"* Corporate greed or misbehavior from business leaders will be more closely scrutinized from consumer groups, sometimes impacting the level of trust people have built in a brand. Nobody knows yet the impact of the investigations around Martha Stewart, Andersen, WoldCom, or Imclone on their brands, but this lack of perceived business ethic will motivate grassroots movements to ask for more clarity and honesty in the way corporations and their brands behave. Brands have become families of a sort, social leaders, and have encouraged and become a basis for people to meet and bond as we have seen with Harley-Davidson and Saturn. When SC Johnson found through research that people trust family corporations much more than faceless "public" ones, it changed its brand strategy accordingly to emphasize the family history of the brand and the integrity of its founder, Sam Johnson. Brands have to understand this unique need to project a sense of humanity–to give everything we possibly can a recognizable human touch. Being a corporate family is a strong concept particularly if you invite people to join your family. *As a Citizen Brand you suddenly find yourself faced with entirely new criteria and rules about how to communicate to people.*

Becoming a Citizen Brand is about taking into consideration the impact every decision could have on people either internally or externally.

Becoming a Citizen Brand is about taking into consideration the impact every decision could have on people either internally or externally. *Citizen Brand* will address how certain companies are responding to this challenge, refocusing their priorities, and taking responsibility for the impact their decisions have on the people of the world. They have discovered that the basic tenet is simple: People in the corporate world and people as buyers are really the same–building together solutions for their lives.

The Ten Commandments

The Ten Commandments of Emotional Branding were introduced in my first book as a way of conceptualizing the radical change in perspective necessary in moving from a traditional functions- and benefits-based marketing approach to the Emotional Branding strategy. They represent, in a nutshell, the essential elements required for creating a powerful emotional brand–and they have proven to be enormously popular with marketers. Updated and imbued with the Citizen Brand concept, they will make up the structure of this book, with each chapter devoted to a particular commandment. However, I want to point out that this is not a "step-by-step" process–each and every commandment is necessary to create a brand that speaks to people on an emotional level. With the exception of chapter 1, "Evolve from Consumers to People"–which because it addresses current consumer trends and the perennial, highly crucial question of how to understand the consumer on an intimate level, is, of course, the place to start in any branding program–the chapter ordering is not sequential. All Ten Commandments are in fact facets of the same diamond and there exists a certain overlap between them as connected elements of a holistic Emotional Branding strategy. This means that the placement of some of the issues addressed and examples used is at times somewhat arbitrary. The attempt here is to capture that elusive formula for touching people's hearts from a branding perspective.

As with human relationships, a brand/consumer relationship is certainly not a science. It is, above all, an art. With the Ten Commandments, we have ferreted out the most important keys to achieving greatness in this art; they are an attempt to place this often intuitive process within a framework that will yield both inspiration and a practical way of rating a brand's emotional potency and honing in on the specific areas where a brand is weak.

As stated in *Emotional Branding*, the Ten Commandments are:

1. From Consumers → to People
   Consumers buy. People live.
2. From Honesty → to Trust
   Honesty is expected. Trust is engaging and intimate.
3. From Product → to Experience
   Products fulfill needs. Experiences fulfill desires.
4. From Quality → to Preference
   Quality for the right price is a given today. Preference creates the sale.
5. From Notoriety → to Aspiration
   Being known does not mean that you are also loved!
6. From Identity → to Personality
   Identity is recognition. Personality is about character and charisma!
7. From Function → to Feel
   The functionality of a product is about practical or superficial qualities only. Sensorial design is about experiences.
8. From Ubiquity → to Presence
   Ubiquity is seen. Emotional presence is felt.
9. From Communication → to Dialogue
   Communication is telling. Dialogue is sharing.
10. From Service → to Relationship
    Service is selling. Relationship is acknowledgement.

1

The First Commandment: Evolve from Consumers to People

Consumers buy. **People live.**

Just like in any really great relationship based on love, it all starts with understanding. You have to know who your customers are–what their daily lives are like, what gives them joy, what their problems and worries are, and, most importantly, what their deepest desires–their dreams–are. People know when brands are speaking directly to them with the right voice, a voice that speaks of their brand's commitment to touching their lives in meaningful ways–through products and services intimately tailored to their needs, through supporting the causes that are important to them, and through marketing efforts that sound just the right emotional note. The fact is that the effort to really know your consumers, not just to understand how to motivate them to buy your brand–but to know them in a holistic manner–is in a sense an action of generosity. It is about going that extra step (or mile!) to gain insight from a truly humanistic perspective. This effort pays off tenfold, because once that deeper understanding is made, many unforeseen connections between people and your brand can also be made. The difference is a long-term, deep approach, versus a short-term, quick-profits oriented approach. Once strong emotional associations are built with a particular brand, they tend to last a very long time. The real bottom line has always been and always will be that consumers respond overwhelmingly to being known and loved for who they really are! We all learned a lot from the 2000 census. My first book, which came out before those results were in, focused a great deal on emphasizing the importance of recognizing demographic groups that have been growing rapidly in importance and were previously largely ignored, such as women, gays and lesbians, and minority groups, including Latinos and African-Americans. The census proved once and for all that these groups indeed are growing in numbers and cultural influence in America. In this chapter I will briefly touch on a few salient new realities for each one of these key groups, using one or two examples in each case of a brand or communications campaign that really "gets it." First and foremost, however, I would like to further explore the big, overall consumer trends that are currently affecting everyone, such as the "Tribal trend."

The Big One: Love Instead of Fear

All of the trends and "sub-trends" I am about to discuss are intimately related to the dualistic concept of "Love and Fear," a new way of looking at brands from an emotional perspective. In almost every system of both psychology and religion, fear and love are said to be the two most powerful emotions of man from which every other emotion is a derivative. In other words, every human emotion has the potential of falling into either the category of "fear" or "love." There are vast volumes of interesting literature on this subject, but for our purposes here we will explore this complex idea from its most basic premises. For starters, fear has to do with death and love is about hope. Let's take the emotion of jealousy as an example. Jealousy has two parts, one having to do with fear and the other with love. Jealousy from the point of view of fear is based on hatred—despising someone because they are more powerful, smart, or beautiful than myself. But jealousy from the point of view of love is based on envy—admiring people for their qualities and wishing that I could be more like them. While this experience of envy may not be particularly pleasant (it is a huge misconception that emotions based on love always "feel good"), it has the power to lead one forward toward good feelings and inspire positive growth, whereas hatred, of course, is pretty much a dead-end, with the possibility of leading only to destruction of some sort. In this same way all of the basic human emotions can be divided into two categories based on either love or fear. The box section entitled "The Six Primary (or Universal) Emo-

In almost every system of both psychology and religion, fear and love are said to be the two most powerful emotions of man.

tions" (see below) will show these basic delineations. It is by no means complete, but it can serve as a launching pad for thinking about what motivates people and how emotions can best be used in the identification of a brand's personality.

The Six Primary (or Universal) Emotions

Emotions are complicated collections of chemical and neural responses. They are biologically determined processes that affect the body and the mode of operation of numerous brain circuits. They are part of the bioregulatory devices that help us to survive. For example, they can provide increased blood flow to arteries in the legs so that muscles receive extra oxygen and glucose in the case of danger and a necessary flight reaction. Although learning and culture alter the expression of emotions, the universal emotions remain highly recognizable across cultures despite the variations in the precise stimuli that induce an emotion. (This is why Darwin was able to catalog the emotional expressions of a very wide variety of species and find consistency in those expressions.) Most psychologists, philosophers, and spiritual scholars speak of five or six basic types of emotion, very similar to those I have listed below along with brief descriptions. As I have said, the two major emotions are fear and love, and the other four basic emotions are based on this primal duality, meaning that the emotion can become distorted by fear or grow toward love. Interestingly, in Western society children have traditionally been taught in many subtle unconscious ways that it's wrong to experience/express natural emotions. Now that our society seems to be largely undergoing this "emotional revolution," mentioned in the Introduction, many habits of emotional repression—based on fear rather than love—may be collectively unlearned.

1. FEAR: The purpose of natural fear is to create caution—to ensure survival. Fear actually expresses our love of life. If it's not expressed in a healthy way, it will become panic.
2. LOVE: For a healthy life we must learn to express love without inhibition or embarrassment. Love that is continually repressed becomes possessiveness, which is unnatural.
3. GRIEF (or SADNESS): Grief is about saying goodbye in the natural cycle of life. It can be a beneficial experience that allows one to move through the sadness quickly. For example, when chil-

dren cry over the loss of some small event, this is natural and said to be healthy. When expression of grief/sadness is repressed it leads to chronic depression.

4. ANGER: This is also a natural emotion. It is about saying "no" to something. Again, it is said to be healthy for us to express this emotion. When anger is repressed, it becomes rage.

5. SURPRISE: Surprise is a response to the unexpected. Growing in the direction of love it can become awe or delight, but if infused with fear, it can become dread or shock.

6. ENVY: As we said previously, this emotion is about the recognition of something one does not yet have. If tempered by love, it can inspire admiration or ambition, and if it is repressed, it becomes jealousy.

From a marketing standpoint, and from the perspective of Emotional Branding, I believe that although fear and love are both powerful motivators, it is much more useful to attempt to inspire positive emotions rather than to create fear-based communications, because love, quite simply, has much more staying power and overall potential to inspire. Fear, by its very nature, is about adopting a defensive posture in order to avoid something negative–and once the threat is gone, the emotional association is no longer valid. For example, children respond better to a positive stimulus than to a negative one–children may eat their vegetables under threat of no TV, but if parents really want to inspire a self-perpetuating vegetable eating behavior in their children, they may have to talk to them, learn which vegetables they like best, and try to prepare those in a way their children will enjoy. The smart parent will take the time to do this because he will be well informed about the physiology of children and will know that children's taste buds have been scientifically proven to be more sensitive than the time-dulled adult taste buds, which is why they object so strongly to eating certain foods (talk about knowing your target consumer!). The smart parent will also emphasize that those vegetables will make the child grow up to be big, strong, and intelligent–and maybe even offer some kind of clean plate reward. Of course, this approach might still fail, but I think it has a much greater chance of success.

A company is stronger if it is bound by love rather than by fear.

Herb Kelleher, former CEO of Southwest Airlines, illustrated this principle in his extremely successful approach to management, saying simply, "A company is stronger if it is bound by love rather than by fear."[1] This is certainly the reason why he was able to build the kind of loyalty among employees that caused them to organize on their own, immediately following September 11, a volunteer giveback effort that was so successful that it allowed Southwest Airlines to be the only U.S. airline to report a profit for the third quarter of 2001! Southwest's new CEO Jim Parker also did his part by declining his paychecks for the fourth quarter. Other airlines requested giveback donations from employees but have had lower and varying degrees of success because of years of difficult labor relations. And this is no different than the relationship a brand has with consumers, especially in uncertain times when a whole new "culture of fear" seems to develop and people need, above all, to be reassured.

An example of fear-based advertising is an ad for an online dating service, Match.com, which attempts to encourage those who would never consider looking online for romance to give it a try. Match.com's research showed that most people in this category eschew an online dating service because they have a romantic notion that "fate will take care of it." The ads Match.com created in response to this insight show the haphazard cruelty of fate with the underlying message that if you leave it up to fate, it'll never happen. The ads attempt to tap into that "I'll never meet someone" fear, but in a way

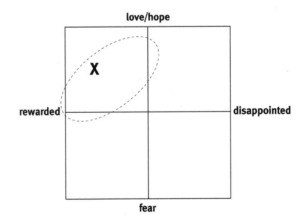

A company is stronger when it is bound by love rather than by fear.

that is so heavy-handed and negative I doubt they are sending lonely singles flying to their keyboards. One ad shows a man and woman looking at one another with romantic interest from across the street, but as the man crosses the street to meet the woman, he is hit by a passing bus. Another subway print ad states, "Mr. Right is not on this train." Now there's a happy thought to start a single woman's day!

These ads are clearly trying for a wry humor, but they end up achieving more of a condescending tone than anything else. "I know better than you. How could you be so silly as to think you might meet the love of your life on the street or subway. Ha!" If Match.com wanted to be funny on a subject as "near and dear" to people's hearts as this one, they should have gone all out, with a wacky humor that avoids cynicism at all costs. It would have been more interesting to investigate the whole crazy process of dating. It could be very funny, for example, to do a cheeky, over-the-top ad showing a "regular date" (in black-and-white, film noir style, depicting a situation that is boring or awful) and then a Match.com date (a gorgeous techno-color date with some fabulous person in a fabulous setting).

Or, it may be even better to focus on showing what dating online (a process which the company's target group is unfamiliar and uncomfortable with) is like and the role fate might play in it from an emotional, romantic aspirational perspective. Match.com could show the sense of adventure, the excitement, the fun, the way online dating is streamlined and faster, with a greater potential for meeting a Mr./Ms. Right from a sheer numbers perspective—and in this way motivate and empower people around the idea of "taking fate into their own hands." A campy, or even irreverent humor could be great, but the campaign should stay away from scenarios that imply "if you don't buy our service, it'll never happen for you . . ." Fears can be exposed without being manipulated, and this, too, can be very powerful because if it is done well it can be a very loving gesture. We all love to laugh about our fears from time to time, both real ones and the more neurosis-inspired ones.

Above all, the brand communication must be absolutely sincere—based on essential human truths—and rendered interesting and original through creativity. I want to make one thing clear here: creating brand strategies based on love instead of fear certainly does not mean leaning in the direction of sentimentality. We are not talking about a cheesy "Hallmark-ish" approach that overtly tries in every stereotypical manner to pluck at the heartstrings. This kind of clunky approach is not only unoriginal, but it is often very opportunistic and manipulative, too. Emotional Branding is about developing a real sensitivity to what people want, and then finding a unique way to give it to them. And this is an art!

Now that we have explored the concept of Love/Fear as a basis for understanding emotional motivation, let's take a look at the major current trends affecting our world and, most importantly, our emotional lives.

The Six Fundamental Trends of Our Times

1. Tribal Fires: A Tribe to Call My Own
2. Sweet Home: There's No Place like Home
3. Child Quest: Inner Child Revealed
4. Reality Check: Hold the Saccharine, Please!
5. Down Home: Small-Town Sweetness and Psychic Hugs
6. Awakening: Soul Seeking through Sensation

TRIBAL FIRES: A TRIBE TO CALL MY OWN

Tribes are like a home of sorts. A place to be yourself and commune with those special people belonging to the same "inner sanctum" who share a similar passion or outlook on life. Being with one's tribe, like being in the cozy safety of one's home, can make one feel a deep, unnameable comfort. Most likely, this trend initially began as a tribute to and natural longing for the distant memory of extended families living under one roof within tight, well-defined communities. Tribes are a response to our fast-paced, fragmented modern lives where we increasingly live separated from one another. The movement toward globalization has created an awareness in people of belonging to an "earth tribe"—a collective sense of the commonalities among all people and a desire to bond on a global level. However, at the same time this has created a greater need for people to define themselves on a more local level—to discover and explore their own individual cultures lest they be swallowed up into the vastness of a more homogenized global culture.

Tribes are a response to our fast-paced, fragmented modern lives where we increasingly live separated from one another.

This is the same dynamic that we see, for example, in retail; when large chains start to take over the landscape there is always in tandem a movement toward more intimate niche retailers who, if they are savvy, can win tremendous loyalty from people who are seeking an intimate experience alongside the convenience of big stores. Tribes are extremely important to our times; as I mentioned in the Introduction, in a world rendered increasingly uncertain I believe that this trend will only continue to gain importance.

How Does This Affect Brands and Branding?

For some time now many smart brands such as Harley-Davidson have understood the powerful role the tribal instinct can have in creating a strong brand. Harley, with its vast network of membership clubs and events and cult/mythlike status among consumers who want to belong to the Harley dream, is a quintessential "tribal brand." Apple computer has built the same kind of passionate exclusive "club culture" around the idea that Apple users are iconoclastic, smart rebels. It is the Apple tribal instinct that motivates 85,000-plus computer fans to attend the MacWorld Expo, an annual four-day event in San Francisco every year. There are many other examples, but the real point here is: inspiring people about the idea of belonging to a "brand club" is not only a huge opportunity—it is almost a necessity today. *People want to feel the warmth of the tribal fires around the brands that they trust and love.* The Tribal trend is about bringing people together for a positive experience. If emotional brands wish to evolve into Citizen Brands, the experience they provide must have more and more to do with helping people and making the world a better place. For many years, Avon has done a great job of galvanizing women, organizing walkathons around the world for the cause of breast cancer. Avon could benefit from going beyond this program, which in effect creates a "tribe for a day." It could incorporate the Tribal trend further into its brand by creating an entire network of clubs and meeting places for these women to forge friendships and fight for this cause under the Avon brand.

Citizen Brands will also recognize that a tribe needs a place—or places—to convene (this is, I believe, one of the reasons for the success of the Starbucks—it provides a cozy, warm place of connection for people). More and more brands will find creative ways of bringing people together on a regular basis at specific physical places for a tribal brand experience. Online communities are also great exam-

WAN2TLK?

abbreviations and acronyms
for fast talkers

EMOTICON	MEANING
AAM	as a matter of fact
AB	ah bless!
AFAIC	as far as I'm concerned
AFAIK	as far as I know
AFK	away from keyboard
AKA	also known as

ASAP	as soon as possible
ATB	all the best
B	be
BCNU	be seeing you
Bwd	backward
B4	before
BBFN	bye bye for now
BFN	bye for now
BRB	be right back
BTW	by the way
BYKT	but you knew that
C	see

Gen Y has created a new language—their own "Code Talk."[2]

ples of the Tribal trend from this perspective. They delineate within the vast, somewhat cold world of cyberspace a particular niche "place" that has emotional relevance to the surfer. iVillage.com and its sister site, Women.com, are examples of well-conceived online communities, and this is the reason they are so successful. They are places where women can make friends, seek advice, and feel the solidarity of other women.

If a tribe needs a place, it also needs a language. To talk to a tribe, a brand will at least need to understand, and hopefully speak, this cultural language meant for the "insiders" of a particular tribe. A fascinating example of this is the "code talk" Gen Y has invented to communicate via wireless devices. Shortcut letter/symbol combination phrases—"CUL8R," short for "See you later"—are doubtless contrived not only for speed and small digital spaces, but also for privacy from any potential parental prying eyes that would just see gibberish in these messages! Someone has even published a manual for this new language, a sort of twenty-first-century Gen Y dictionary, and some smart fashion and consumer product brands that would like to

cul8r

9

woo Gen Y have begun using these symbols in their brand names, logos, and packaging designs.

If a tribe needs a place, it also needs a language. To talk to a tribe, a brand will at least need to understand, and hopefully speak, this cultural language meant for the "insiders" of a particular tribe.

In the tribal environment brands can also be seen as a shortcut for people to find other like-minded people. Increasingly, we see people using brands to define themselves and as a way for strangers to get to know one another. There is even an *extreme* example of an online dating service in Holland that uses the term "brand dating" where subscribers describe themselves only according to their favorite core brands. Ads read, "SWF, Mercedes, Tiffany's, Gucci– NOT Diesel or Tommy Hilfiger seeks Porche lover . . . etc.!" While this may be a silly, over-the-top anomaly, its mere existence says something about people's passion for using the brands in their lives as touch points for creating relationships with others!

Finally, this trend signals an important collective understanding of the power of groups. Increasingly, there are "clubs" or groups being formed to bring a greater economic or social force to individual members. Some municipalities now issue their own currencies to encourage local spending and rebuild communities without relying on more traditional methods of raising support, such as lobbying Washington.

SWEET HOME: THERE'S NO PLACE LIKE HOME

Seemingly in conflict with the Tribal trend is what I will call the Sweet Home trend, which is all about enjoying the pleasures of creating a beautiful home environment and spending high quality time recreating there. This trend, which has been on the rise since the mid-Nineties, signals the increase of home-based activities such as family meals, home entertainment, decorating, gardening, shopping online, and so on. Many of these activities hearken back to simple, "do-it-yourself" or homespun pastimes, such as crafts and baking. This trend is the reason we now see a flurry of new college courses such as one called "Retro Fun" at North Seattle Community College, which teaches sewing, bicycle repair, pie baking, etc. Although this trend is about doing things in and around the home, it does not exclude the Tribal trend; in fact, it only emphasizes a greater need for a tribe. Of course, every tribal base has its "tepees," and as cabin fever inevitably sets in from time to time, it will be all the more important to have tribal events or gatherings to escape to. And, of course, select members of tribes may visit individual tepees for more intimate bonding within the context of dinner parties, etc.

How Does This Affect Brands and Branding?

This trend is the major reason why brands like Pier 1, Home Depot, and Williams-Sonoma are currently meeting analysts' expectations, reporting overall sales and profits that were stronger than a year ago in an environment of economic recession. According to a recent study by Unity Marketing, for the past two years consumers spent more on home furnishings than they did on clothes. Abigail Jacobs, public relations manager for Kmart, has said, "People are not only staying home more, but they are giving home entertaining gifts."[3] Besides beautifying the home and entertaining others there, this trend is also about an ongoing quest for hobbies and entertainment that can be enjoyed on a regular basis from one's home. It is clear that online shopping will benefit from this trend and sales are also strong for companies like Blockbuster and Hollywood Video and for arts and crafts retailers, such as Michael's Stores and Hancock Fabrics. Games of all sorts–from decidedly low-tech, low-end old-fashioned board games to expensive pool and foosball tables to the most sophisticated video games–are seeing a sharp upturn in popularity. As even the wealthy forgo fancy vacations, we are seeing increasing sales of ultra-luxury games such as The Sports Authority's "Bass Fishing Deluxe," a refurbished arcade game that costs around $9,000 and lets you find out who is better at the sport of fishing, you or twenty-four different breed of fish!

Herb Silvers, who sells vintage pinball machines, jukeboxes, and other game-room items in Arleta, California, says his business has doubled since September 11. "People just don't want to leave their homes right now, but they want to be entertained there," he says. Before September 11, dealers such as Silvers or Lou Marschak, who restores antique billiard tables, used to get calls only from collectors, but both are now receiving inquiries from people who want to outfit a family game room. As we rediscover and reinvent the classic game room, it would seem likely that the most popular games would be those that are most social in nature in keeping with the Tribal trend.

Of course, we do not know how long this trend will last, but it has been building quietly for some time (witness the huge success of Martha Stewart) and once people develop a taste for home-based activities, they are likely to continue with them for some time. Most of all, it would seem that *this trend is about "grand living at home"– an active exploration of all of the wonderful things and activities we can bring from the outside world into our home,* as opposed to the old idea of cocooning or of the couch potato who only wants to escape or avoid the pressures and responsibilities of the outside world. It is a celebration of home and family.

Time-starved people, looking to enjoy the comforts of home, may rebel against using that time for chores, and we may see the advent of more services.

The brisk sales of an entirely new category of lounge wear that is a step up in style, fabric quality, etc., would seem to imply that people are not slouching around their homes in sweat pants with holes, but that there is an altogether new collective conception of home presence. Perhaps people want to test the limits of what they can experience from the comfort of their homes. We have long been morphing toward a society where telecommuting will become if not the "norm," then a close second. And as many laid-off or unemployed people channel their disenchantment with the corporate world into their own entrepreneurial projects, particularly Gen X (see later section on Generation X), both home offices and telecommuting will become all the more prevalent. But as the elements of work and entertainment are increasingly added to our concept of home, we may find that other things, such as everyday chores, are taken away. Time-starved people, looking to enjoy the comforts of home, may rebel against using that time for chores, and we may see the advent of more services like the valet laundry services P&G and Unilever are currently testing in certain markets. P&G's service, called "Juvian," is a valet laundry and home fabric-care service that is being positioned as a "spa experience for clothes" that delivers meticulous attention to every piece of clothing. For a minimum order of $17 per bag of clothes (about two loads of laundry), Juvian will pick up, clean, fold, and return customers' dirty clothes. Consumers can pay extra for special treatments such as "aromatherapy" and "color and tone preservation." Meanwhile, Unilever is preparing a test launch of a similar service, modeled after its "MyHome" laundry and cleaning service started last year in the United Kingdom. Along the same lines, the British supermarket Tesco has had enormous success with its online business of delivering groceries to customers' doorsteps in a cost effective manner. But as people become more interested in reexperiencing certain home-based activities, such as baking bread from scratch or planting a garden instead of hiring a landscaper, it will be interesting to see which activities we pay others to accomplish for us and which ones we keep as a part of our home routines. Clearly, those activities which are the most repetitive and boring, such as laundry and food shopping, will be the first to go!

CHILD QUEST: INNER CHILD REVEALED

It is a natural human impulse toward comfort to periodically revert back to a "childlike state," especially in times of crisis. This trend signifies a desire to return to a simple life. *This trend represents a healthy impulse for coming to terms with an increasingly complex and tense world.* It is a way of both escaping from and, in some cases, attempting to restructure our adult reality. D. W. Winnicott, the esteemed psychoanalyst, developed a theory around what he called the "area of transitional phenomena"—a zone between dreams and reality (or fantasy/emotion and reason), which is populated by games, teddy bears, things that remind us of our childhood and safety. He believed that this intermediate space for play, creativity, and imagination was essential for a child to develop normally and come to terms with reality. The "childlike state" I am referring to here has to do with seeking comfort by pursuing simple pleasures and indulging in the zany antics of play. From this point of view, you could say that it is about both "teddy bears" and "trampolines."

First of all, let's talk about the need for "teddy bears." People are seeking the "familiar" in this new uncertain world. Sincerity and authenticity have become very important. Focus groups have recently said they'd like to see the return of Coca-Cola's famous "I'd like to teach the world to sing in perfect harmony . . ." commercial because they have warm memories of it as a positive, inspiring message of global communion. *This trend signifies a definitive end to our love affair with the complexities of hedonism, conspicuous consumption, indulgence, cynicism, and a preoccupation with shallow/trivial matters of all kinds.* This is not to say that sophistication and luxury will disappear—they will just become a bit more streamlined, oriented toward comfort, ease, taste—an elegance that can be festive in the celebration of life, but that is less about flashy self-indulgence. Designer Joseph Abboud has said, "Fashion reflects what's happening in society and now it will become less pretentious and showy . . . people are looking at the quality and comfort of their life and the clothes that reflect it. Clothes will become more user-friendly with softer, touch-and-feel fabrics."[4] In the same vein, sexual expression, I believe, will also tend toward a softer sensualism, avoiding a harsher, more aggressive tone.

Now we will explore the "trampoline" aspect of this trend, which expresses the need for our "inner child" to not only seek the comfort of simple pleasures, but to also be allowed to come out and play–to explore, to go wild, and maybe even drum up a bit of mischief in the process. First of all, although we rarely think of it this way, play is a basic need, proven to be absolutely crucial to the healthy development of both humans and animals alike. Dr. Stuart Brown, physician and naturalist, said in a recent *National Geographic* article, "Play may be as important to life–for us and for other animals–as sleeping and dreaming." Brown goes on to say that play helps animals become adept at hunting and winning mates. For humans, lack of play can lead to antisocial behavior. He cites a study of twenty-six convicted murderers in Texas where 90 percent of them showed either the absence of or abnormal play as children. "Play is an important part of a healthy, happy childhood, and playful adults are often highly creative, even brilliant individuals," says Brown. Play provides us with an outlet for our emotions. There are many forms of therapy, for both adults and children, that use forms of play as a medium for people to express and gain understanding of feelings that are normally hidden. Play is also vital as an outlet for dealing with all manners of stress.

Our increasing need for play is the reason why Las Vegas, the great playground for adults, has become so incredibly successful, and it is the reason that other concepts for entertainment will continue to merge in new and creative ways with retail, restaurant, and travel/leisure industries. It is interesting to note that of the 56 percent of those who gamble, 97 percent prefer to do so in over-the-top settings. This trend is the reason why theme parks are booming, with annual revenues of over $6 billion. And when we travel/explore/recreate, we are looking for the unusual and exotic, in every possible way, such as the Australian hotel that offers upscale tree-houses for $900 a night. Unusual vacations, such as "storm-chaser" trips that allow thrill-seekers to learn all about tornadoes by chasing them at a close distance with the experts, will also continue to be popular.

The difference after September 11 will most likely be a rise in more "purposeful" adventures–for example, "volunteer vacations" where you can help environmental scientists study nearly extinct wolves in Montana, or help build homes for families in a third world country. This trend is also the reason we will continue to see the development of technology that emphasizes fun and accessibility. Techno-gadgets have **People of all ages need to continually revisit and explore that "free space" of simple pleasures and creativity that exists in our unformed youth.** clearly become toys, to the point that we are now beginning to see "robot toys" for all ages, such as the adorable robot dogs that can be taught to obey commands. While the technology that touches our daily lives is often about work, it also must increasingly help us to play–and preferably to somehow combine the two so that our work will be less cumbersome, boring, or repetitive. Feeling enslaved by our high-tech, high-demand society, people may increasingly reject technology as a "cold master" that disseminates information they must understand and process, responding more to technological wonders that portray warmth and are malleable to their needs. Gadgets and technological equipment that exude accessibility, personality, and fun, either in their design aesthetic, such as Apple computers, or in their actual functions, such as games, will be successful because they allow us to play.

Above all, this trend–whether from the "teddy bear" or the "trampoline" aspect–reminds us that people of all ages need to continually revisit and explore that "free space" of simple pleasures and creativity that exists in our unformed youth, perhaps to find ourselves again, or perhaps to reinvent ourselves.

How Does This Affect Brands and Branding?
First of all, brands will need to secure their relationship with loyal users. Winning new customers away from the competition has always been a challenge, but in the current environment it will be all the more difficult. Brands with a heritage to leverage will greatly benefit from taking a retro approach, such as recent Ivory ads that emphasize the brand's purity ($99^{44}/_{100}$ percent pure) through images that convey the idea of family and the simplicity of an earlier time. One such ad features a modern sepia-toned photo of a mother bathing her infant, along with a drawing from an old Ivory ad showing a mother bathing her child with copy that refers to the "ties that

bind." Secondly, brands will have to find out how their own unique value proposition can simplify people's lives, reassure them, and appeal to the "inner child," either through comfort or fun. A Bang & Olufsen sound-systems catalog portrays a mixture of playfulness and sleek, adultlike aesthetic that belies a very serious approach to design. The copy tells the true story of one customer's very personal day-to-day relationship with music and finishes by telling us simply to "Always Nurture Your Inner Child."

As a wonderful example of creating products that appeal to this human need one has only to look at the colorful, playful household designs of the Alessi design house. Alberto Alessi believes that in our deepest beings we respond to and have an urgent need for uncomplicated and often quite childish objects. His work is about exploring people's emotional relationships with everyday objects, and the magical quality of these objects speaks eloquently to our need to make our world friendlier and more fun. Alessi designs bring alive one of the most important aspects of play—that of surprise. An ordinary object such as a bottle opener becomes a cartoon-like character with the jagged gap that opens a bottle forming the mouth.

This trend toward the comforts and simplicity of childhood is also the reason Wal-Mart is organizing a $25 million plus "Frosty the Snowman" holiday promotion. The silly, affable, nostalgia-inspiring Frosty couldn't be a more comforting cultural icon, particularly for Baby Boomer parents who've seen his Christmas special aired every year since the mid-Sixties. It is also why Coca-Cola introduced for the first time an animated version of their 1930s Santa Claus character in a commercial for the holiday season.

A commercial for Webster Bank is a perfect example of a service brand's response to this trend from the perspective of "emotional comfort." This commercial, which illustrates how Webster frees people up for "the little things that make up the big things in life," shows a father and son fascinated by watching an ant transport a rock, a coach teaching kids how to tie shoelaces, and a woman watching old home movies with her parents. Another commercial in the financial arena (we particularly need comfort and simplicity in this area at the moment!) for Charles Schwab shows an elderly African-American mother talking about all of the things she likes to cook for her grown son when he comes home to visit. At the end of her long list of pies, etc., the sweet, smiling lady throws in a complex, jargon-ridden phrase about the financial portfolio update that, of course, she will also be preparing for him. . . . Then, the punchline: "Wouldn't it be nice to receive financial advice from the person you trust the most?" Positioning your brand as "mom" couldn't be more comforting, but what makes this commercial really work is the humor–a jaunty little "we know how you feel" wink that addresses fears through a love-based approach.

Goodyear Tires recently aired a commercial that was a creative and intelligent appeal to this need to simplify in an increasingly complex world, and that also implicitly addressed the issue of safety, which has so plagued the tire industry since the Firestone fiasco. The commercial shows children from all around the world–America, Russia, Tibet, Africa–on a family road trip asking exasperated parents, in their native languages, "Are we there yet?" emphasizing with gentle humor the universality of childhood. The fact that it shows parents and children cozy and comfortable on a trip, with the parents' biggest concern being to keep the impatient children occupied until they reach their destination, implies "safety" in a much more powerful way than an overt statement would. The commercial also succeeds in creating an emotional connection among people around the world from very diverse cultures on the basis of one simple, basic human truth: Children everywhere get fidgety in cars and drive their parents nuts!

This trend certainly does not signify an end to our ever-expanding need to explore new, challenging territory. The real challenge here will be, however, how to explore that fresh territory and keep enough of the comforting elements of the brand equity in play. Humor as an expression of this playful spirit will be all the more important, but it will be a return to an uncomplicated, kinder, gentler humor that does not thrive on irony or the putting down of others. Edgy, mean-spirited humor is definitely on its way out. We will see humor that is silly to the point of slapstick and more self-effacing honesty in humor that encourages us to above all laugh at ourselves, the quirks of our own tribe, or the common elements of human nature. A great example of this fresh approach to humor can be found in a fall 2001 ad campaign created to encourage tourism to New York. The campaign created by BBDO and the New York mayor's office celebrates the "New York Miracle." These delightful commercials feature celebrities fulfilling a dream in New York City with childlike gusto. In one spot, Barbara Walters sings off-key and tries her best to dance to a number from *42nd Street*; in another we see Woody Allen ice skating in Rockefeller Center, doing double and triple Lutzes and then turning to the camera to say, "You aren't going to believe this. This was the first time I put on skates in my life!" The spots are funny in a gentle, sweet way; they make us laugh because they reveal the little child in us all who wants to live a dream, like Henry Kissinger running the bases of Yankee Stadium. And, they show that our inner child, like all children, is willing to risk looking silly doing it, as in the spot where Yogi Berra conducts a completely atonal symphony and then turns to the camera and asks, "Who the heck is this Phil Harmonic?" This nutty commercial taps into the true spirit of the inner child we all want to unleash in the most lovable way.

REALITY CHECK: HOLD THE SACCHARINE, PLEASE!

This trend signifies disenchantment with a flowery, unrealistic perception of the world. People today know better. We have seen the sky crumble, literally. And while this trend is not about negative or depressing imagery, it is about seeing things as they truly are and recognizing the consumer as an empowered, intelligent, and keenly aware member of society. It is particularly salient with members of Generation Y because of their savvy grasp of marketing as the generation that has been marketed to "from the crib" and because of their high regard for the attribute of intelligence. In a world where so much information is available to all, one way of dealing with it is to talk about it—honestly. This bringing of the truth "out into the open" can actually be very therapeutic and, perhaps, this trend simply signifies a collective need to get some things off our chest. *The plain truth is that people want to know the truth.* As uncomfortable as the "reality of the situation" may be, from one point of view this trend is actually more about comforting ourselves than about anything else, because in acknowledging the problems, sicknesses, and imperfections of the world, we are in a sense releasing ourselves from the enormous pressure toward an unattainable ideal of perfection.

The plain truth is that people want to know the truth, as uncomfortable as the "reality of the situation" may be.

How Does This Affect Brands and Branding?

A brilliant print ad by The Body Shop, a long-time advocate of reality-based communications, attacks societal views of female perfection head on. The ad shows a plump doll (à la Barbie but with a good thirty or so extra pounds) with a tag line that reads, "There are 3 billion women who don't look like supermodels and only 8 who do." Similarly, a Benetton ad simply showing a happy child with Down's syndrome with no tag line continues the Benetton tradition of communications that address real issues, but with more sensitivity and a subtle flavor of optimism that is new to their approach. This trend perhaps signals a kind of optimism that is not about "everything working out okay" but is still very powerful because, presented within a framework of "reality," that makes it believable. Take a recent Rite Aid campaign for example. The campaign is a series of commercials based on real-life experiences between Rite Aid pharmacists and consumers. One commercial shows a worried-looking middle-aged woman who is clearly very sick opening her Rite Aid bag of medicine. She takes a card out, reads it, and looks shocked. Her daughter asks her what is wrong and she replies, "It's a card. From my pharmacist. She says she hopes I feel better. I didn't know people did things like that anymore." The ad is quiet, with no music, with average-looking (not "commercial beautiful") people and visuals that are not over polished—all of which contributes to a sense of authenticity. We have no idea if the woman is going to get well or not—this is not implied at all in the spot, but we know something about her emotional connection with her pharmacist at a difficult time. Another recent commercial for John Hancock Life Insurance tackles a tough subject—that of an aging parent with Alzheimer's. In the commercial we see a middle-aged woman with her mother who does not recognize her, which of course saddens the woman. But she asks her mother if she is happy and has everything she needs, and so on. The mother replies yes and the daughter says, "I'm glad you are happy, Mom," clearly relieved that she is able to care for her parent. The situation portrayed here is, of course, one of life's harsh realities and one we would all prefer not to have to think about. However, the commercial sounds the right note emotionally by addressing the core of the situation: how difficult it is emotionally, and how much more difficult it would be if there weren't enough money to care for the parent. Another parent/child commercial addresses the real challenge of staying in touch through the years with the obstacle of physical distance. The commercial, for AT&T, shows a father and son playing catch. As they throw, the distance between them increases and the boy grows. The man turns to chase a particularly high toss and a stand with a phone appears. As the man turns away from the ball and picks up the phone, the copy says, "Stay Connected." Anybody who has ever experienced the pain of falling out of touch with a loved one can relate to this commercial, but again, the brand is offering itself as a solace–if not an overall solution. Another facet to this trend has been the growing popularity of "insider" ads or entertainment industry shows. The idea is that people, particularly young people, are interested in the authentic inner workings of media.

Along these lines, Budget car rental produced a series of funny ads that pretend to reveal how Budget's campaigns are produced. The ads show ridiculously unrealistic ideas that Budget executives keep rejecting. MTV's "Behind the Music" is another very creative execution of this idea. "Everything is reality; people care about the process," says Christina Norman, senior vice president for marketing and on-air promotion at MTV.

It is fantasy that pretends to portray reality that may well fall under attack given the Reality Check trend.

Whether a brand chooses to address this trend or not depends to a large degree on the brand image. It is not a trend for all brands, and it certainly doesn't mean that consumers are no longer interested in escapist fantasy; clearly, the need for soothing–or forgetting entirely the sharper edge of reality–will always exist. It is *fantasy that pretends to portray reality* that may well fall under attack given the Reality Check trend. I will talk more about the reality/fantasy dynamics later in the Gen Y section within the context of Gen Y's passion for truth, which often translates into a disdain for advertising or even in anti-marketing activism.

Regardless of where an individual brand stands on this issue, it is above all key to be aware of the trend and to understand that, in general, people's emotional tolerance for hype, overly fabricated fantasy, or corny sentimentalism is waning. People are looking inside themselves for the kind of hope and resolve that comes from realism and truth. Remember, what endeared Rudolph Giuliani so much to the American people during the terrorist crisis was not only his unfailing dedication and leadership during a difficult time, but also his honest, "straight shooter" style mixed with a genuine expression of heartfelt emotion. He sounded the right note at that moment.

Down Home: Small-Town Sweetness and Psychic Hugs

This trend is a continuation and intensification of the ongoing trend toward individuality or customization. "Down Home" is about empowerment in the Emotional economy; a way for people to regain control of their lives and a sense of self that can be missing in a cold, ultra–high-tech society. Part of the trend is our need to personalize the world not only for ourselves, but in order to feel connected to others. The sharing of personal stories is key. For example, the reason that the Dunn, North Carolina, *Daily Newspaper* has a market penetration of 112 percent within a highly diverse community with a lot of access to other media, is that the paper prints "down home" stories about the people that they can't get anywhere else. Stories about the readers themselves who love to see their names in print. Other small-town newspapers follow the same formula, portraits of high school kids, photos of homeless cats and dogs, etc., forging a brand relationship with people by printing these local stories. When the problems of mass customization–both the hassles of inefficient systems and the tough economics–are finally solved, this trend will really kick into high gear. It will be the powerful, unseen "ace in the hole" that changes the entire game.

Micro or niche brands such as these have captivating personal stories that invite the consumer to be a part of the "brand story."

How Does This Affect Brands and Branding?

Big companies will have to learn to speak with a personal voice in order to win the hearts of consumers, and design will be a powerful tool for communicating that personal touch to their employees and consumers. This trend is the reason for the huge success of micro, or niche, brands such as Jones Soda or Khiel's, because these are brands with captivating personal stories that invite the consumer to be a part of the brand story. Jones Soda, the hip mom-and-pop soda company (which had revenues of $19 million in 2000) puts customers' photos on its labels and runs a chat room on its Web site that is immensely popular with kids. Jones Soda became an "in" brand through marketing efforts, such as stocking the colorful sodas (red, yellow, purple, green, blue) in unusual and highly intimate venues like record stores, hair salons, and tattoo parlors. People love companies that do "only one thing" and do it well and this is why, when beloved cult brands such as Ben & Jerry's or Snapple are purchased by large corporations like Quaker Oats, it can be very difficult for them to keep status with consumers who perceive them as sacrificing their unique personality on the altar of the masses. Brands like this must be handled with kid gloves, as Quaker Oats learned after the brand plunged 23 percent over two years.

The "Down Home" trend is the reason why Burger King wrote letters of apology to parents when their Pokémon promotion ran out of merchandise and why SC Johnson has decided to launch a highly unusual $450 million two-year corporate branding campaign to appeal to consumers (and not investors) on the basis of being a "family company," with ads that trade on their heritage by featuring Samuel C. Johnson, the seventy-three-year-old chairman and great-grandson of the founder. Recent FCB research has shown that no less than 80 percent of consumers believe family owned companies make products they can trust, versus 43 percent who said that of publicly traded companies! Creating internal communications that bring people's personal stories to the forefront, such as a human-interest newspaper, is also a huge opportunity to motivate and bond *employees* in a way that will serve to solidify the brand's emotional message.

AWAKENING: SOUL SEEKING THROUGH SENSATION

This trend is about the impassioned need people today have to actively seek sensations to feel their "aliveness" and gain a deeper sense of themselves, whether through the wild adventure of extreme sports or relatively tame activities that involve indulging in experiences that wake up the senses—and everything in between. I spoke about this trend in the Introduction: physical work is very minimal in our machine-age lifestyles and therefore we need to create powerful "sensorial scenarios" in order to experience our own physicality. This trend relates strongly to the Child Quest trend since the play-oriented quest of seeking the inner child often includes sensory experiences. But here the focus is entirely on the sensory experiences people are craving. It is about seeking out visceral experiences like the adrenaline rush from practicing a dangerous sport or the profound relaxation of a spa. Because it emphasizes a strong universal human need, this trend cuts across all boundaries of generation, background, and class, although it is expressed very differently among different groups. In keeping with the Tribal trend, however, these different groups are often opting to experience their sensorial highs together in a group setting or, at the very least, to form clubs and clans around their chosen activities. This is why we see such powerful cultural influences forming around radical fringe groups like motorcross riders, surfers, snowboarders, skateboarders, etc., and around the whole extreme sports movement in general. This group is tightly bonded through a collective statement to society about our careful way of life that Kristen Ulmer, an avid extreme sports fan, aptly sums up in the book *The Extreme Game: An Extreme Sports Anthology*. Mr. Ulmer writes, "There's always this notion in America that nobody should take risks. The toilets are clean, the hamburger meat is cooked to X degrees, and there are a lot of lawyers. American culture is scaredy-cat culture, and people are sick of it."[5]

While extreme sports may be the sensation-seeking activity of choice for many in the Gen Y and Gen X demographic, for the older, often more affluent groups, there are many other,

People will pay $5 or more for a beautifully packaged aromatherapy soap that will relieve our stress or energize us in some special way.

albeit milder expressions of this trend. For example, there is a new demographic target group in the United States called the "Bobos," according to David Brooks, author of *Bobos in Paradise: The New Upper Class and How They Got There*, who are looking for unusual and exciting experiences. The name comes from the "bo" in "bohemian" and the "bo" in "bourgeois." This highly educated group embraces bohemian values and rejects vulgar displays of wealth. All choices, specifically consumer ones, must extend from some higher purpose. This being said, extravagant consumer purchases are justified as long as they fulfill the Bobo's need for life-enhancing authenticity. Their purchases and experiences need to be stimulating for the brain and body alike, unique and customized. The manager of marketing communications at BMW of North America, Baba Shetty, says that there's been a shift in marketing to affluent consumers. "What makes for a successful life now are experiences, both exciting and enriching."

How Does This Affect Brands and Branding?

To start with, all brands must appeal to the senses, from product development to brand communications, in order to rise above the status of mere commodity to become an emotional brand. Take, for example, the fact that people will pay just $2 for a four-bar pack of Ivory soap in any supermarket, while paying $2 for one bar of scented, colorfully packaged soap at Bath & Body Works and $5 or more for a beautifully packaged aromatherapy soap that will relieve our stress or energize us in some special way. The spiritual and sensorial have clearly become important parts of our lives when purchasing brands, and the promise associated with any product needs to be relevant to these aspirations. A recent series of TV commercials for Land Rover Discovery II is a good example of this trend from a brand-communications perspective. The spots offer a decidedly different, completely visceral perspective of the SUV in action, opening with the view of looking straight down onto the top of a Land Rover from a few feet above and then quickly swinging down and outward from the vehicle and underneath into the ground or under water and then coming up on the other side of the planet for another scene with another Land Rover. GSD&M agency created the series of three spots of scenes to convey a sense of discovery of the different parts of the world and reflect the current theme of "Land Rover: the most well-traveled vehicles on earth." The final effect is that the viewer is traveling around and through the world itself.

Another great example of leveraging our thirst for thrill seeking to dimensionalize a brand experience is the NASCAR Cafe in Las Vegas, which appeals to a wide range of people, those interested in race cars as well as the general public. Just like any café, the NASCAR Cafe offers food and drinks but there are many exciting additions to the

$2 $1 $4

The values given by people to brands vary according to their sensorial and emotional character.

"menu," including a roller coaster that starts inside the café itself! And this ride is not for wimps—in fact it's probably better to eat after jumping off. Aptly named SPEED—The Ride, the NASCAR Cafe's roller coaster reaches 70 mph. The first roller coaster of its kind in the western United States, SPEED uses LIMS (Linear Induction Motors) to quickly reach high speeds through magnetic force. SPEED begins inside the NASCAR Cafe, where a high-speed launch propels passengers along the Las Vegas Strip. SPEED carries passengers through an underground tunnel 25 feet below the surface, a breathtaking loop, an exhilarating straightaway, high-speed turns, through the Sahara Marquee, and up a dizzying degree incline that ends 224 feet above ground before returning the passengers on a backward route through the same path.

In addition to the SPEED ride, visitors to the NASCAR Cafe can climb into a real model stock car and experience the realistic sights, sounds, and motion of an authentic (but simulated) NASCAR race through a 20-foot wraparound screen that projects an authentic visual replica of the Las Vegas Motor Speedway—each car is equipped with a 16-channel, 15-speaker sound system, which ought to be enough to get most people's adrenalin going!

We Are Family!

First of all, the 2000 census showed us that the family structure as we've known it in the past is in the process of changing dramatically. People are marrying at older ages, or not at all. Adoption rates are up, and interracial marriages are up. The number of young adults flocking back to the nest is also up. The numbers of both single mothers and single fathers are growing. In fact, according to the 2000 census, the traditional family–married couples with children younger than eighteen years–constituted just 24.1 percent of all U.S. households in 2000, down from 30.9 percent in 1980 and 40.3 percent in 1970.[6] Married couples without children have been on the rise for the past decade, first equaling the percentage of families with children, but now surpassing them at 28.7 percent. "Other" family households, which includes the rapidly increasing number of unmarried couples living together, single mothers, and gay and lesbian families, increased to 16 percent from 10.6 percent in 1970. One of the fastest growing subsets of this group, single mothers, soared 25 percent in the past decade to 7.6 million. Alongside this, the social roles of men and women have shifted; women are no longer the obvious choice as custodial parents. The number of households headed by single fathers also increased greatly–a full 62 percent in the past decade from 1.3 million in 1990 to 2.2 million in 2000–and even though the numbers of single dads are still small compared with single moms, this is still a socially significant increase. And then, of course, there are the singles: 10.7 percent of men living alone and 14.8 percent of women; for the first time, one-person households outnumbered married families with children. All of this means that we are evolving into a more flexible definition of the notion of "family." If you are thinking that the movement toward clans of friends and family as represented by the Tribal trend has something to do with these changing family structures, I would have to agree with you. *What all of this means is that the notion of "family" is expanding to include a myriad of new formats, and brands will need to respond to these new models of how we live.*

Lipton's recent commercials reflect an understanding of the daunting task of portraying today's American family through humor. The commercials show "families," around mealtime, exhibiting classic family mealtime behavior (arguing brothers and sisters, a flustered mom trying to get dad to help set the table, etc.–the usual stereotypical family dinnertime behavior, which in any traditional commercial would only convey the "expected"). The caveat here is that the "families" are bizarrely mismatched from all walks of life, ages, and races normally considered to be inconsistent with the concept of family. One "family" consists of Mr. T as "dad" and Loni Anderson as "mom" and Olympic star Mary Lou Retton and George Hamilton (who could be her father!) as a bickering brother and sister. The tagline says it all: "When you cook, you're family."

Women: The Ones You Want

As I pointed out in *Emotional Branding*, women are without question the most influential consumer group in America because they directly purchase or determine purchasing decisions for no less than 80 percent of all products sold. Strangely enough, although this statistic is well known, it is shocking to realize that many brands do not seize the opportunity of marketing specifically to women. In my first book I outline the key differences between women and men to be aware of when creating a brand strategy with emotional relevance for women. Here, I want to talk about some of the most recent discoveries from the 2000 census and how some brands are learning to talk to women based on a real understanding of their lives and needs. Brands and their communications have yet to catch up with the demographics–specifically in relation to the mammoth numbers of single women and single mothers. Charles Schwab Corp., one of the few to advertise along these lines, has created a commercial for its online stock research arm that features Sarah Ferguson, the Duchess of York and a divorced mom, in a spot created by Omnicom Group. The Duchess is telling her daughter a "Cinderella-esque" bedtime story, and following the traditional "and they lived happily ever after" end, she adds, "Of course if it doesn't work out, you'll need to understand the difference between a P/E ratio and a dividend yield, a growth versus a value strategy. . . ."

Nike is another company that has clearly begun to grasp the importance of the woman's market, and it is making a concentrated effort to better understand and woo women. Nike, realizing that men's and women's approaches to both sports and sportswear are vastly different, has developed a new strategy to address the differences between how women and men conceive of sports and celebrities. Unlike men, many women do not think of themselves as athletes unless they are involved in a professional sport–they are more interested in the process from an experiential and personal perspective and less interested in the external achievement. A recent advertisement celebrates "everyday women" showing a runner sprinting through the city with copy that reads, "I am not Marion Jones." Nike's new woman's Web site, *www.nikegoddess.com*, states, "It's not about perfection and not about winning or losing. It's about human potential. It's the feeling you get when you finish your first marathon, 10k race or walk around the block . . . It's small, personal victories as well as large public ones." Showing an understanding of the extreme time crunch women experience both as breadwinners and as those chiefly responsible for their families and households, the site goes on to state, "It's about making time for ourselves in the midst of many other priorities." The site offers many helpful tips for how to get more out of "that precious time you reserve for being active, including more fun." Nike, opening women's Nike stores in Los Angeles area first, is also trying to broaden its brand's overall appeal to women by designing more trendy, fashion-forward shoes with less emphasis on sports. The company is seeking a younger, active, fashion-conscious consumer. In terms of product development, Nike is infusing its traditional lines with "out-of-gym worthy styles," which busy women won't have to change into or out of in order to workout.

Through positive aspirational brand strategies and messages, brands can actually enforce and accelerate trends that cause the advancement of social causes. In this way, advertising–like Nike's celebrating the power of women in their ad imagery–can actually encourage broader social roles for women, as opposed to just being a reflection of societal viewpoints of the times.

A big idea in terms of the empowerment of women and one that brands could tap into is in the bonding that happens quite naturally between women as great community-oriented communicators.

Similarly, Avon has been working hard to create an image that projects a new feminine strength, using role models like Venus and Serena Williams, the powerhouse tennis stars, to represent the brand. Avon calls itself (and seems to truly be) "The Company for Women." One hundred fifteen years ago, Avon was one of the only companies around that gave women a chance to make money even before they could vote. The company has kept its heritage as a grassroots, community-oriented company–continuing the excellent work it is doing to fight breast cancer (more will be mentioned about this in chapter 2)–while updating its image to be relevant to women today. No longer the door-to-door "ding-dong the Avon lady is calling" company, now they give women in countries like Japan, China, Poland, and Russia a chance to become representatives and improve their lives. Their new product line, "Becoming" is based on a brand imagery that stresses female empowerment and the reinforcement of self-esteem and confidence with the tag line, "Celebrating who you are and who you are becoming."

Dockers advertising expresses the bonding that happens between women.

A big idea in terms of the empowerment of women and one that brands could tap into is in the bonding that happens quite naturally between women as great community-oriented communicators. "Brand clans" for women in some cases could be so powerful–helping to generate the kind of success with women that the "Ladies of Harley" club has for that brand. *Women instinctively understand the strength they have in numbers*, and this is why we see the advent of organizations, such as the Single Women's Alliance Network (SWAN), that have tapped into the 40-million-strong U.S. population of single women to negotiate products and services at a discount for its membership, based on its members' extraordinary purchasing power. As a Citizen Brand, a brand needs to find positive ways to help women to connect to the things that are meaningful to them: community, connection, intimacy, meaning, and from a practical point of view, a balanced lifestyle that includes all of these things alongside a successful, strong professional life. As a final note about women, from the Citizen Brand perspective it is crucial to remember that because of this holistic, big-picture approach, women are particularly concerned with what a brand stands for, and they very often will not support a brand that does not demonstrate good corporate citizenship!

Women Warriors: No More Nice Girl!

It is rumored that Caesar warned his soldiers that, while facing a Celtic warrior in battle was fearsome, what they should truly be terrified of was the prospect of facing their wives, who fought alongside their husbands on the battlefield. In the ancient Celtic matriarchal society the concept of womanhood as a powerful, unfettered force to be reckoned with was very real and today, as our society turns more toward a matriarchal structure, we are seeing a resurrection of this idea in our own culture. The difference of course is that the "battlefield" today is splintered—to be found from boardrooms to bedrooms and everywhere in between, as women claim their right to define and express themselves on their own terms in both their professional and personal lives.

As women continue to explore this concept, brands will need to open new dialogues with them about the nature of this strength they are seeking. Is it about the kind of strong woman we see on one of the most highly rated shows among women, *Survivor*? Tom Ford seems to think so and is using this concept as the inspiration for his collection: "This spring's Gucci girl will be a strong warrior type. A survivor. I think that's right for now," he says. Reebok seems to agree with this angle. Their series of ads running during *Survivor* in the fall of 2001 played off the James Brown hit "It's a Man's World," naming the spots instead, "It's a Woman's World," and showing powerful women like WNBA player Jennifer Azzi, tennis star Venus Williams, and Survivor II winner Tina Wesson in typically male situations with the men playing the traditional female roles, such as that of the cheerleader. The campaign was supported by the Web site, Womendefy.com.

In addition to an exploration of physical toughness, there is also a growing sense that women want to explore the boundaries of the traditional Western woman's role in plenty of other ways. Apparently, after centuries of being told, above all, to be "lady-like nice," it's finally really and truly okay for women today to frown, pout, sneer, curse, act as wild as they wish, and say what they think, whenever, however, and to whomever they want. Really. You don't believe me? Well, maybe it's not yet 100 percent OK, which is why there is a need for all the self-help styled books currently on the market, like *Getting in Touch With Your Inner Bitch, Kiss My Tiara: How to Rule the World as a Smartmouth Goddess*, the workbook/journal *Be a Bad Girl*, or *Bitch: In Praise of Difficult Women*, to help lend that extra dose of courage to women as they hurdle over hundreds of years of societal conditioning to expressive freedom. In France, Nike smartly tapped into this trend by producing a series of cheeky little books last year called *Ras-le-bol!* (loosely translated as "Fed-up!" or "Enough is enough!") that play on the tough-girl theme and give tips like, "Be less liked and more respected." Certainly, "Bitches," "Bad girls," "Wild women" (including the ever-popular "evil temptress" types), as well as women who just plain speak their mind no matter what anybody thinks of them, are nothing new as icons in our popular culture. What does seem to be new, though, is this recent fascination women have with the power of taking control of their right to show their "bad selves" whenever and however they choose. Call it the mainstreaming of the "bitch," a reaction against marginalization throughout the ages, and a defense against potentially devastating setbacks to the feminist movement as recent as the *The Rules* craze in the mid-Nineties, which had scores of women once again preaching the necessity of playing all sorts of manipulative, deceptive games in order to land a husband. No self-respecting woman warrior today, especially not a Gen Y "bad-girl," would be caught dead reading such 1950s drivel!

But once the war is truly won and she is accepted, will the bitch still be bad? I am convinced that the real idea of "No more nice girl" isn't necessarily about being "mean"—it's just about being yourself and overcoming "toxic niceness," a long simmering syndrome which, according to the *Be a Bad Girl Journal*, can be a serious impediment to the assertiveness needed to get what you want in life. Take the words of my friend Hilka, an executive at Deutsche Bank, regarding the perils of having to be tough and demanding in a male-dominated industry without being labeled with the *b* word and yet retaining her more compassionate feminine side without being labeled as too soft: "What I really want, is to be a 'nice bitch.'" She wanted the power to be able to be both, along with the freedom from any sexist labels about her behavior. What I think this is really all about is the power of choice women are insisting on having today and their understanding that strength comes above all from being true to themselves.

Gen Y: Get Ready, America—Here They Come!

The 72 million members of Generation Y (born from 1977 to 1994), many of whom have reached, or are about to reach, their twenties, are today facing an enormous challenge–their first major challenge and perhaps the biggest one they will ever face. We cannot know yet what response this generation, which has grown up in times of peace and prosperity, will have to its first major catastrophe and to the economic fallout of our times; it may mean that many of them will graduate into very unstable, job-poor situations. What is certain, however, is that the effects will be significant on this generation, which up until present was largely sheltered from the shocks that previous generations have borne, such as the devastating appearance of AIDS for Gen X or the assassination of John F. Kennedy and the Vietnam War for the Baby Boomers. Will Gen Y–called "Generation Yes" by some for its very positive, "I can (and will!) change the world," attitude–become more cynical now that it has had such a rude wake-up call into the world's harsher realities? Or will it persevere in its optimism, working all the harder to effect the change it views as essential?

For starters, it is important to recognize that Gen Y has, of course, not been sheltered in the same way previous generations have been sheltered. Their age is, after all, the Information Age. So, in a sense, they have never really had an "age of innocence," at least not on a psychic level, because they have always known so very much about the world's ills. And they have always shown a great desire and aptitude for affecting their environment for change. The fact is, Gen Y has exhibited the most social activism since the Baby Boomers in the 1960s, and they are likely to base much of their consumption on the values they ascribe to the companies providing goods and services. In fact, according to a Cone/Roper survey, *67 percent of teens pursue purchases with a cause in mind* and 80 percent plan to tell their friends about those companies. As a very large and increasingly affluent generation, Gen Y's consumption habits will clearly make their mark–changing dramatically the entire consumer landscape. Already, their influence is making itself known. Gen Y is preparing

The fact is, Gen Y has exhibited the most social activism since the Baby Boomers in the 1960s.

to leave some pretty-well-feathered nests; their Boomer parents' affluence continues strong. And as teens grow older and take on part-time jobs, they are beginning to have considerably more money to spend. In 2000, teens spent $155 billion, $2 billion more than in 1999. An average teen spends $84 a week. So brands beware. This is a generation you will, sooner or later (and the sooner the better!), want to know well.

But getting to know Gen Y is not easy. Gen Y is a tough target for marketers–savvy and highly intelligent (a recent survey showed that "intelligence"–even beyond clothes!–is the number one thing teens today want to possess). Very nearly half of all American college students today have taken marketing courses and "know the enemy." They are well aware, and they pride themselves on being able to dissect and remain impervious to marketing messages.

Gen Y is extremely motivated to have their voice heard in terms of business ethics and their vision on globalization. Their ideas are grassroots, very popular, pervasive, and not without merit.

From a Citizen Brand perspective the most important thing to recognize about Gen Y is that a large portion of Gen Y is extremely motivated to have their voice heard in terms of business ethics and their vision on globalization. Their ideas are grassroots, very popular, pervasive, and not without merit. Seeing how their voice might not get any representation because of the merging of media corporations and the greater power of global corporations is frightening for them. Anti-consumerism based on the negative impacts of our "mall culture and television" on young people is a serious subject for this group. And how the culture of branding is a rich nation's game that excludes or tramples on the needs of poor people is a very sensitive topic. They object to the manipulation of information by some corporations and are very adept researchers into the truth. Labor practices, environmental abuses, and racism are among the top issues around which Gen Y is organizing and looking to have its voice heard. Many university professors support these concepts with books and articles and most universities today have real, vital hotbeds of activism. Take a look at a couple of these recent Gen Y activist campaigns on college campus that were overwhelmingly successful:

1. Yale University: Students forced Yale and one of its corporate business partners, a pharmaceutical company, to relax a patent on an

AIDS drug. Yale and its partner now allow the production of a generic version of the drug, royalty free.

2. Pennsylvania State: After a series of anonymous death threats aimed at African-American students who only make up 4 percent of the student body, students took over the student union in a ten-day sit-in demanding that the administration address the climate of racial intolerance. The school's president promised to establish an Africana Studies Research Center and create $350,000 in new minority scholarships.

3. Harvard: Students staged a three-week occupation of the president's office to put a national media spotlight on the low wages the nation's wealthiest university pays its custodial and food-service workers. Harvard promised to raise wages.

4. University of Michigan: Student pressure forced Nike, who had a licencing agreement with the university, to agree to improve working conditions in a Mexican factory and reinstate workers who had been fired for striking.

5. University of Wisconsin: Students created Ecopledge, an organization that attempts to persuade corporations to be more environmentally conscious. 9,000 students have signed the pledge vowing not to work for, or purchase from, certain corporations.

One of the biggest goals of Gen Y activism is to fight for what one activist Canadian magazine, *Adbusters,* calls "the birth of mental environmentalism" or the manipulation of our minds through advertising, viral marketing, and the growing role of brands in schools and universities. As a solution, *Adbusters* proposes nothing short of a cultural revolution through, among other things, "cultural jamming" tactics like the doctoring of billboards and designing mock ads that feature reworked slogans such as "Do it Just." A recent issue of the magazine claims, "Our business is to topple existing power structures and forge a major rethinking of the way we will live in the twenty-first century. We believe culture jamming will become to our era what civil rights was to the 60s, what feminism was to the 70s, and what environmental activism was to the 80s." In this well-executed magazine you'll find impressive listings of numerous activist events and protests such as "The Toronto financial district shutdown," "The Trade Justice Carnival" in London with Naomi Klein as a speaker, and major anti-corporate protests in Nice and Gothenburg, as well as the next EU challenge in Brussels, and events surrounding the national "Buy Nothing Day."

If we are to experience a rite of passage for an entire generation, it seems to me that a strong understanding of what that means is crucial here, especially since the target of this movement includes big businesses and advertising agencies.

Generation X: The Lost Generation

From "slacker" to dot.com fortune and fame to ?–a big question mark. Generation X (born from 1965 to 1976)–the perennial "middle-child generation" of our era with a population of a mere 40 million–has been through a very tough time recently from living through and taking much of the brunt of the fallout of the Internet start-up fiasco. But Gen X has responded to the situation with its own particular, famous flair: a combination of individualism, flexibility, and bravado. First of all, *many Gen Xers are finding that they still don't want to work within the system* and they still don't quite know what they want to do when they grow up or maybe (wounded as they have been professionally) they just don't want to work at all–at least not for a while, at least not in the traditional sense. Maybe they'll just reinvent the whole notion of work in their usual highly creative, entrepreneurial manner. What is certain is that they will do whatever they do on their own terms.

Many (but certainly not all) a Gen Xer can be found at their folks' house these days, or in other more modest digs, reinventing their lives and redefining what they value most. Many have found that they don't mind living more simply in order to have more time for endeavors other than work. Sociologists have called the phenomenon "downshifting." While this does imply less work activity, it would be a mistake to think that this group is doing less. They are very engaged in their lives, they are simply reevaluating–once again–the American Dream. Some marketers have taken to calling them Generation disconneX because of this hiatus period, which is also tending to influence this once tech-enamored generation to be less wired constantly to their communication devices and focus more on simpler, even old-fashioned modes of communication and entertainment. The fact is that members of *this generation, who have always defined success in far greater terms than economics, are now reaching the pivotal age when they will be focusing more on building families, which seems to be taking a front seat for the moment in terms of priorities.* Whatever they choose to do, we can be sure that Gen X will do it in an interesting and inspiring way that, as the oftentimes powerful cultural influencers they are, may very well inspire both their younger and older Gen Y and Baby Boomer "brothers and sisters."

Baby Boomers: Living Large

In more ways than one, Baby Boomers today have truly hit their stride. According to the 2000 census, there are more than 83.8 million people between the ages of 35 and 54–up 32 percent, or 20 million, from the 1990 census. The "baby boom" propelled the largest percentage increases of any age group in the 1990–2000 decade. By 2005, more than 85 million Americans will be older than fifty and the median age of Americans will be 36.6 years, the highest ever. Well, not only are they the biggest generation of all, they are also the wealthiest. And, in contrast to Gen X's hiatus, they are not showing any signs of slowing their work or living pace whatsoever. In many ways, this huge generation seems to be picking up speed as they age. They are putting off retirement indefinitely for the moment. They continue to work and, according to an AARP study, a full 80 percent of Baby Boomers plan to work part-time during their retirement years. This means that they will have higher incomes longer into their lives–a boon for many a brand if they can learn how to appeal to Baby Boomers. And even when Baby Boomers do retire, you have probably heard that most of them don't plan on just sitting around. Well, they don't. For one thing, they will go back to school and begin entirely new endeavors. A Del Webb Corporation survey found that 28 percent of the Baby Boomers they questioned plan to go back to school when they retire.

The trick for many marketers will be in trying to understand how to advertise to them as a specific age group without being obvious that you are trying to reach them because they are getting older; because that in and of itself is, of course, a big turnoff.

But if they are working hard, they also continue to play hard. There has been much talk of this generation showing us all a new meaning of aging in America. And so far, they are succeeding in their mission to redefine age with plenty of aging celebrities–from Viagra-chugging Hugh Hefner to fabulous-fifty actresses like Cheryl Ladd, as well as regular Boomers, like your sixty-year-old neighborhood motorcycle-riding mama–to give evidence that members of this generation are simply refusing to accept the limitations previously ascribed to their age. They often look to Gen X and Y for inspiration and are not afraid to jump in and try the cultural and sports trends of the younger generations, such as snowboarding, which, to the chagrin of many a hip snowboarder, has largely been co-opted by mom and dad!

The trick for many marketers will be in trying to understand how to advertise to them as a specific age group without being obvious that you are trying to reach them because they are getting older; because that in and of itself is, of course, a big turnoff. This proud generation will not want to be treated as "different" and yet will want, and be able to afford, plenty of special treatment! A study by the GE Center for Financial Learning found that 55 percent of Boomers expect to "perform basic tasks independently well into their eighties" and that means that brands will have to help them find a way of doing this. We are already seeing lots of ingenious ergonomic product developments and designs based on this idea, and it will only continue. I will explore the topic of ergonomic design and its enormous potential for helping brands connect with people powerfully in their everyday lives in chapter 7, "Evolve from Function to Feel."

Ethnic Trends: The New Faces of America

Marketers everywhere are trying to figure out how to respond to the seismic shift of "mainstream" America toward an ethnic majority, both in terms of sheer numbers that were bigger than anyone expected, and in terms of cultural influence which, though more difficult to measure, is clearly a big new trend.

As a general note, the Census 2000 data on race are not directly comparable with data from the 1990 census or earlier censuses because in 2000, for the first time, respondents could report one or more races. This is an important difference, reflective of an entirely new societal structure from an ethnic standpoint. As Roger Selbert, vice president of strategic planning at the Hispanic agency LatinWorks, says, *"The future of diversity is not multiculturalism–separate and distinct ethnic enclaves–but a mixing, blurring, and blending of racial and ethnic traits."*[7] As we learned from the census, by 2040, minorities (African-Americans, Hispanics, Asians) will collectively outnumber whites in America . . . hence the term "Emerging Majority." The question marketers are facing is whether to market to members of the Emerging Majority as part of the mainstream (i.e., multicultural advertising) or to target them as a specific niche. On the one hand, if we are working toward a truly integrated society, then images and marketing messages of unity are important; people of color are part of the mainstream, not isolated or on the fringe. And yet, culturally targeted ads have been and will continue to be more relevant to ethnic audiences in some instances; when and how to execute such campaigns is an important and delicate issue.

It seems to me that the youth will lead the way to answering these questions, as they themselves are representatives of ethnic blending both in terms of their own ethnicity and in terms of youth culture itself, which is fed strongly by cross-cultural influences. In the 2000 census the people who reported more than one race had a significantly younger median age (22.7) than those reporting just one race (35.6). About 25 percent of Americans are younger than eighteen and more than one-third of those youth are Hispanic or black. This growing segment of the youth population is the trend-driver that is largely helping to form mainstream America's taste in music, clothing, and everything cultural. *Ethnic culture = urban culture = youth culture: the cool factor.* Many fashion/lifestyle trends originate in urban centers and are quickly absorbed into general popular culture, and Generation Y is extremely interested and adept at appropriating urban style. In a nutshell, marketing and branding professionals would do well to keep a close eye on the urban/ethnic demographic! This is why Chrysler is trying to build a hipper image through mainstream advertising that features attractive young Latin- or African-American people. As Jeff Bell, director of the campaign at Chrysler says, "It's not a matter of majority and minority. It's a matter of major influencers in popular culture."[8]

GENERAL TRENDS IN THE AFRICAN-AMERICAN MARKET

Census 2000 showed that 36.4 million people, or 12.9 percent of the total population, is African-American.

Let's take a look at a few of the major trends for this group:

•   African-Americans are more affluent than ever, with an 85 percent gain in buying power since the 1990 census, bringing their total spending power to $572.1 billion per year, or 8 percent of U.S.

buying power. As African-Americans earn more and spend more, the ostentatious display of wealth and status popularized by hip hop artists in the late Nineties has been taken up by the larger urban and, finally, mainstream culture–big jewels, big furs, expensive clothes, and cars are *de rigueur* (for now), in spite of the sinking economy.

- Suburban African-Americans are leaving urban centers for the 'burbs, with 39 percent now residing there. Marketing to this affluent segment is not the same as marketing to white suburbanites, because suburban African-Americans still strongly identify as urban. Also, they are more eager to enjoy their money (see above) and are heavy consumers of luxury goods. Branding/marketing campaigns stressing images of luxury and affluence will win with the majority of black consumers, though many luxury-goods marketers are oblivious to the potential. The majority of specifically African-American targeted marketing is for lower-ticket items such as fast food and sneakers.

- One of the biggest trends in the African-American market (primarily Gen X and Y) for 2001 was the phenomenal success of Motorola's 2-way pager. African-American and Latino youth have always been early and eager adopters of mobile telecommunications technology; urban youth were the first nonmedical professionals to carry pagers, and helped jump-start the cellular-phone boom. While Motorola and Star Tac are the top two cell-phone brands in the African-American market, Motorola was first to capitalize on urban thirst for the newest/latest telecom tool–hence the ubiquity of the 2-way, a tool now as common among urban youth as cell phones. They are, in fact, hot and cool, and their prominent use by music-industry figures solidified their cool factor with the kids in the 'burbs. The key benefits they represent for this group are: instant communication, constant accessibility, portable email.

- Internet: 43 percent of African-Americans are now online; of those online, 54 percent have made purchases, compared to 74 of the general population. African-Americans are more likely to use the Internet to leverage their careers. Fifty percent of African-Americans use the Internet for job hunting, compared to 24 percent of general-market users, who were more than 95 percent white. African-Americans are more likely to use the Internet to network with other professionals. The study also found that 16 percent of African-American users have taken online classes, compared to 9 percent of the general market. Online African-

Americans are younger, wealthier, and more educated than African-Americans who remain offline.

- African-American members of the Boomer generation differ from their white counterparts in key ways: Black Boomers insist, even more than white Boomers, on buying products because of their social value. Cause-marketing strategies and visible corporate community participation are very important to this group. African-American Boomers still hold the injustices and hardships of pre–Civil Rights America close to their hearts. Because many of them experienced segregation first-hand, they tend to view products and services as not being "for them" unless they have a specific reason or invitation to use the product and service, because in the past, they were not included. Specifically targeted ethnic marketing seems to be highly appreciated and important for this demographic.

As with any ethnic group, the most important (and increasingly obvious) thing to do is to bring the culture of that group into the brand culture itself. *As with any ethnic group, the most important (and increasingly obvious) thing to do is to bring the culture of that group into the brand culture itself, either through hiring the people representative of the ethnic group you are trying to reach, or by hiring a great ethnic or diverse branding agency.* Toyota learned the hard way about how important it is to understand their African-American customers and market to them appropriately. When the automaker produced a promotional postcard that showed a smiling mouth displaying tooth jewelry with a gold inset of its RAV4 sports utility vehicle, Rev. Jesse Jackson and the Rainbow/Push Coalition, feeling that the ad was demeaning to African-Americans, called for the company to pull the advertising. Toyota did and issued a public apology. Jackson demanded that Toyota hire an African-American agency and add more minority dealers and minorities to its board. Rev. Jackson claims that Toyota ignored his urging in a 1999 letter to hire more diverse ad agencies and "avoid culturally insensitive" campaigns when in early 1999 Toyota published an ad in *Jet* magazine with a headline that said, "Unlike your last boyfriend, it goes to work in the morning."

No brand today can afford to make that kind of mistake–it makes one wonder about the future strength of the Harvard "brand" after the institution offends and loses a top African-American scholar, Dr.

Cornel West, through an elitist attitude that criticized Dr. West's recording of a rap CD. Even seemingly impervious institutions like Harvard can be very seriously damaged by the kind of press and negative public perception that results from a situation such as this one!

GENERAL TRENDS IN THE HISPANIC MARKET

Higher-than-expected Hispanic growth in the 2000 census has resulted in many marketers jumping to alter their plans and grappling with questions about how to reach this powerful group. By 2005, Hispanics will be the largest "minority" group in America.

- Hispanics have $630 billion in purchasing power. The Hispanic middle class grew 80 percent between 1979 and 1998.
- Hispanics as a group indicate that having a brand name is very important when purchasing almost every type of consumer item. Hispanics are more likely than everyone else to be brand-loyal. Fifty-two percent will stick with a brand they like, compared to 43 percent of non-Hispanics.
- Eight-five percent of Hispanics have computers at home, and 75 percent have Internet access. Thirty-one percent of these users have shopped online.

Of particular significance are Hispanic youth, which have been the largest group of minority children since 1998. Gen Y minority youth, Hispanics included, are more likely than earlier generations to see their ethnic identity as only part of who they are. They have "multiple categories" for themselves. They may consider their heritage as being more or less central to their identity, but it is not their only identity, and they shouldn't be marketed to as if it is. Nevertheless, heritage is very important to this group. Researcher Peter Roslow notes: "I'm always amazed by the 'Hispanicness' of Hispanic teens. They're speaking Spanish at home, both [languages] with friends, English for college and the Internet, but they're very much into Hispanic culture. Even when they're born in the U.S." Earlier generations were more focused on "total assimilation."

One of the core values among Hispanic youth that set them apart is "familismo," or strong family orientation. Hispanic teens are more likely to watch television with their parents, while 50 percent of Hispanic girls and 27 percent of Hispanic boys say they admire their mother more than anyone else in their lives. Hispanics are more likely than any other group to take their children with them while traveling.

Advertising in Spanish-language media does the trick for reaching Hispanic adults, but unlike prior generations, messages targeted to today's Hispanic teens do not have to be in Spanish to be understood. All the same, marketers who use the language in their ad messages may reach them on a more emotional level. Today's Hispanic youth are very proud of their culture, are very likely to be bilingual, and want to see Spanish-language advertising in both Spanish media and mainstream media. But be careful, using Spanish language messages isn't everything. It's also important to be "in-culture," a term coined by Hispanic marketing strategist Isabel Valdés. Research shows that in-culture and in-language advertising messages outperform English-language messages. Among Hispanic teens, English ads are 28 percent less effective than Spanish ads in terms of ad recall, and 54 percent less effective in terms of persuasion.

Fisher-Price has made clever use of its understanding of the importance of the Spanish language for this market by developing bilingual versions of its Baby Smartronics line. The toys will be able to speak in both Spanish and English; parents will be able to decide which language their child will hear by flipping a switch. *People* magazine's highly successful *People en Español* edition is also a great example of a brand reaching the Hispanic market through intelligent product development. The magazine is also region specific, with its west-of-the-Mississippi issue more Mexican related while the east-coast issue is more oriented to Puerto Rican, Cuban, or international stars. Kraft has a terrific bilingual food Web site called ComidaKraft.com, which includes Latin-inspired recipes along with traditional American recipes and can switch with a click of the mouse from Spanish to English, allowing the user to compare recipes in both languages. The culturally relevant content includes information about and recipes for Hispanic holidays, as well as information on heath issues, such as diabetes, of particular concern to the Latino community.

Gay and Lesbian Markets

The census stated that there are more than 600,000 gay and lesbian families. However, this number is a matter of much debate; the

Human Rights Campaign estimates that this is undercounted by 62 percent. Regardless of their number, this group is clearly extremely important: first of all, as a major cultural influence, above all on younger generations, but also increasingly in mainstream America (witness the huge success of prime-time gay-themed TV shows like *Will & Grace*); and secondly, in terms of their affluence and demonstrated brand loyalty. One of the most important things to note about this group is that couple-hood and family-hood are big areas for these groups that are underserved by brands. The census revealed that a full 50 percent of all respondents who identified themselves as "gay or lesbian" were in partnered relationships. About 13 percent of these couples have children under eighteen in the home. Obviously, advertising/marketing/branding needs to let go of the stereotype of the young, single gay male. The financial and insurance industry is already reaching out to same-sex couples, whose planning and investments needs are often differentiated by their inability to marry. "Celebrating diversity" is certainly an important step for brands to take today. But Brands also need to take the next step (or several steps!) beyond this initial level to begin to understand how to target gays and lesbians from an emotional perspective. In other words, after decades of treating gays as an invisible minority, brands are now acknowledging the importance of this group. But the perceived attitude is often very much self-congratulatory: "Look everybody— we're tolerant!" What is called for is a more personalized approach. Some key trends concerning this group:

- Whether "gay vague" or forthright advertising is the best way to reach this market is the subject of some debate. Some members of this demographic view "nudge and wink" vague advertising as cowardly. "Gay Vague" is a term coined by analyst Michael Wilke of CommercialCloset.org. It refers to advertising featuring gay innuendo designed to reach both gay and mainstream audiences. Generally with these ads, mainstream audiences see ambiguity, while gay audiences see a direct sales pitch.
- Coors, Amazon.com, AOL, AMEX, Johnson & Johnson, Smith-Kline Beecham, Subaru, Levi's, MTV, GM, and Travelocity.com are some of the increasing number of big brands that are doing gay-specific advertising (as opposed to gay-vague ads).
- Ad spending in gay publications is up 25 percent, while "gay vague" advertising in mainstream publications is becoming more and more prevalent. As social prejudice for this group begins to

dissipate, corporate decision makers are increasingly responding to a community they once preferred to ignore—even with mainstream advertising campaigns that once were avoided for fear of alienating less tolerant consumers.

• "Genderation Inspecific" is a marketing term coined by journalist Tyler Brûlé. It refers to Generation Y's preference for ambiguously gendered advertising. Younger demographics today are choosing to go the sexy, fun route—embracing all lifestyles and points of view (gay, straight, bisexual, curious . . .). To reach Gen Y, marketers have to understand this spirit of openness and aversion to gender labeling. What is certain is that at a minimum, discrimination-adverse Gen Y will want your brand to treat this group with respect.

• Seventy-eight percent of lesbian and gay e-shoppers prefer to buy from companies that advertise directly to them.

As a final note, *from a Citizen Brand perspective it is crucial that, before seeking to market to this group, a corporation make certain that their internal policies reflect well on their desire to have gays and lesbians as customers.* Otherwise, a company will be viewed as a hypocrite and there is nothing worse for this community who wants to be accepted for themselves and not just for their wallets! Ford was very smart in deciding not to do any direct marketing to the gay community until it had its internal policies in place. Ford first resolved simmering employee benefits issues, waiting until after the "Big Three" Detroit automakers (who were petitioned by the gay community) established employee benefits to same-sex partners under a joint agreement with the United Automobile Workers before setting in motion marketing plans concerning the gay community. Ford has also taken other interesting steps to show its sensitivity to the gay community, such as its support of Beverly Hills Ford, a gay dealership with an all-gay staff. The idea behind Beverly Hills Ford is to make buying a car easier by discussing financing situations in terms of same-sex couples; so far, it has been a big hit with the gay community.

From a Citizen Brand perspective it is crucial that, before seeking to market to this group, a corporation make certain that their internal policies reflect well on their desire to have gays and lesbians as customers.

This community also greatly appreciates brands that show social conscience for both gay-related causes and non-gay-related causes.

Another car company, long a favorite with the gay community, Subaru, really understands how to play the role of good corporate citizen in the gay community. Subaru sponsors the Los Angeles gay pride festival and events organized by the Human Rights Campaign and was a founding sponsor of the Rainbow Card, an affinity credit card program–Subaru gives up to $3,000 discounts to cardholders. "We are clear that we support the health and civic-mindedness of the gay and lesbian community," said Tim Bennet, director of national marketing for Subaru. "We were the first to offer domestic partnership benefits. We're not just here to sell you a car as an exploited segment."[9]

2

The Second Commandment: Evolve from Honesty to Trust

Honesty is expected. ***Trust is engaging and intimate. It must be earned.***

This commandment is about moving beyond the expected business principles of basic quality assurance and honest business practices (without forgetting about them!) to an approach that seeks to engage people within the context of a relationship based on trust. While quality products and services and a business based on integrity are certainly a part of building trust with people, the focus a Citizen Brand must have on creating trust indicates a fundamental "mindshift," which is sometimes subtle in execution. This "mindshift" means moving from a philosophy of "show and tell"—where a company in the active role simply tries to show and tell the people, who are in a "passive" role, that they are an honest and trustworthy company—to an approach that understands that *the true dynamic of trust is based on a continuous, reciprocal "give and take" principle that recognizes the very powerful, active role of the consumer on a continual basis.* This means that corporations must actively earn the consumer's trust. Once it is given, and the corporation is enjoying the consumer's patronage, the corporation must continue to give valid reasons for the consumer to trust, remembering always that it can be taken away at any moment.

From the perspective of the necessity today of becoming a Citizen Brand, the material we will address in this chapter will be critical because it directly addresses the issue of trust and how it can be established between corporations and people through a corporate culture and agenda that demonstrates a real sensitivity, understanding, and, ultimately, commitment to social responsibility. The following eight commandments in this book will continue with this theme but are more focused on the executional aspects of a Citizen Brand strategy, each one contributing a necessary element to the overall emotional relevance and strength of the brand.

From the perspective of the necessity today of becoming a Citizen Brand, the material we will address in this chapter will be critical because it directly addresses the issue of trust.

Just like in any real relationship, trust is the foundation—leading to respect and longevity. The 2001 corporate reputation survey conducted by Harris Interactive and the Reputation Institute for the *Wall Street Journal* polling 21,630 respondents found, once again, that "emotional appeal," defined as "trust, admiration, and respect" was the ultimate driving force in how people rated companies. Furthermore, the study showed very clearly that while advertising can certainly help convey a message to people, it doesn't necessarily change fundamental opinions. For example, despite Philip Morris's massive $250 million corporate advertising campaign in 2001, highlighting its charitable activities, the company's overall rating remained second to last, just above Bridgestone/Firestone. Many of the poll's respondents felt that the company should have spent its ad budget "more on philanthropy and less on publicity." The previous year's results were very similar. Sixteen percent of respondents familiar with the company said they had boycotted its products in the past year, with several respondents saying that they simply don't believe the sincerity of the company's efforts in the face of all of the smoking-related lawsuits. This means that people perceive Philip Morris as merely a "show-and-tell" company that they suspect of manipulation. When spending money for causes, it is important to change and correct what is perceived as negative practice. Charitable activities only work strategically if they are a reflection of a larger corporate strategy that includes people-driven policy changes. Is it possible for a company like Philip Morris to gain the "give and take" quality of trust of a true Citizen Brand, or does the very nature of their business prevent it from doing so? This is one of the very thorny questions I will attempt to address in this chapter. One thing is very clear, however: Not only is trust precious—it is fragile. The 2001 survey also highlights the point I have just made about how difficult it can be to regain trust once it is lost, regardless of the amount of money a company may spend on communications to rectify a broken trust situation. Exxon Mobil is a case in point, with many of the people surveyed still expressing hostility toward the company more than ten years after the Alaskan oil spill.

First Things First: Building a Company As a Community

Howard Shultz, CEO of Starbucks and an innovator in the art of Emotional Branding, says it very simply and clearly: "The brand has to start with the culture and naturally extend to our customers . . . If we want to exceed the trust of our customers, then we first have to build trust with our people." Seems simple–a "no-brainer," really. But however simple this core concept to building an Emotional Brand may be, the execution of the philosophy presents manifold difficulties, to the point that it's even hard to tell in many cases that the good intentions of this philosophy exist somewhere in the layers of the corporate creed. I believe that this is because as human beings we need constant reminding, constant inspiration, constant care/nurturing, and this–once again, simple–fact is often forgotten. Starbucks was one of the first companies to take this rhetoric and make it tangible for their employees in real, practical ways, such as offering part-timers stock options and health benefits. Of course, many companies are now endorsing similar initiatives, some with more integrity and style than others. For example, Nucor, the steelmaker company known for its commitment to the environment and recycling, builds trust with its employees through a unique company benefit tailored to its people's needs: Nucor provides every child of every one of its employees (most of whom are not college educated) with a $2,500 per year scholarship for higher education. Nucor has not laid off any employees due to lack of work since it entered the industry in the 1960s. In response to the recession, Nucor reduced work schedules and implemented travel restrictions. CEO Dan DiMicco explains, "A lot of our mills are in rural communities, and you can decimate the communities by laying those workers off. . . . How can you build loyalty when you pat people on the back when times are good and when times are tough you show them the door?"[1] Nucor illustrates the degree to which it values its employees by listing all 7,500 of their names in its annual report.

> **How can you build loyalty when you pat people on the back when times are good and when times are tough you show them the door?**

The symbolic gesture of the name listing in Nucor's annual reports serves to emphasize the idea that *a corporation is a living organism, composed of and influenced by the people who work there more than we can even begin to realize.* Corporations either form organic, constantly changing communities that can be healthy, inspirational places for people and their ideas to thrive, or atmospheres that are rigid, corrupt, and stifling. The art of great management has to do with balancing a strong corporate/brand foundation with the right amount of flexibility and openness to people's changing needs. Because the people in a company come, go, and continually change, the first step toward creating a solid corporate community is to create a strong, emotionally relevant brand vision that will provide an ongoing framework. A strong brand vision not only helps customers understand the brand, but can also give an enormous sense of mission, passion, and direction inside the company. For this to happen, it is vital not only that employees understand the brand's values, but that they also embrace them, and this means that the brand vision must be unique and have enough character to be very clear to everyone, without losing a sense of elasticity that allows employees to feel that they can contribute their own individual personality to the brand vision. Uniting people behind a strong, emotional brand voice can be especially powerful today in light of the Tribal trend and the need people have to create communities. *In fact, many people today feel closer to coworkers than to neighbors because of the time they spend at work,* where we now have day-care centers, gyms, and so on–they are seeking the warmth of tribal fires in the office place, and when they find it, it can inspire both loyalty and creativity. Unfortunately, few find this kind of supportive atmosphere. Walker Information, a customer- and employee-satisfaction researcher, says that fewer than one in four workers are truly loyal to their companies and committed to staying. And the evidence for the importance of this loyalty from a business standpoint is pretty conclusive. For example, a study by Watson Wyatt of 750 companies showed that *companies with excellent recruiting and retention policies provide an 8 percent higher return to shareholders* than those that do not–with those who have a strong commitment to job security earning an additional 1.4 percent for shareholders. In addition, JResearch suggests that loyalty continues to matter a great deal even in a time of heavy layoffs since it shapes people's choices not only about where to work but also about "how long, hard, and wholeheartedly they apply their mental energies–the fuel that drives today's economy." As Peter Drucker said in a recent article for *The Economist*, where he emphasizes the incredible value of these mental energies in business, "The management of knowledge workers should be based on the assumption that the corporation needs them more than they need the corporation. They know they can leave. They have both mobility and self-confidence. This means they have to be treated and managed as volunteers, in the same way as volunteers who work for not-for-profit organizations."[2]

Treating employees with the same consideration as one would treat volunteers may seem extreme to some, but I would agree with it in principle because the statement emphasizes not so much the "benefits package" perspective to treating employees well, which, although important, does not fully address the issue of how to connect with employees. It's an expression of gratitude toward the employees' contributions that recognizes their value. I would add to this that the new expectation will be to *treat employees not only as much needed, highly valuable workers, but also with a humanistic, emotional sensitivity that demonstrates an understanding of the employee as a whole person.*

The gulf between those companies that understand this idea and those that do not is currently widening. September 11 was a litmus test for many employers and it is very interesting to see how different corporations responded and what effects those responses had on their employees. Those employers who failed to show sufficient compassion and sensitivity to the emotional impact of an event of this magnitude lost a lot of loyalty ground with their employees. In some corporations, employees were criticized for failing to focus on work that day, and for watching too much TV instead. Some were not given permission to leave early, or if they were, the company begrudged them the time off, which in some cases was tallied up as part of their vacation time! A marketing manager of one such firm, who is considering leaving her position as a result, said simply, "I expected much more compassion."[3] *In the face of such intense primal emotions, these companies could have forged a deeper relationship with their employees, inspiring loyalty.* The potential for damaging that relationship is also

> Chappell has organized his entire company around this principle of putting social and moral responsibilities at the center of his business instead of operating from the traditional "numbers game" perspective.

great at such moments because when emotions run high and people are very sensitive, it is easy for the corporation to become a focal point for feelings of frustration and anger. A consultant at a Chicago consulting firm remarked, concerning her senior supervisor's insistence that everyone "return to business as usual" that day, "What we needed was to stop and say, 'OK, we're going to take a deep breath and think about this.'" She says that when the time comes for her to make long-term plans, "I will remember this situation and how my firm dealt with it."[4]

Clearly, an empathetic management philosophy is missing from these scenarios, but, even more important, a core Citizen Brand philosophy is also missing from those corporations that do not seem to understand the importance of the role they play in people's lives. A great example of a company that practices this Citizen Brand philosophy is Tom's of Maine. Tom Chappell, the CEO, is the author of the book *Managing Upside Down*,[5] which attempts to reverse the values of business by making social responsibility a prerequisite of conducting commerce. Chappell has organized his entire company around this principle of putting social and moral responsibilities at the center of his business instead of operating from the traditional "numbers game" perspective. This means that decisions, such as whether to move an entire division of the business to Vermont in order to save half a million dollars a year, are made very differently than they would be in a traditional company. In this case, Chappell decided not to make the move because Tom's of Maine's commitment to its community and the state of Maine is a fundamental part of its mission statement. It also means that the products themselves completely reflect Tom's commitment to totally natural, environmentally sensitive ingredients.

Chappell has found that the rewards of running his business from a people-first philosophy has paid off in the long run, not only in terms of having a very clear, unwavering brand mission that people can take pride in and cleave to, but also in terms of the creativity that is fostered through a people-first credo. Tom's of Maine strives to flatten the business hierarchy as much as possible in order to encourage creativity. Chappell says, "When you are working to empower people in your organization, you're really giving people permission to be who they are, and to use their gifts to solve problems."[6] After implementing his "Upside Down" management approach, where individuals at all levels come up with ideas that they then "champion" through the process of measuring them against company objectives and consumer needs, Chappell found that product development took off at an incredible rate. "We have changed our new-product delivery system at such an exponential rate I can hardly count the progress," he says. This kind of unleashing of creativity not only creates new products, or course, but also happier employees–and it should come as no surprise that 83 percent of employees who enjoy their jobs, also have a "strong sense of loyalty" to their employers, according to a recent Ipsos-Reid poll.[7] Through a strategic tool developed by one of our principals, Peter Levine, my company approaches projects through a very democratic, collaborative brainstorming process with our clients where everyone's ideas contribute to the concepts explored. This innovative approach, which we call *Brand Focus*, fosters a true spirit of partnership and inspires the kind of creativity that leads to unexpected solutions.

How do very large companies foster the same kind of open forum creativity among the full scope of their employee force? Some larger companies such as Voyant Technologies have had great success with programs like their "Bright Ideas" project, which encourages employees to submit ideas for new products or marketing strategies on their Web site for discussion and eventual approval. CEO, Bill Ernstrom says, "We want everyone to act like an owner and entrepreneur."[8]

Interestingly, another very important element to creating the kind of trust that results in employee loyalty is a company's commitment to good business ethics and demonstrated efforts to play a role in supporting social causes. *A Roper Starch Worldwide study showed that 61 percent of employees are more likely to feel pride and a strong sense of loyalty when their companies support social issues.* This kind of loyalty can translate into nothing less than greater job satisfaction, higher retention rates, and better overall performance, including customer service–what every company wants to achieve!

Home Depot: Home Is Where the Heart Is

I was very interested in meeting with Home Depot, the successful retailer, with a track record that is staggering. As customers, my wife and I have always felt inspired shopping there. The atmosphere

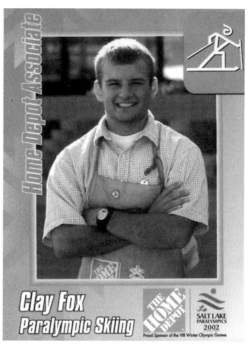

Home Depot associate and Olympic hopeful Clay Fox.

is unpretentious, and the warehouse design that characterizes the concept supports their claim of being a dependable quality "professional" store. A couple of weeks before this book's due date, I was very pleased to get the opportunity to meet with their very articulate and passionate former CMO Dick Sullivan. Dick is a sincere advocate of the company's policies concerning community involvement and his generosity in sharing the Home Depot vision meant that our meeting went well beyond its allotted time—at the end I was lucky enough to be treated to a full tour of their historical museum and vast communications studio. The brand is religion there, and "people" is all they think about. Home Depot encapsulates in many ways the true vision of a Citizen Brand.

First of all, Home Depot recognizes the impact their business has on the economy and the communities in which they operate. They will create over 40,000 jobs in 2002 and with $50 billion in revenue they are one of the fastest growing retailers in America. In 2002 they are, so far, bucking the general trend toward layoffs, and

I must say I clearly saw a connection between their financial success and the care they show for their employees. "Some secretaries are millionaires" in this company, mentioned Dick, affirming that everyone can become and think like a stockholder in the company.

Their corporate story is of course not picture perfect—they have been criticized in the past for using materials that hurt the environment, but they have gone a very long way to improve their way of doing business, and I am convinced that they will continue to make progress in this regard. Home Depot is, all in all, an example of good ethical practices. I asked Dick what kind of programs they felt the most pride about, and among their most impressive to me is their support of talented potential participants in the Olympics by paying promising athletes full-time pay for half a day's work so they can train. Their group of "disaster volunteers," who are always ready to move and help people in times of crisis is one of the most interesting concepts I found in the context of the idea of becoming a Citizen Brand. Most important, perhaps, are Home Depot's initiatives; the company gives the power to a decentralized management to make quick decisions. In helping New Yorkers during the September 11 tragedy, thousands of hats, gloves, and flashlights, among other needed items, were sent to the site of the tragedy by the regional stores in the shortest amount of time. That's how deep "the trust" runs in this company, where associates are permitted to provide the impetus for these kinds of actions.

Part of what makes this company good is also its modesty, a sign of supreme confidence, and a rare quality with successful brands. I had to coax Dick for more than thirty minutes to discuss in greater depth their community activities because, at Home Depot, it is not something they brag about. These practices are part of their culture, part of their DNA. Home Depot leverages its expertise and products to support communities wherever they can. They build or refurbish hundreds of schools in the country, build habitats for communities where youth are at risk, and are on alert for any disaster where their help can make a difference. Home Depot has, in fact, contributed over $100 million in cash and products and millions of volunteer hours to such programs. The Casa Verde youth building program of Austin, Texas, is one of the thousands of community-based programs supported through their "team Depot program," which taps into what they call their "sweat equity." The volunteerism spirit of the place gets people to work together on lofty projects in ways that allow them to get to know each other and trust each other. In this way, people can start sharing the same passion for what they do, which will most definitely show in their work. This is a culture with heart that connects with people. *There is this idea that advertising or branding programs are the only way to reach people when the power of a culture that cares is more potent!*

The creation of this kind of spirit among the 250,000 associates requires formidable communications programs. This is the role of the "HDTV television channel," the Home Depot internal communications vehicle that allows, among other things, associates to hear what Bernie Marcus, the founder, has to say about being "orange-blooded," the term the company has coined in reference to their corporate color of orange. Through this program, associates hear the latest brand news, learn how to handle such things as special plumbing orders, meet other associates, and watch new stores give their best and loudest Home Depot cheer. Employees can call in live during the broadcast to join in a discussion with the executive vice president of human resources during his live broadcast.

This corporate brand culture started with a people-first approach that has touched every associate with an "orange-blooded philosophy." In a culture that prides itself in being nonbureaucratic or political, where the status quo is not acceptable, and where challenging a boss is permitted, people can only grow and make a difference for themselves and others inside and outside the stores.

Home Depot embraces all the positive attributes of a "can do" attitude. Dick Sullivan explains, "We are in the self-esteem and confidence business, not a retail business. We have an enormous heart," he says, "because we touch people's emotions. We understand the feel and the look of their most precious emotional asset, their homes."

Home Depot's sensitivity to the importance of endorsing change, diversity, and community involvement is well rooted. In Alaska, for instance, Home Depot works with local suppliers and vendors, reflecting their goal to support the economy of the different regions they serve. The philosophy of Home Depot is interesting in terms of how they feel about their role in the economy. They know that 78 percent of the economy is consumer-driven and that consumers sustain businesses, create jobs, and protect our way of life. So they regard branding as an important asset to protect and use in order to trigger desire and stimulate demand. They even partner with suppliers to leverage the Home Depot brand and their brand's credibility to help sell excess inventory.

The power of this brand from a corporate-citizen perspective is in how it blends citizen responsibilities, employee responsibilities, and business practices into the social fabric. Their emotional identity is strong because it is in their heart and is lived passionately by everyone in the company. They may be a very big retailer, but they are also one with a big-hearted philosophy.

Building the Road to Trust: Be a Good (Global) Neighbor!

The concept of the corporation with an active social conscience is clearly an idea whose time has come. As a *Washington Post* article puts it, "the social conscience market is hot,"[9] and today there is hardly a company that does not have as a part of its corporate agenda an extensive network of corporate philanthropy and cause-marketing programs. The success of these programs from a business perspective has been widely acknowledged—with 83 percent of consumers saying that they have a more positive image of a company that supports a cause they care about and a full two-thirds saying that if price and quality are equal, they will purchase a brand associated with a good cause.[10] In a survey of 1,000 consumers in twenty-three countries, *six in ten said that a company's social performance, including its labor practices, business ethics, and environmental impacts plays a vital role in the forming of their impressions of a company.*[11] In fact, a good number of academic studies have found that there exists a correlation between responsible business practices and not only employee satisfaction, but also overall positive financial performance. As Unilever's chairman, Niall Fitzgerald put it, "This is more than altruism—it makes good business sense."[12] And now, Wall Street is definitely paying attention. The Enron fiasco has shown us clearly that financial performances in the long term are influenced by ethics, and firms not showing a clear commitment to the people side of the business on a global level will be much more severely scrutinized in the future. And the trust level corporations may have enjoyed with people in the past has been severely damaged as well. In a recent Golin/Harris survey, a ratio of seven to one respondents said that they intend to hold businesses to a higher standard of behavior and communications. In this same survey a full 52 percent said that they

In fact, a good number of academic studies have found that there exists a correlation between responsible business practices and not only employee satisfaction, but overall positive financial performance.

are only "somewhat" confident that corporations will make business decisions "in my best interest," and 30 percent were only "slightly or not at all" confident![15]

Clearly, from an Emotional Branding perspective there is still a certain kind of leap that needs to be made by many of these companies, even by some of those who are the most active in the area of social responsiblility! *The leap that must be taken today is to move beyond the concepts of philanthropy and "cause marketing" to that of building a comprehensive brand mission that incorporates ethical/social values in manifold ways and infiltrates everything the company does,* including any social programs it supports. In other words, corporate responsibility must be written into the business model itself and the brand values need to evolve beyond merely being the "face" of the brand to inform the core operations of the business, which must become totally transparent. A recent *Fortune* magazine article says, "If the 1980s were remembered for greed and the 1990s for shareholder value, it is likely that this decade will be remembered for one in which business models changed indelibly toward social outreach and a complete about-face in defining what the bottom line means to a company."[14] Shareholders today are asking about these issues and requesting more transparency, as in the case of shareholders in Amoco, General Motors, and Ford asking their companies to report on carbon emissions, and shareholders in Kraft and McDonalds requesting that the companies stop manufacturing products that contain genetically modified products. And when we look at fiascos such as Enron, the once stellar example of successful Old Economy/New Economy transitions, we see the need for a real, viable substance of integrity to back up the brand promise. Enron's various shady transactions have come crashing down around it serving up a brutal (and, I hope, instructive) lesson to Wall Street of the importance of looking a little further beyond opaque, intentionally complex financial statements, even when the numbers look great. The tolerance people have for situations like this, where employees' retirement accounts suddenly vaporize while Enron's former executives are sitting pretty now with the hundreds of millions in income they made in the last several years on stock options, is clearly dwindling rapidly. Other CEOs of major corporations such as Lucent, Kmart, and WorldCom have also clung to their wealth while their companies stumble financially and employees lose jobs. The model of the future will be more along the lines of the gesture PepsiCo CEO, Roger Enrico, has been making since 1998 by giving his $900,000 salary over to the PepsiCo foundation for scholarships for the children of employees who make less than $60,000 a year.

Everywhere we look we see evidence of this trend toward a fundamental shift in corporate values and consumer's expectations, and this will likely continue to intensify as Generation Y, very concerned with social causes, as we saw in chapter 1, comes into the full bloom of its cultural and economic power. This new atmosphere is the reason we see trends such as a consistent growth in socially responsible investing. *In the year 2000 a total of $2 trillion in assets under management in the United States were in portfolios that had some form of screening for social responsibility criteria, as compared to $600 million in 1995.* And, in the first six months of 2001, a dozen social and religious indexes and mutual funds hit the market as compared to six introductions in 2000. People want to invest in companies that are in tune with their own social values. Acquisitions such as the purchase of Ben & Jerry's by Unilever, Aveda and Mac by Estée Lauder, and Stonyfield by Dannon are also bringing a new set of corporate values that will, hopefully, influence the corporate culture of the acquirers. Besides buying a great business, they are also purchasing a very valuable Citizen Brand feather for their "corporate caps."

In the year 2000 a total of $2 trillion in assets under management in the United States were in portfolios that had some form of screening for social responsibility criteria, as compared to $600 million in 1995.

On a global level, I am fascinated by increasing moves by corporations to share their know-how or resources with emerging nations, as in the case of Ted Turner of CNN's gift of $1 billion dollars to the United Nations, and Coca-Cola's efforts to help with the HIV/AIDS epidemic in Africa. In the case of Coca-Cola, its efforts have little to do with traditional philanthropy or cause marketing—it is an altogether different sort of endeavor that may well be a harbinger of future corporate programs. Coca-Cola is contributing the trucks of their vast distribution network, which reaches into the most remote village, as a way of helping with the very difficult problem of transporting educational materials, testing kits, and condoms to these areas. In this very practical, hands-on way, the company is playing an important role—as a partner in the well-being of the lives of the people to whom it sells its product. In addition, Coca-Cola has pledged to pay for full medical coverage, including drugs, for any of its 1,500 employees in Africa or their immediate family members who are HIV positive. This is also a wise business decision if Coca-Cola wishes to continue to have a strong presence in Africa. Another Coca-Cola project in underdeveloped nations in Africa and South America that deftly combines business objectives with an attempt to play the role of good corporate citizen, is its current project to develop a supplemental drink for children, to be called Vitango, that contains twelve vitamins and minerals chronically lacking in the diets of people in developing countries. The company is striving to make the drink taste good to children and keep it affordable for those who need it most. This product will in turn help Coca-Cola to establish relationships with governments and schools, which will serve as a positive platform for the company and all of its products. The project got its start when a group of marketing and innovation executives visited Coca-Cola in Ecuador and realized, as part of a program for advancing the Coca-Cola brand through schools, that the children were poorly nourished and inattentive in class. This is a case of a company being in touch with its market and finding a way not only to help its consumers on an ongoing basis, but also to create more opportunity for brand contact at a grassroots, people-to-people level. The beauty of this initiative is that Coca-Cola is not promoting this program on a public-relations level.

The Globalization Quagmire

However, these efforts by Coca-Cola can serve to help to polish the company's reputation on a global level, which is increasingly important today. In fact, there has been a profound shift in the way the corporate world at large views the issues of globalization. In the past several years, we have begun to see protestors' ideas making inroads in mainstream business culture. The protests in Seattle and Genoa and elsewhere have had a growing effect in serving as a wake-up call for governments and corporations alike, and many have begun to listen to the complaints of these activists in a way that was previously unimaginable. For example, Shell's Chairman, Sir Mark Moody-Stuart said last year, "Because we, too, are concerned at the requirement to address those in poverty who are excluded from the benefits that many of us share in the global economy, we share the objective of the recent demonstrators in Seattle, Davos, and Prague."[15] The

World Bank has even begun to show signs of embracing the protestors' goal of "sustainable development," edging away from huge infrastructure projects like dams, showing some degree of agreement that economic growth alone isn't enough to reduce poverty. Harvard economist Dani Rodrick says, "We've moved from a situation where the professional technocrats would pooh-pooh the protestors as a bunch of know-nothing retrogrades to one where that line has completely evaporated. . . . Intellectually the battle is really won."[16] The French and German governments have announced that they will meet to discuss ways of better managing globalization and the potential fallout, with former Prime Minister Lionel Jospin declaring that France was "delighted to see the emergence of a citizens' movement at the planetary level," and the German Chancellor Gerhard Schroder saying, "These people are not just cranks . . . their concerns about unequal trade relations or financial speculation that bring entire economies to the brink of ruin are real."[17] And recently, in Monterrey, Mexico, at the Global Development Conference, the number-one message conveyed by all the international economic institutions was about the fight against poverty and the reduction of global inequality. Indeed, according to the IMF (International Monetary Fund), in twenty years the number of poor people living under $2 per day has increased by 50 percent–to 2.4 billion, or 40 percent of the global population.[18] I believe that on a global level there is a growing awareness of the suffering in poorer countries and a sensibility of objection to these conditions. Brands such as Gap, long under attack for sweatshop conditions in its factories worldwide, would do well to pay critical attention to this trend. The Gap has a labor-compliance department made up of 90 people who it claims work relentlessly to monitor and improve the conditions in these factories, and even admits that at times they were unaware of poor conditions in factories, but now they say they are on top of the problem. However, a certain "big-brand arrogance" can be detected in their refusal, for example, to settle a suit against them from the garment workers in Saipan for $8.75 million. Other companies named in the suit, such as Sears and Calvin Klein, agreed to pay. Global Exchange, an organization focusing on improving global living conditions, has been waging a campaign asking Gap to improve factory working conditions and is particularly offended by the company's nonsettlement of this suit. Leila Salazar, corporate accountability organizer at Global Exchange said about their refusal to settle, "The Gap continues to deny they are involved in any wrongdoing. They continue to question us on our definition of sweatshops."[19] This kind of attitude is danger-ous to a brand in today's climate. Could this attitude be the reason for the Gap's lack of success with Gen Y? The problem could be largely more of an ethical problem than of being or not being on the mark with fashion. Instead of taking a defensive posture in these sit-uations, they should "go above and beyond the call of duty" to approach these problems with innovative solutions. They should make it their aim to become known as a "good neighbor brand!"

The problems of globalization are not easy problems to even begin to solve. Even when governments or corporations are trying by all inten-sive means to "do the right thing," there are manifold, intertwined issues involved, not the least of which is the challenge of dealing with developing countries' own policy failures. And, of course, just figur-ing out what that "right thing to do" is can be a daunting task, to say the least. For example, there are those who say that pushing for labor standards in developing countries could even be damaging to those countries if it discourages corporations from doing business there, because the multinationals actually pay 10 percent more than local companies and they provide much needed jobs. This rationale still seems unfair to me, and may to many other consumers as well, but it is one point of view on the problem. The complicated, hydra-like issues surrounding globalization are far too complex to address ade-quately here, and this book makes no pretense of tackling in-depth political and economic issues. However, one thing is for certain; the tides are changing and these points cannot be shrugged away–they are *the* crucial issues for our times, and from a branding perspective both the opportunities and the dangers that loom are huge.

Do What You Say and (. . . Then) Say What You Do

One of the biggest problems facing corporations today will be a lack of consistency–either perceived or real–in terms of their policies, programs, and public rhetoric surrounding social responsibility ver-sus their actual business practices. Companies that develop an exten-sive system of philanthropic/cause-marketing programs and yet manufacture their clothing in sweatshops in developing nations are missing the point. While there is no such thing as perfection and the issues at hand are very complex, I think that today's savvy, hyper-informed consumers are beginning to have a strong distaste for such blatant contradictions, because it smacks of hypocrisy and can make the consumer feel foolish, or worse, guilty for having believed and participated in a brand that does not practice the values it preaches. This is the problem we mentioned earlier, which the Philip Morris corporation faces in terms of its image. What good is all of the good it is trying to do through its charitable endeavors as long as these deeds are ultimately associated with a company perceived in a negative manner by the public? This perception is clearly the reason behind the recent change of the parent company's name to "Altria" (derived from the Latin word "altus" meaning high or high performance), transitioning toward a new image with less of a connection to the tobacco business and more emphasis on other businesses, such as Kraft and Miller Brewing Co. This effort could be extremely smart if it signals real change. How it is communicated and the degree of commitment to the truth will determine whether this program succeeds. If this approach is just graphic and cosmetic, it will make the nontobacco divisions feel better about not being associated with tobacco internally, but it will not have an impact on the outside world. The first advertising messages about the new identity have not yet stressed the real reason for the change as an answer to a public expectation. If this is only a symbolic gesture–helpful though it may be in improving the company's image in certain sectors–it will be seen by many as simply dressing a "wolf in sheep's clothing."

What can tobacco companies do to improve their Citizen Brand status? Some of these companies, like RJ Reynolds and Philip Morris, are beginning to spend more of their resources researching ways of making their products less toxic, which is a good sign of a true Citizen Brand move. This is following the success of some natural tobacco brands such as American Spirit, the reputedly toxic-free brand whose sales have tripled since 1997 (and which was just purchased by RJ Reynolds) and Brown & Williamson Tobacco Corp.'s "Advance" brand with a special toxin-reducing filter. Philip Morris is also currently developing a new cigarette brand with "a significant reduction in potentially harmful smoke constituents."[20]

There also seems to be more understanding on the advertising front about the value of emotional sensitivity to the issues surrounding smoking. Recently, British American Tobacco, Japan Tobacco, and Philip Morris all voluntarily agreed to scale back their advertising around the world–they are working together to ban ads that show models who appear to be younger than twenty-five; that involve product placement; that link smoking to athletic, professional, sexual, or social success; or that make use of celebrities. Moves such as this can only help their companies grow in the direction of Citizen Brandship.

If the challenges tobacco companies face in becoming true Citizen Brands are great, those that face pharmaceutical companies are truly daunting. This much maligned industry has, in the same way as Philip Morris, been attempting to overcome its poor image with the public through aggressive public relations and extensive programs devoted to social responsibility. It would take all day to list the various causes each of the major pharmaceutical companies supports and one could spend hours, as I have, on the Web sites of Merck, Pfizer, Eli Lilly, and so on, perusing the material about their philanthropic endeavors. These efforts are truly impressive! But still, we see in popular culture a veritable parade of allusions to the "evil drug companies" from the pharmaceutical company portrayed in *Mission Impossible II* that creates a deadly virus and begins intentionally infecting people so that it can make money selling the cure, to the ultimate monolithic corporate villain in one of John Le Carre's most recent novels, *The Constant Gardner*,[21] which is portrayed as using poor Africans as guinea pigs to test dangerous drugs.

Maybe this "villainization" is highly exaggerated and therefore undeserved, but one does have to wonder when one hears stories about pharmaceutical companies locking in vaults the data from studies whose research results come back unfavorable, and requiring researchers to sign agreements stating they will not publish any data without the company's approval. Many have even gone so far as to say that because drug companies provide huge sums of money to universities and researchers know that negative results will be harmful to these relationships, much of the research is generally tilted in the favor of the pharmaceutical companies. The number of cases accusing drug manufacturers of suppressing research that shows that certain medications are addictive or harmful, as well as accusations that some drug companies have tried illegally to extend patents on drugs, depriving lower-income people of the drug's benefits, is currently on the rise.

As the pharmaceutical companies move more into a "consumer-product" mode with the ability to advertise their products directly to consumers since regulations were softened in 1997, they also must learn to be more responsible and sensitive to people's needs, and assiduously avoid just selling them products that may or may not be helpful–or which could even be harmful. There is a growing suspicion among many consumers that we are "overdrugged" in Western society as victims of overzealous marketing by pharmaceutical companies (working in tandem with doctors and medical associations). This is a particular point of view, which you may or may not agree with, but it is somewhat shocking to realize that today there are regions in North America where nearly 20 percent of kids are being treated with stimulants. Similarly, *PR News* reported that media references to "social anxiety disorder" increased from fifty in 1998 to one billion in 1999, following promotions by Paxil manufacturer, GlaxoSmithKline. The fear, in particular with the murky area of mental-health drug advertising, is that the ads appeal to the ultimate emotions of happiness we all want to have (and the feelings of sadness we all want to avoid) and don't differentiate well enough between normal feelings of anxiety, or sadness, and the kind of more dangerous conditions that would require treatment–and in the process may serve to create a need that does not really exist. As an *Adweek* editor put it, "By being intentionally general, they pull us in– and the emotion clouds the specific details that follow about who might need the drug."[22]

This *Adweek* article suggests that ads immediately following the events of September 11 may have really crossed over this line of trust with consumers, playing on their fears too much with commercials like a Paxil spot showing anxious people saying things like "I'm always thinking something terrible is going to happen. . . . Your worst fears . . . the what ifs . . . I can't control it . . . It's like a tape in my mind. It just goes over and over and over." This seems to be a manipulative use of the power of emotions in light of the fact that it was the way that many, if not most, people felt after such a terrifying event, and not representative of a more serious long-term condition requiring medication!

On the flip side, the expertise and products of pharmaceutical companies are needed by society and serve to increase the quality of life for many. The fact is these companies have many opportunities to play the role of a true Citizen Brand by the very nature of their business. For one thing, some of their promotional efforts that offer solid information regarding health conditions can play a decisive factor in encouraging people to visit their doctors and address health issues that otherwise might go undetected. For example, Warner-Lambert created a $1 million campaign for its cholesterol-fighting drug Lipitor, which included cholesterol screening events and lectures in concert with the American Heart Association. Pharmacia has funded print ads for the American Cancer Society to educate the public about colon cancer, outlining facts that are crucial for early detection. The idea here is to create a relationship with the consumer through education, with the focus on consumers and their needs and experiences–as opposed to pushing the product itself. Pfizer has done an excellent job with creating an emotional identity for Viagra that has been helpful to men in dealing with the problem of impotence, which Pfizer calls "erectile dysfunction," as a way of lessening some of the embarrassment involved by showing that the drug company understands the way this problem can affect a man's life and his relationship with his spouse. Pfizer's communications are increasingly strong in terms of a brand image that speaks in a youthful, energetic, positive voice and gives men who are often reluctant to address this issue permission to do so. Increasingly, pharmaceutical companies seem to be aware of a new Citizen Brand role they can play in people's lives. Recently, GlaxoSmithKline, Pfizer, Novartis, and Eli Lilly all announced that they would offer medication at deep discounts to low-income elderly people.

On the flip side, the expertise and products of pharmaceutical companies are needed by society and serve to increase the quality of life for many.

The true power of pharmaceutical companies to help people is seen in many of their charitable endeavors, such as Merck's Mectizan Program that has treated, for free, over 25 million people in thirty-one countries for river-blindness disease with the drug Mectizan. This touches on another very sensitive topic for drug companies. Pharmaceutical companies are also under fire for not doing enough to help underprivileged populations gain access to their products–they are accused of blocking this access because of the patents that allow them to make their products so expensive. The drug companies claim that the patents are necessary to defend the years of exclusive rights for a medicine so that they can recoup the vast research-and-development costs for a new drug, and therefore, they have consistently fought for their right to keep the patents. Passionate debates have resulted regarding nations like Brazil and South Africa where patented drugs are too expensive for most victims of AIDS and other life-threatening diseases. In light of this state of affairs it was interesting to see that Bayer, which charges pharmacies more than $4 a tablet for Cipro, had to be threatened by a patent override by the U.S. government in the face of the anthrax scare in order to agree to lower the price to just under $1 each. The anthrax "epidemic" seems thankfully thus far not to have truly surfaced; meanwhile, just think of what positive brand associations this brand may have been able to build with a vulnerable, frightened public had there been more willingness on its part to play a Citizen Brand role in a time of need.

The pharmaceutical industry is first of all a business that needs to compete and excel while reporting positive quarterly results to the financial market. Reaching beyond the short-term, limited economic scope of the industry to stretch the imagination toward trying new ideas is certainly a step in the right direction. Why not, for instance, create spin-off companies in poverty-stricken countries with a public-service mission that would directly create and sustain the necessary infrastructure of distribution and doctors and simply sell the medicine in those countries very cheaply? This long-term approach might present less immediate rewards, but I guarantee it would present immense long-term benefits. It would help the first pharmaceutical company to do this to gain a true foothold as a helper in these communities, not to mention the overall positive impact of being a true Citizen Brand. This idea is not mine. It actually is the idea of a good friend of mine who was previously a high-level executive at a major pharmaceutical company, which he conveyed to me as a potential creative solution to the dilemma!

Eli Lilly: Reconnecting with the Public

I had the opportunity to interview Sidney Taurel, the chairman, president and CEO in what was a fascinating meeting. The Eli Lilly brand was founded by the Lilly family with the goal of building a business with strong values of "people, integrity, and excellence." The brand is still around today because of its commitment to innovation, honesty, and quality.

In the past two years, Eli Lilly has embarked on a branding program to connect the company better with medical professionals and consumers in an emotional way that reaches beyond its products.

The problem was that Prozac was known but Eli Lilly was not.

The biggest challenge in this was to create an internal culture more "attuned to the need of the consumers." Eli Lilly wanted to convey their empathy, personality, and dedication toward their mission to deliver on a promise. They needed to let people know that the consumer for them is at the center of the equation. The result of this program led Eli Lilly to create a real forum for a dialogue with its consumers—where employees spend time with patients and attend sales meetings where patients come to discuss and share their experiences with various brands—to prove that, as Sidney says, "most importantly, our responsibility is not to push pills but to help patients."

In this important effort to reconnect with people, Eli Lilly is recognizing that their compassion is the key to their success. They are affirming that their business saves lives and that this is the most important thing to them. Their efforts are sign of a larger industry trend where pharmaceutical companies are realizing they must radically change the structure of their businesses in order to understand and share information with the public. They are seeking to show us that they realize that they need to become part of a greater solution.

The Brave New World of "Mission Branding": What Works!

Here, we will take a look at a few exemplary "cause-marketing" and philanthropic programs executed by various brands that I feel are particularly effective and lead toward a more holistic Citizen Brand philosophy that can inspire long-term trust. First of all, as we've said, cause marketing is an increasingly popular marketing strategy with over 85 percent of corporations in the United States now participating in some type of program. A study by the Promotion Marketing Association and the Gable Group also shows why: Fully 100 percent of the companies surveyed said that their expectations were met and rated their campaigns as extremely successful.[23] According to a Roper Starch survey where consumers were asked to cite the issues in which they most want to see companies involved, public education, crime, and the environment were the top three (in that order). However, the most important thing for a company to consider in supporting a cause is brand relevance; *the cause must emanate from, be reflective of, and eventually contribute to the overall brand mission and core corporate belief.* Secondly, something about the way it unfolds should be innovative; otherwise, the efforts can so easily be lost, or even seem trite, in a sea of cause-marketing programs. Lastly, and perhaps most importantly, the programs should be used as a real opportunity to create a team of brand ambassadors within the community. This is a great opportunity to fortify the brand experience in the consumers' everyday life on the basis of the issues that matter most to them. And, from this perspective, the brand is actually giving people–the employee and the consumer alike–the chance to have the profound emotional experience of making a real difference in the world. As Kraft Foods president Robert Eckert says, "Consumers are yearning to connect to people and things that will give meaning to their lives . . . they want something to believe in, whether its family, a set of values, or some passion they can pursue. It's a kind of spirituality."[24]

BRAND RELEVANCE: START A BRAND CRUSADE

Obviously, one of the best known, and first, examples of successful long-term cause-marketing campaigns is the Avon Crusade against breast cancer, which has raised approximately $110 million since 1993 to fund access to care, especially for underprivileged women, and to the search for a cure. It is the perfect cause for a brand like Avon, which, as we saw in chapter 1, is all about empowering women through a strong grassroots network. This originally door-to-door program that began with selling pink ribbons has truly taken a shape of its own and become a powerful, highly integral part of the brand equity, and this is where we begin taking cause marketing further, more into the all-encompassing realm of "mission branding." Their recent promotion "Kiss Goodbye to Breast Cancer" sold a line of lipsticks with names like "Triumph" and "Strength" for $4 with one dollar going to Avon's breast cancer charity. Avon has set a new, very ambitious goal to raise $250 million for breast cancer research by end of 2002.[25] Avon was a true pioneer in teaching the value of the person-to-person, "brand-bonding" aspect of cause related programs!

Another great, although lesser-known, example of supporting causes with intrinsic brand relevance is International Paper's award winning long-term program of habitat conservation for the endangered red-cockaded woodpecker on the company's forest lands in the Southeast. This is the first time a private landowner has taken steps to expand and enhance the species' habitat on his land rather than just maintaining the birds' populations or relocating them to public forest lands. International Paper was also one of the first forest-products companies to have an independent third party verify the sustainability of its forest practices through the internationally recognized standard known as ISO 14001 and the industry's Sustainable Forestry Initiative (SFI). International Paper's approach embraces the theme of environmental protection, economic growth, and social responsibility as mutually reinforcing goals, as opposed to businesses whose practices do not include or are against this credo.

Programs such as Quiksilver's Reef Check program also deftly combine service to a very brand-relevant cause and at the same time capitalize on the opportunity to gain access to a valuable field of knowledge and contact with surfers around the world, which is very important to the brand's image as a surf authority. Quiksilver, the international board-riding and fashion company, has also developed a program called Quicksilver Crossing, a seven-year circumnavigation of the world in support of the United Nations Environment Program (UNEP), which funds the Reef Check program. Reef Check is an extremely ambitious global ecological survey that utilizes thousands of volunteer scuba divers, led by marine biologists, to determine the global health of coral reefs. The importance of coral reefs cannot be overstated: They are often called the "rainforests of the sea" because they serve as a vital link in the food chain for numerous marine species. They are facing an unprecedented crisis due to pollution, overfishing, and global warming. The Quiksilver Crossing voyage has three main objectives: to find surf, to respect local cultures, and to contribute to the scientific knowledge of the world's coral reefs through the Reef Check global coral reef monitoring program. While searching for new surfing locations–to provide the latest, best insider's information to their customers–the Quiksilver Crossing's seventy-two-foot exploratory vessel also serves as a floating research station, allowing Reef Check scientists to survey reefs that would otherwise be inaccessible. Since 1999, the Crossing has hosted nearly three hundred surfers, scientists, and media on board, and has covered 46,944 nautical miles. The director of Reef Check, Dr. Gregor Hodgson, says, "Since the launch of the Crossing, thirteen Reef Check marine scientists have surveyed nearly fifty remote coral reefs that hadn't previously been assessed by scientists, and most of these reefs show some signs of human impact. By getting the local communities involved in reef management, Reef Check is one solution to the problems." This collaboration between Reef Check and Quiksilver has received many accolades as an example of corporate environmental vision from the UN, The World Bank, and the scientific community. It has been a great success from a public-education/public-awareness and conservation point of view, as well.

Starbucks' efforts toward social responsibility are also carefully crafted to be in cohesion with the brand's image. Starbucks formed the Starbucks Foundation in 1997 with an initial $500,000 contribution from company founder and CEO Howard Shultz, with literacy as its main focus. Starbucks has many wonderful programs for literacy that take place in its stores, allowing people with little or no access to educational assistance the opportunity to take free reading or writing classes led by writers, to contribute to publications, and to give readings–all of which also contribute to the overall brand image as a true coffeehouse, a center for cultural endeavors. The foundation also provides support to CARE as its largest North American corporate contributor. CARE is an international relief organization that directs funds to grassroots programs in developing countries. Starbucks has established various programs to improve the developing economies where its coffee is grown, harvested, and processed. The company is increasingly committing to buying more coffee beans from certified importers paying small farmers above-market prices, as defined by the Fair Trade standards.

IMAGINATION/ORIGINALITY: "THE CAUSE" AS A MESSAGE OF INNOVATION

An innovative new effort to support a worthy cause is seen by Heineken USA, which has donated $3 million to start a nonprofit organization. The Heineken Foundation will seek to raise funds for music education programs for schools in urban markets. What is unusual about this effort is that the way the money will be raised is through a new CD label, Red Star Records, based on the red star of the Heineken label–but intentionally not directly associable with the beer brand. Heineken is, in fact, creating a separate but related brand for its charitable endeavors through this program that should also lend a cachet of coolness to the brand.

Ben & Jerry's, the perennial Citizen Brand favorite, which gives back 7.5 percent of its pre-tax earnings to the community through corporate philanthropy and which was much mourned by its die-hard fans when it was purchased, has recently shown that it still understands a thing or two about the movement it helped create. For one of its recent promotions for its "Concession Obsession" Hollywood-themed flavor, the company decided that the real stars in the world are the good citizens. Ben & Jerry's launched the brand with a campaign called "Citizen Cool," which searched the nation for the twelve most civic-minded civilians and created a documentary about citizenship, featuring man-on-the-street interviews about citizenship. So far, since the launching of the campaign, the flavor has enjoyed double-digit growth.

There are also many creative ways to directly involve consumers in the process of supporting the causes they most care about, such as Target's loyalty card program. There are also many creative ways to directly involve consumers in the process of supporting the causes they most care about, such as Target's loyalty card program, which donates one percent of a shopper's purchases to the schools of the shopper's choice. This is a very practical, easy way for people to feel good about supporting a cause with which they are intimately concerned and for the brand to gain status with the consumer as a helping neighbor.

Sometimes the best programs come from a concept as simple as Target's. Another example is the program created by leather goods maker Etienne Aigner (owned by Hartstone Group, with $170 million in sales), which plays off the signature letter *A* on its products. The company created an outreach program with the National Education Association to encourage kids to read, a cause near and dear to the hearts of its customers, many of them mothers. The double-entendre tagline for this program—"What Does it Take to Get an *A*?"—plays off an overall theme of excellence, whether it is the Aigner products or the process of striving for educational achievement. The program, which has created reading aids, raised funds for books for schools, and established reading corners in their stores for children, has been an enormous success.

EMPLOYEE INVOLVEMENT: CREATING BRAND COMMUNITIES THROUGH BRAND AMBASSADORS

Clairol's program, "StyleWorks," offers a perfect example of how beautifully this concept can work in the real world. StyleWorks provides free makeovers, image consulting, and mentoring to women making the transition from welfare to work. Clairol's own employees volunteer, from the clerical to the executive ranks, helping the women transitioning out of welfare to deal with issues such as business etiquette, organizational skills, balancing work and parenting, and financial management. Each Clairol employee works with a StyleWorks client for one year, meeting once a week. The outreach program has been a tremendous morale booster for employees, proving that people really do love it when their company gives them the opportunity to volunteer and participate in a meaningful cause. Maureen Buckley-O'Hora, a senior product manager who is mentoring a twenty-four-year-old single mother, says, "We all feel good about the program . . . we all want to give back and feel like our work life is about more than selling hair color."[26] It is hard to say who gets more out of such programs, the helper or the helpee. And the brand, meanwhile, creates a very memorable and emotionalized association for these women. Offering people from different worlds the opportunity to come together around an important cause is really one of the very best things a Citizen Brand can do—it touches on that deep craving human beings have for spirituality and meaning.

As a conclusion to this chapter, I would like to offer a case study of one of the greatest Citizen Brand companies of all time, The Body Shop, which gives us a very inspiring vision of how a company can embody all of the principles we have discussed here.

The Body Shop: A Role Model for Citizen Brandship

I had the good fortune of being able to interview The Body Shop's very articulate, intelligent head of communications Steve McIvor, who explained to me in depth the philosophy and practices of the company's Citizen Brand strategy. The Body Shop is, of course, founded on the concept of corporate social responsibility, having practically invented the idea, which was not in the least widespread at the time of its inception. This company, long known for its animal rights, environmental, and human rights activism, does not practice philanthropy but is, instead, very actively engaged from a business perspective in making the world a better place. The way the company is run completely reflects the idea that corporate responsibility should be at the core of a company's mission and not a "side activity" executed for appearances' sake. The entire company revolves around its passion for making a strong positive impact on the world, and the ways that they attempt to do this are both innovative and highly intelligent from a practical point of view.

Around its ideals, the company has created a true culture where the excitement level is high. Steve McIver told me that last year a full 93 percent of the employees in their head office were involved in volunteer programs; the company gives half a day's pay each month for their participation. Employees very often go in teams to volunteering activities, which cements people to community, to the company, and to one another. Interestingly, they have found that their most successful managers are often very actively involved in The Body Shop's initiatives; they are "believers" with strong ethics. The Body Shop also actively recruits people from the not-for-profit sector, people who, like Steve himself, bring their beliefs with them and don't just leave them at the door. These are people who undoubtedly bring new ideas and challenges with them to the company, keeping The Body Shop's credibility at a strong, healthy level.

Steve explained to me that The Body Shop is set up and run by a series of "Business Ethics Teams" that oversee various aspects of the business, like marketing campaigns and community affairs programs, from a social responsibility perspective. These Business Ethics Teams look at how The Body Shop can work with various community groups and not-for-profit groups as a business, seeking always to actively listen to their "stakeholders"–their employees, customers, and shareholders. In the true spirit of a company that seeks the truth and does not wish to hide even its own flaws, but wishes instead to learn from them so that it can improve its performance, The Body Shop is conducting a series of independent, publicly published surveys with these groups, for honest feedback on how they are doing with their initiatives.

The Body Shop is set up and run by a series of "Business Ethics Teams" that oversee various aspects of the business, like marketing campaigns and community affairs programs, from a social responsibility perspective.

One of their more recent endeavors was to launch the "Human Rights Award," the second largest award of its kind after the Nobel Peace Prize, a year-and-a-half ago. The award, a $300,000 grant, is given once every two years to up to four leading community-based organizations and is decided by a jury comprised of representatives from a wide range of human rights disciplines. In its first year, the award focused on child labor rights, specifically on the education of children, and in the second year, the award's focus was on housing. It is interesting to note that The Body Shop at first resisted calling it "The Body Shop Human Rights Award," but the jurists insisted on the use of the company's name because they felt that equity associated with the brand would lend the award even more credibility.

In another initiative, The Body Shop is partnering with Greenpeace to fight global warming by sponsoring renewable-energy use instead of fossil fuels (for more information, take a look at their Web site: *www.choose-positive-energy.org*). Steve explained that this unique partnership is the harbinger of future business/NGO (nongovernmental organizations) collaborations. Greenpeace and other NGOs are more and more willing to ally themselves with businesses in seeking solutions. *Because the not-for-profit sector is seeing that businesses are more influential than government in many ways in bringing about change, the professional, compromise-based approach can more often reach practical solutions more effectively and quickly than can the traditional NGO approach. Although ethics and business have historically been seen as opposing forces, this is now changing.*

Steve cited as an example that the environmental activist Catherine Fuller has joined the board of Alcoa. In this scenario where the "lion and the lamb lie down together," as Steve put it, can be found many powerful solutions. Similarly, Greenpeace and N Power Energy recently partnered in developing a product called "Juice," a totally renewable energy source for domestic consumers. As Steve so aptly put it, "both the problems and the solutions lie in business." This opinion was recently echoed at the World Economic Forum by UN Secretary General Kofi Annan, who said, "In many cases, governments only find the courage and resources to do the right thing when business leaders take the lead."[27]

The Body Shop is certainly one of those businesses taking the lead— in their own very unique, smart way. They are a strong advocate of what they call a "positive-engagement approach," which is a sometimes messier but more constructive approach to solving problems. This approach seeks to find out how business can become a truly progressive force in an everyday, practical manner. This means that when The Body Shop realizes that a supply chain company has a problem, it works with that company to help it meet The Body Shop's standards. The Body Shop uses its purchasing power wisely in order to influence conditions in supply chain factories. The issues involved

Hydrating shea butter is Community Traded too, which means your hands and feet aren't the only ones to benefit.

COMMUNITY **TRADE**

Shea butter & honey.

AFRICA SH
HANDS & FEET HONE
5.6 OZ (160 g)

Brazil Nut
DAMAGE CARE
SHAMPOO
DRY, DAMAGED & CHEMICALLY
TREATED HAIR
Maintains color and shine
SHAMPOOING
TRAITANT
à la noix du Brésil
CHEVEUX SECS, ENDOMMAGÉS
OU TRAITÉS CHIMIQUEMENT
250 mL (8.4 US FL OZ)

Buying directly from small manufacturers and artisans as opposed to buying indirectly from mass manufacturers.

...ns Brazil nut oil to replenish natural oils in dry, damaged ...air. Adds shine and leaves hair feeling soft and smooth. ...t fading in color-treated hair. COMMUNITY **TRADE** ...er and rinse. Follow with THE BODY SHOP Brazil Nut Damage Care ...

...ent de l'huile de noix du Brésil qui contribue à redonner ...ux cheveux secs, endommagés ou ayant subi un traitement ...e l'éclat et donne une sensation de douceur. Des écrans ...er le fermissement des cheveux teints. COMMERCE ÉQUITABLE ...er dans les cheveux mouillés en massant et rincer. Faire suivre ...du Brésil LE BODY SHOP. Éviter tout contact avec les yeux.
...Brasil

with this approach are very complex. The fact is that many kids actually have to work to support their families in some communities, so instead of revoking the contracts as soon as a problem is uncovered, and depriving all of the factory workers and the community of their livelihood, Steve believes that to help effect real and lasting improvements in the conditions, companies should invest in initiatives such as educational programs that will provide a better future for children.

The Body Shop also has a terrific, very extensive "Community Trade Program," where the company buys directly from small manufacturers or artisans as opposed to indirectly from mass manufacturers. In Third World countries this can mean the difference between getting by and building a sustainable community. The company buys as many of its materials as it can, such as cocoa, shea butter, baskets, and paper, in places like India, Nepal, and Africa, cutting out the middleman and guaranteeing prices regardless of market fluctuations, with an added premium given for community benefits such as education and sustainable community projects.

The Body Shop has seen the real business advantages of this approach, especially in terms of a fierce brand loyalty from their customers. Steve explained that this is one of the most powerful stories a brand can tell: "Where did my product come from?" Consumers today want to know how their products were made and if anyone was harmed in making them. "Business has largely become a homogenized process," he went on to say, "but this is about individual lives—individual people and the relationships between them, and making a very real tangible difference in people's lives. . . . The emotional attachments people form to The Body Shop products is very strong." In fact, they have to be very careful when making decisions to discontinue certain products because the customers often become very upset.

When I asked him for advice for companies seeking to increase their level of corporate social responsibility, he said that it was very important for those companies to begin by integrating the concept into their business practices before jumping on the bandwagon, as any misstep will be detected and can be used to undermine their overall aim. His caution was to be careful how quickly you try run into this area, where the issues are extremely complex, and to *be careful how much you hype and promote what you are doing.* As a company that has taken a strong stand in this area, The Body Shop has been subject to much criticism any time there has been a perception of an incongruity with their message, and the world's media is very quick to publicize any problems. *Most importantly, he advised, "Don't think about just looking good–it's a long-term endeavor." He adds that "companies need to learn to work in a consultative or advisory capacity."* One very provocative and interesting theory he offered was that striving for ethics stretches conventional thinking and puts you in a different creative arena. This different perspective, he noted, can be very powerful in helping a company find a different, more exciting solution than its competitors.

3

The Third Commandment: Evolve from Product to Experience

Quality for the right price is a given today.
Preference creates the sale.

This commandment addresses the question of how to expand beyond a mere product-offering status to create an exciting, emotionally relevant brand experience that will bring the brand alive for people in a way that truly contributes to their lives. Because brand experience is about a direct, visceral interaction with the brand, this chapter will focus primarily on brand "museums," or "theme parks," retail environments, and promotional campaigns that function as innovative sources of inspiration to people in the course of their daily lives. From a Citizen Brand perspective brands entertaining people bring fun and pleasure to commerce. And, as we will see, they can do so much more than this too!

Magical Brand Worlds

For the past several years we have seen the trend of "brand destinations," which take the form of theme parks or museums, grow exponentially. The idea, which was groundbreaking at its inception, is that when a brand becomes a physical place, it can leverage and express its huge emotional character in a positive way. The concept of people "visiting" their favorite brands for a mixture of entertainment, education, and fun has clearly taken root with great success for many companies, such as Coca-Cola, Kellogg's, Legos, and Hershey's. These theme parks follow the formula of Disneyland and Las Vegas to offer people a veritable smorgasbord of experiences, from restaurants to shops to rides and exhibits. This is a wonderful way to build a relationship with consumers, by offering them an outing so special that it will become an unforgettable brand experience. Coca-Cola is generally credited with beginning this trend with its World of Coca-Cola brand museum located outside Atlanta. The idea at the World of Coca-Cola is to allow visitors to be able to "See, hear, and taste the magical story of Coca-Cola." Located in a three-story pavilion, World of Coca-Cola encompasses the rich history and progress of the beverage, which was created in Atlanta over 110 years ago and which first served at a small pharmacy soda fountain near what is now Underground Atlanta. World of Coca-Cola captures all the excitement of this world-famous product, not only through its exhibits, but also through its unique architectural style. Visitors pass under an enormous three-dimensional Coca-Cola globe suspended eighteen feet over the entrance, then step into a spectacular three-story, sky-lit atrium. From there visitors can move at their own pace through an easy-to-follow series of fun and fascinating exhibit galleries. At the late 1930s Barnes Soda Fountain, an old-fashioned soda jerk will demonstrate how an early Coca-Cola was prepared. The International Video Lounge gives a fascinating perspective on the global reach of The Coca-Cola Company's activities with the "Tastes of the World" exhibit, offering an international sampler of soft drinks distributed by The Coca-Cola Company but not available in the United States.

Hershey's, another classic American brand has had great success with its own brand destination, "Hershey's Chocolate World" in Hershey, Pennsylvania. Hershey has made its visitor's center, which is free, into a complete entertainment center, including a factory tour ride and a 3-D theater where visitors can explore the art of chocolate-making on a simulated factory tour ride that concludes with a delicious sample. The center includes wonderful "Everything Hershey's" shops and a "Hershey's Chocolate Town Café," where visitors can relax after their tour.

The best of these brand museums/theme parks incorporate into their mission a strong dedication to playing a community role in the true sense of a Citizen Brand. Kellogg's Cereal City, a nonprofit themed family attraction operated by the Heritage Center Foundation to help support their local Battle Creek Community Foundation, succeeds in this aim. Much like the World of Coca-Cola, Kellogg's Cereal City

Kellogg's Cereal City branded theme park understands the importance of the role the brand plays in bringing entertainment to the community.

Getting Around

- Four Theaters
- Cereal Production Line
- Photo-on-a-Box
- Historical Museum
- Cereal City Interactive Area
- Kids Play Space

aims to provide visitors with a sensorial brand experience that will allow them to "See, hear, smell, and, yes, of course, taste" Kellogg's cereal. Visitors learn exactly what goes into the making of Kellogg's Corn Flakes through a video tour, graphic panels, and hands-on exhibits and pass through a simulated cornflakes production line in operation where they can sample the warm flakes as they "come off the line."

However, Kellogg's goes far beyond the concept of sensorial entertainment in its commitment to the consumer by focusing on providing educational experiences for children that emphasize both historical and practical knowledge. Cereal City celebrates the cereal industry in an educational, historical, and highly entertaining manner with fun, interactive ways to learn about the history of the cereal industry and the many aspects of Americana it has touched. Cereal City offers educators custom-tailored field-trip plans and develops ongoing interactive, multimedia exhibits to teach kids about history, health and nutrition, and food economics, such as the "$nack$ & Cent$" exhibit where kids learn about scarcity and choice as they experience a kitchen from an ant's eye perspective and listen to the story of cereal as told by the Kellogg characters and famous folks like brothers Dr. J. H. and W. K. Kellogg, C. W. Post, and the "Sweetheart of the Corn." Another ongoing multimedia exhibit, called "Cereal Bowl of America," teaches about Battle Creek of the late nineteenth and early twentieth centuries and explores the cereal story and its relation to American social and cultural events of the era with artifacts and memorabilia. Kellogg's clearly understands the importance of the role the brand has played as an American cultural icon and Cereal City capitalizes on the opportunity of communicating this brand equity through sharing a love of history. "A Bowl Full of Dreams" is a wonderful, colorful presentation exploring the marketing and advertising efforts of Kellogg Company. Visitors can also see original artwork by Norman Rockwell, Vernon Grant, and others who created the early Kellogg's print ads. There is, of course, a factory store, play areas for kids, and a "Dig 'Em's Diner." As a final gesture upon leaving, Kellogg's Cereal City provides an individual box of cereal for each guest.

Apart from, or in addition to, brand theme parks, there are many creative ways that brands can bring their own unique historical heritage to people to enhance the brand experience. Ivory recently found a very novel way to do this by partnering with the Smithsonian Institute. As part of an effort to celebrate the 120th anniversary of Ivory soap, Procter & Gamble developed a new retro packaging similar to the nineteenth-century design that was launched as a part of an exhibit at the Smithsonian's National Museum of History. P&G donated Ivory advertising materials dating back to 1882 and hired a sculptor at the event to create the portrait of Uncle Sam out of a huge eight-foot square block of Ivory soap. Children were also invited to learn the art of soap carving and sculpt figures out of chunks of Ivory soap. The program was widely covered in the news, connecting a successful brand to the nation in a more intimate fashion. According to Alexandra Lipinsky, marketing director for personal cleansing at P&G, the campaign will help bring history to the forefront of consumers' minds, which is especially valuable at this time when people are thinking

As a part of an exhibit at the Smithsonian's National Museum of History, P&G donated Ivory advertising materials dating back to 1882.

about simplifying their lives. This warm message from a brand beloved through time connects to an audience on a personal level.

Brands that do not have 100 plus years of history to mine can still find a myriad of ways to connect with history and build their own heritage while offering people an experience of history. Ralph Lauren has done just that at the Smithsonian by sponsoring the ongoing restoration of the original American flag project, which visitors can observe taking place in a huge glass-walled room where the enormous time-worn flag is being painstakingly pieced together again.

As more and more brands realize the great potential of these kinds of museum exhibits and brand theme parks, people's expectation of discovering their favorite brands in these exciting and interactive venues will surely increase. Parallel to this development, at the retail level, stores themselves will become more and more interactive and

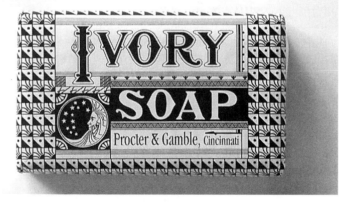

P&G's promotional vintage packaging for Ivory Soap.

experiential; *places where culture, social gathering, and commerce will mingle.* In fact, the distinctions between stores and entertainment venues are already beginning to blur, just as the distinctions between restaurants and recreational venues are merging, as with the GameWorks locations that include full-service restaurants with bars and videogames (can stores be far behind in developing similar offerings?). Certainly, Las Vegas is at the forefront of this trend—it can no longer be considered primarily as either a casino, theme park, shopping-mecca, or entertainment center, because it is a conglomeration of all of these. Moreover, it is fast becoming a veritable cultural center, with world-class museums as well.

The Evolving Tale of Retail: When Selling Becomes Storytelling

Even when the economy has hit "bottom," there are always great opportunities for retail. This is indeed a very exciting time for retail, when we are seeing the exploration of great new ideas. First of all, as I just mentioned, the merging of entertainment and retail has been taking place for some time now and malls are becoming as much about visiting brands like Microsoft as they are about visiting a traditional store. In *Emotional Branding,* I explored some of the most cutting-edge experiential retailers, such as REI and Discovery Channel, which offer consumers the opportunity to experience their products in the most exciting, interactive ways imaginable—such as in-store rock climbing or strolling through interactive "sound zones." This approach to retailing is rapidly becoming par for the course, with recent developments such as the merger of The Mills Corp. and the William Morris Agency. Mills Corp. is the major mall developer, famous for its Discover Mills and "shoppertainment" centers that are virtual tourist destinations, with stores such as Bass Sports, replete with fishing ponds; William Morris Agency is the world's top talent- and literary-agent group, with celebrity and corporate clients like Whoopi Goldberg and Anheuser-Busch. We are sure to see other new and very exciting executions of this concept. Mills and William Morris have joined together to form a consulting company called Venue3D, which will provide unique strategic business consulting and corporate advisory services in the emerging area of venue-based branding and marketing. In total, Venue3D's initial client portfolio offers marketers strategic access to more than 200 well-known consumer destinations in North America, and more than one billion consumers per year. Venue3D's services will include creative venue representation, brand experience concepting and development, naming rights and identity acquisition, strategic alliances, and sponsorship sales. Some of its initial clients include The Rouse Company (South Street Seaport, Faneuil Hall Marketplace, New Orleans Riverwalk, Harbor Place in Baltimore); Urban Retail (Water Tower Place in Chicago, Houston Galleria, Century City Shopping Center in Los Angeles); Vornado Realty Trust (Penn Plaza in NYC, Chicago Merchandise Mart, L.A. Mart); and Fairmont Hotels and Resorts. Venue3D will also service the entire portfolio of the Mills Corporation, which includes twelve major market retail and entertainment destinations in ten states. "This new, venue-based medium is extremely powerful, connecting with consumers where they work, live, shop, play, eat, recreate, and transact,"[1] said Steven H. Kram, COO of The William Morris Agency. He goes on to say, "Venue3D is going to offer a way to bring products into consumers' lives in the same way that you're seeing integrated advertising on television. . . . Just like on television, products can be integrated into a story line at the shopping center."[2]

However, as we catapult ourselves into this spectacular future of high-tech, ultra-entertaining, attention-grabbing retail venues, it is important to remember that there are many different ways to enchant consumers and tell a story. One of the problems with the "entertainment mecca merger" concept is that time-starved consumers visiting retail venues (as opposed to theme parks or casinos) are not always looking for an escapist adventure. Sometimes they just want to browse a little and purchase products in a time-efficient manner without having to make their way through an Alice in Wonderland–like maze of fantastic new retail concepts. The concept of storytelling is certainly not new to retail and it will be important to remember all of the more low-tech, subtler branding tools of the past, which are still incredibly effective–sometimes even more so.

The most important thing is that a retail concept be "people oriented" and that its execution be well designed. Design indeed transcends technology–it is about ideas that you can see–and it can be very powerful in creating a total brand experience at retail level whether through high-tech or low-tech solutions! People may be happy to spend time exploring via technology at certain times, like when they're visiting a store for the purpose of entertainment or when they are surfing the Web from the cozy comfort of their homes, but at other times it could be unappealing. It is important to be sensitive to these differences.

The challenge in retailing of the future is to balance both the desire for escape and entertainment with our more practical need to find and purchase products. The solution is to be extremely flexible and creative in providing a little of both whenever and however possible and in knowing when and where consumers will favor one over the other.

The challenge in retailing of the future is to balance both the desire for escape and entertainment with our more practical need to find and purchase products.

Of course, to be able to do this, it is crucial that we really know people and what they are looking for from a shopping experience in a given location. Teens are more likely to want to engage in a deeper interactive, entertainment-oriented experience, since shopping, to them, is largely about socializing and exploring trends and they have–or will make–the time to try something new. The same often goes for families, since the shopping outing often includes the goal of spending quality time bonding. But for time-crunched working mothers, for example, the challenge of balancing the practical exercise of shopping with entertainment is more difficult. However, it is important not to generalize or limit the possibilities for any demographic. If the brand experience offered has an intrinsic added value for working mothers, such as relaxation or education, or is just so completely enticing as to become a destination in and of itself as part of her "time-for-herself" rituals, then it can really work. As a part of their new, more upscale "white" (without the signature red and white checkered awnings) store concept, Bath & Body Works is now offering spa services–massages, facials, manicures, pedicures, and so on–along with a new collection of spa products called "True Blue." In tangent with this, Bath & Body Works is also developing an extensive aromatherapy line. CEO Beth Pritchard says Bath & Body Works is expanding its pampering concept to include, "not just soaps and lotions, but a total sense of health and well-being."[5]

Bath & Body Works could develop a real Citizen Brand effort around this new holistic concept by offering seminars, or even a series of courses, with certificates in aromatherapy, health, and beauty. In this way, the stores themselves could become more like communities that bring a variety of people together for shared brand experiences.

Along these lines, Aveda offers a series of "Lifestyle Workshops" such as "Stress Less," "Baby Massage," and "Perfect Sense," which teaches aromatherapy methods. Another clever retail concept that allows for plenty of "brand bonding," albeit in a much more frivolous setting, is Star Shoes in Hollywood, which sells an incredible collection of vintage shoes in a cocktail-lounge atmosphere where people can order drinks, wear the shoes all night long around the fabulous digs, and even take a few turns on a dance floor–essentially partying while they shop!

Bath & Body Works could develop a real Citizen Brand effort around this new holistic concept by offering seminars, or even a series of courses, with certificates in aromatherapy, health, and beauty.

Shared experiences and tribal bonding will indeed be the most important opportunity for an emotionally powerful experience at retail level in the future. Stores and, above all, malls themselves, have an enormous capability for becoming a real nexus of a community with the power to bring people together under common causes and contribute to their lives. Many stores and malls have accomplished this in certain ways, but *there is much more that can be done, especially in terms of well-planned youth programs that appeal to Gen Y's desire to contribute to their community.* Canadian Cadillac Fairview Malls has had a great deal of success hosting a series of events to bring youth together in support of SHiNE (Seeking Harmony in Neighbourhoods Everyday), one of the country's leading youth organizations. The kids have loved events such as the "To The Maxx Climbing Challenge," where they scaled twenty-five-foot indoor climbing walls, and the SHiNE Hands-On Pledge Wall, where they were invited to take up paint and a brush and leave their handprints and messages of social harmony on the wall. These lively town-hall style events, which are moderated by special celebrity guests, have also included SHiNE Teen Speak Outs, which provide young people with a unique opportunity to express their views on issues that are important to them. Throughout each event SHiNE teams provide information about the SHiNE organization, community opportunities, SHiNE clubs, and in-school programs.

The Store as Your Best Friend's Home: Hanging Out

Another response to the cold magic of megalithic entertainment-oriented retail emporiums in malls is the retail trend toward an eclectic collection of handpicked cool items in a more intimate, personalized environment. Stores such as Moss, the design "shrine," in Manhattan's Soho were at the forefront of this trend. To visit Moss is to receive a mini-education in modern functional design. The "brand experience," in this case, is the personality behind the choice of the merchandise mix, which initiates the consumer into a knowledgeable insiders' world. Some of these lifestyle stores, which are mostly highly urban/modernist or "bobo" (bourgeois/bohemian) in flavor, are literally designed to look like a hip friend's home—as in, for example, the Manhattan store aptly named, "Apartment." One Vancouver shop named "Bruce" was designed to be, as owner Campbell McDougall says, "an anti-department store." Instead of offering all things to all people, Bruce offers the best of everything to a very select group of style-conscious consumers. The two-level shop sells modern designer fashions, shoes, housewares, gifts, eyewear, art, music, magazines, and a few things in between. Upstairs, a high-design café offers trendsetting shoppers a place to relax over a light meal and drinks. It's a store concept that capitalizes on what some industry watchers have called the single most important retail trend in the last three years: combining various and sundry products that speak to a very specific audience. Another Canadian shop, The Pleasure of Style, in Toronto, is located in an actual apartment and sells a mixture of funky modern and vintage items from around the world.

Hollister, Abercrombie & Fitch's latest retail concept, created for a younger, high-school–aged consumer, builds on this idea of creating an intimate, homelike atmosphere to encourage kids to hang out. The stores are designed to look like a California beach house with Spanish tile roofs and laid-back lounging areas with couches, where kids can read magazines, listen to jukeboxes, and socialize. It is indeed very smart for retailers to offer teens a homey hangout space away from their "parent-infested" homes, and they will surely develop an emotional connection with a brand that understands this need!

Retail's New Story: Stores as Cultural Destinations and "Public Spaces"

Now I want to take you to a new place altogether, to the place of the stores of the future. It is a very different place that in some sense combines all of the ideas we have just seen, but in a new and very exciting way that beautifully reflects the Citizen Brand concept. First of all, one of the most powerful new ideas in retail environments is the creation of environments that are flexible, fluid, and have the capability to be malleable or changeable so that people can have their own unique experiences that are different every time–or they may even affect the environment themselves according to their own mood. DKNY was the forerunner of this trend in the way the store completely changed its look and feel every month or so to tell an entirely new story. If the story was about the concept of "Spring," for example, the theater lighting in the store was adjusted, the store redecorated and completely re-merchandised.

To begin with, I would like to use one of my company's architectural projects, the New York City bar, XL, to further illustrate this concept and show where it is now taking the world of retail. As the most popular new gay bar in New York City, XL owes its success to more than just being a pretty place. David Ashen, the head of architecture in our firm and a tremendous designer and thinker, worked very hard to create an environment that would stand out among others. He wanted to create a place that would attract influential people and that could become a rallying point for activists' activities in the gay community. And he succeeded in this goal. It was appropriately used to promote Mark Green, a candidate for Mayor of New York City and a supporter of gay causes.

David is one of those brilliant conceptual thinkers who can "dimensionalize" a concept in unexpected ways from a sensorial and holistic point of view. The physical space of XL, which was a run-down, former repair shop, came to life as a totally unique, highly interactive space that is defined by and pulses to the mood of the crowd.

David was obsessed by what he called the "change" factor–reaching beyond static walls and decors that are bound to go out of style sooner or later and keeping a level of excitement with people who are today easily bored. He wanted to inspire the crowd. He saw the space as evolving with the mood of the crowd at different times of the night. He also wanted to make every part of the bar a "peek-a-boo" concept where people or things could be identified without complete recognition and where no place would be "taboo."

He responded to the challenge with brio. First, he bet the house on lighting. He used highly creative, colorful lighting strategies to create different moods. Then he used see-through mirrors and frosted glass to bring about a play of reflected shadows and movement that is dreamlike–undefined but present, reinforcing a sense of mystery. From the street, for instance, you can see through a huge blue frosted window highlighting a modern concrete front and see people moving inside without being able to see details clearly. Privacy is respected, but for passers-by on the outside the excitement of the place is clearly expressed in an intriguing manner.

The unisex bathrooms are open around a huge, beautiful aquarium, and the separations of the stalls are also in frosted glass . . . private but mystical. A VIP room with a two-way mirror allows you to meet with friends or have a corporate meeting in total privacy yet be able to observe the scene. The concepts of voyeurism and intimacy are explored in an interesting and playful way through a balance of privacy and mystery that brings an overall sense of wonder. XL has become so hip that it is starting to attract straight people as well–it is a magical place where anyone can feel comfortable. I am convinced that David has brought a new concept in environmental work that could be translated in offices and stores with great results. David is now designing his latest bar project, the redesign of the famed Limelight nightclub which is situated in a former church. There is nothing religious about this project, except that the place is sure to be divine!

I wanted to talk about the bar XL in this chapter because of the fact that David succeeded in his aim to create a dynamic and "changeable" space that is responsive to the way people want to use it, allowing it to transcend the definition of "just a bar"–it's a great example of where retail trends are now headed. The transformation taking place in the world of retail goes far beyond the idea of entertainment. It is about creating public spaces where people can exchange ideas and have a myriad of different experiences each time they visit– life-enhancing cultural experiences of art and design with commerce taking the backseat. *The idea that stores can become a public space for people–especially in a crowded urban environment where public space is at a premium–is a brilliant one!* The best public spaces, while they have their own distinct design personality, are also very open and flexible with the ability to be altered constantly according the whims and needs of the people who use those spaces.

The original location before the new architectural design.

At XL, lighting helps the space evolve with the mood of the crowd at different times of the night.

Prada's new store in Manhattan is a perfect example of how this can work. The launch of this two-story store designed by architect Rem Koolhaas has had rave reviews from the press and is currently the talk of the town. It has succeeded in bringing forward the imagination factor of the brand. *What is unique about the store is that it is designed to be a multi-use space: a retail space, a gallery space, a theater space–almost anything you can imagine!* The first floor is an entire city block long and seems to have been designed as a roller-skating rink. Its U-shaped feel gives a sense of something unexpected that will reveal itself to you as you move into the store—already you are feeling the imaginative spirit of the place. On one sliding side of the "rink," stairs have been designed to display a shoe collection, a nice way to showcase a full collection or the fashion of the season. The upper floor presents movable fixtures hung from the ceiling which feel more like showcases than selling presentations, and the walls are used for graphics only. This kind of merchandise display is a great concept for allowing the store to change its entire look every season. The idea here is that the space is malleable. It can be used to host fashion shows, to present new collections, to do a fragrance launch . . . or, and this is where we are headed, to sponsor a cultural event, a gallery-type exhibition.

Germano Celant, Prada's curator, is one of the most respected in the world. Is there provocation in clothing the rich while you support values that despise this exact notion?

Miuccia Prada is known to have been associated with the Italian Communist party and even once used the Communist headquarters in Paris for a fashion show. The Prada Foundation sponsors various cultural projects and is well known for its commitment to the art world. Germano Celant, their curator, is one of the most respected in the world. Is there provocation in clothing the rich while you support values that despise this exact notion? I would venture to say that this very question is inherent in the creative tension the brand expresses. The store materials, for instance, have a factory or industrial look and the technology of both the architecture and clothing manufacture is very pragmatic. No rich marble or materials in the store that bring cues from the world of the rich elite. The message is further emphasized in communicating fashion as a statement for a new society and clothing that becomes a statement of individuality. I doubt very much that Prada's mission is to turn its store into a propaganda machine on behalf of the working class; and, as customers, I doubt people feel they are being asked to endorse a political point of view! But what you can feel in observing people in the store is that they are looking for a different brand language that breaks out of the crowd, and they are finding it here.

Emotions, even if challenging and controversial, create buzz and attract the attention of the public. *In mixing politics, social con-*

sciousness, culture, and art, Prada creates a message that challenges our psyche. The Prada luxury idea is not to exclude, but to provide statements through fashion. The message is fashion. The culture is fashion.

This movement toward culture can be seen budding in retail at the moment, particularly (but not exclusively) in fashion stores. A Hugo Boss store in Manhattan has a Frank Gehry exhibit, while Takashimaya has cleared out all the merchandise on its first floor to create a gallery space. And Diane Von Furstenberg has created a unique retail space that has a small (800 or so square foot) store in front and a huge loftlike space of 20,000 square feet in back that she uses as a gallery space or to host cultural or fashion events that bring together the best talents the city has to offer, including the work of other designers. But, and I've perhaps saved the best for last, the most exciting execution I have yet to see of this public/cultural space concept is in the wonderful new Felissimo store.

FELISSIMO: A NEW WORLD OF DESIGN AND "ACTIVE CONSUMERISM"

In my last book I talked about the incredible Japanese store, Felissimo, and here, once again, I would like to talk about it, because the store has evolved its winning retail formula to make it even better, which is, of course, the sign of a master retailer as a purveyor of experiences that stretch beyond the expected in keeping in touch with people and larger societal trends. Felissimo opened its first store in New York City in 1992. Its vision was to create a three-dimensional space offering unique merchandising in a serene retail oasis for millions of visitors from around the world. The store is located in a beautiful four-story brownstone—which was a very innovative idea for its time and has now been vastly copied. The overall feeling of the store is one of discovery and sensorial experience that is very unique in the retail world. I was a regular at the store, where you can find the most interesting and innovative gifts at all prices always presented in packaging that added to a sense of discovery of the object as a piece of art. The most interesting idea for me was the fact that you could find products there that were to be found nowhere else. This was a new idea at the time and brought a valuable proposition to shoppers used to department stores, which all fight over the same brands—which of them does not have Ralph, Tommy, Estée, Liz, Lalique, etc., etc.? At Felissimo you could always find the refreshing appeal of something unique. But a success story must continually be revitalized to meet people's aspirations, and during my last visit I discovered that, unbeknownst to me, Felissimo had changed its winning formula to one that is completely focused on design. The new brand statement is: "The Felissimo Design House vision is to inspire lifestyle models for the twenty-first century by encouraging dialogue and collaboration between designers, consumers, and enterprise." Furthermore, Felissimo states that its belief is that *"design cultivates relationships between people, nature, and lifestyle. In our model design promotes happiness, well being, and adds value to everyday life.* Felissimo therefore will create, promote, and offer collaborative opportunities for design concepts that improve, inspire, and emotionally move the lives of those that share in our creative initiative." When I read this. I almost cried. It should be my company's mission statement.

In accordance with this new brand mission, Felissimo now has an incredible in-house art gallery where it houses exhibits and hosts charity events. One such exhibition was based on the concept of "peace" with art displayed by more than a hundred artists from around the world.

We may be tempted to think that Felissimo is new at this design-oriented approach, but it is interesting to observe that in 1995 it had already created "Design 21," an international design award as part of the United Nations fiftieth anniversary celebrations. The purpose of this award is to discover and provide opportunities to young talent from all over the world–young creators from different cultures. UNESCO, the United Nations' educational, scientific, and cultural organization, and Felissimo together manage and organize the award.

Consumers today are seeking a personal involvement. This attitude, characterized by the store as "active consumerism," encourages an active engagement from people and is a reality that transcends the ideal. Today, the store reflects this new philosophy entirely. Gone are the frivolous, yet beautiful, scented candles and accessories. The store has been repainted white and has turned itself into a virtual art gallery–a showcase of design concepts you can buy. Felissimo has commissioned Robert Rauschenberg to design a teacup, and the famous architect Arata Isozaki, a world leader in postmodernism, to design a chopsticks rest. You can find innovative ideas such as the "Munidée" collection, a series of cute, miniature-sized clothing articles that serve as bottle covers. These are all great concepts that connect people to design through everyday objects.

What is most important and instructive about this store is the philosophical attitude geared to finding solutions for people, which is in opposition to the passive attitude of the twentieth century. *Consumers today are seeking a personal involvement. This attitude, characterized by the store as "active consumerism," encourages an active engagement from people* and is a reality that transcends the ideal. We are in a new world of total human engagement in the Felissimo store.

Bring the Brand to the People

Beyond enticing consumers to hang out and recreate in stores and malls to experience the brand, brands must also find ways to bring a valuable brand experience to the consumer in other venues.

The best way to make people fall in love with your brand is to bring a useful or fun experience directly to consumers in the daily course of their lives. There are many inventive ways to do this and the best have to do with giving people the chance to interact with a brand in a totally new way. Often, the best way of doing this is to offer people a memorable experience for free, as American Express did when they launched their Blue Card in 1999 with a free Sheryl Crow concert in Central Park, which eventually received three Grammy nominations. Blue cards were marketed at the event and the ensuing sign-ups for the card exceeded Amex's expectations.

Nikon also took its brand to the people with a nationwide highly unstructured, "no rules" photo contest for Gen Y, a demographic that is particularly responsive to this kind of in-the-field brand initiative. Nikon's promotion, called "Coopix 775 Summer Fun Road Tour" was a great success in bringing the experience of Nikon's new Web-enabled pocket-size digital camera directly to its Gen Y consumers in a way that was relevant to their lives. Nikon hired twenty-year-olds to decorate vans and take photos on a cross-country road tour. The photos were posted on a Web site as an interactive diary of the journey. At each of the twelve cities where the vans stopped, consumers were encouraged to use the cameras to photograph unusual events and submit their photos to a "Search for Summer's Ultimate Funny Photo" contest with a grand prize of an all expenses paid trip to New York for the winner and ten friends. As Nikon's VP of marketing says, "This was the first time Nikon has launched a product with a national marketing tour where we actually brought the product to the consumer."[4] In view of the promotion's success (the Web site had 50,000 visitors in the first month!), Nikon says it is planning more similar promotions for the future.

Harley-Davidson has also found a clever way to give people a first-hand experience of its brand and encourage those who may be a bit intimidated by the "tough/Easy Rider" aspect of the Harley image. In a program called "Rider's Edge," Harley-Davidson is offering motorcycle instruction at its dealerships. The courses, which are intentionally not designed as a "selling tool," teach people not only how to ride a Harley, but also focus on overall motorcycle safety, using the same stringent driving and written tests required by the Motorcycle Safety Foundation for motorcycle certification, and gives tours of repair shops and motorcycle warehouses. Lara Lee, director of Rider's Edge says, "We wanted to take the person who felt like an outsider and turn him into an insider, without insiders feeling as if we were taking away from Harley's image, which is a little bit bad and a little bit separate."[5]

The most original and powerful aspect of the Coca-Cola Company's $150 million Harry Potter promotion, Coca-Cola's largest promotional effort ever, is the fact that at the heart of the promotion are measures to encourage children to read. In this case, Coca-Cola is not only offering a brand experience, but is also making a genuine attempt to help people and enrich their lives. The goal of this multifaceted, multimedia campaign—centered on the highly anticipated children's fantasy film *Harry Potter and the Sorcerer's Stone*, which is based on the hugely successful series of Potter books—is to "touch people on a very personal level," rather than simply bombard them with commercials and print advertisements. This campaign, which promotes the film along with the Coca-

This is a great opportunity, a great inspiration, to step it up and focus on reading. If we think of young people as the future of the country, it's more appropriate than ever that they have the right foundation, and reading is a big part of that.

Cola brand and two lines of juice drinks, Minute Maid and Hi-C, includes traditional advertising, charitable contributions to sweepstakes, and grassroots consumer activities. The initiatives will span up to three years in almost forty countries. There are instant-win games, a special Web site (*www.LivetheMagic.com*), donations of books to schools, and a contest for a trip to London for a "Hogwarts Castle Adventure," packages of Coca-Cola Classic and Coca-Cola with "Harry Potter" graphic designs, and converted Coca-Cola trucks that promote reading among children during a cross-country tour. "This whole program is a good example of our desire to deliver experiences to consumers. . . . That's pretty powerful, we believe,"[6] says Suzanne Robbins, senior brand manager for cause marketing at the Coca-Cola North America division of Coca-Cola in Atlanta. "We've done tremendous work in youth development for years," Ms. Robbins says. "This is a great opportunity, a great inspiration, to step it up and focus on reading. If we think of young people as the future of the country, it's more appropriate than ever that they have the right foundation, and reading is a big part of that."[7] There are three elements to the reading programs; two are in conjunction with the organization known as Reading is Fundamental. One element is the Library Collection Program, under which Coca-Cola and the organization will use a grant of $18 million from the company to place 10,000 sets of hardcover children's books in community centers and in classrooms of children who attend kindergarten and grades 1–3. The other element is Story Travelers, which are Harry Potter/Coca-Cola converted delivery trucks that will visit hundreds of sites nationwide in the next three years–sites such as malls, stores, and community centers, as well as urban and suburban schools that take part in Reading is Fundamental programs. Two children's-book publishers, Scholastic Inc., and Troll Communications, are to donate more than a million books to the Story Travelers program so that each visiting child may take home a free book. The Gift of Reading Tour will send oversized books to five cities nationwide and for each signature on the book–which pledges the signer to a commitment to reading– Coca-Cola and First Book, another organization that encourages reading, will give a needy child a book. More than 100,000 books are expected to be distributed during the tour.

This campaign is clearly another sign of Coca-Cola's efforts under Chairman Douglas Daft to build a new image as a good corporate citizen by creating marketing programs that make its products part of consumers' lives rather than simply drawing consumers to its brands. The campaign is well orchestrated and specifically attempts to avoid overcommercialization of the beloved Harry Potter character. For instance, there was no product placement within the movie, Harry Potter was not used as a "pitchman" for the products, and the Coca-Cola graphics on the packaging and trucks are intentionally subtle. Despite these efforts, some people and organizations are criticizing the Coca-Cola campaign for what they consider to be the commercialization of culture, particularly as it involves children. They have even gone so far as to create a Web site called *www.saveharry.com*. Of course, Coca-Cola was smart to build this program around Harry Potter, and it probably could not have avoided upsetting some people. The consumer's emotional landscape today is a minefield when kids are targeted, and what is important to remember in similar circumstances–particularly when associating with a powerful, passionately loved cultural element like Harry Potter–is that a brand must be very sensitive and attempt to evaluate any and all reactions before proceeding. But in the end, one must also remember that varying reactions are a normal and healthy part of the process of interacting with a consumer democracy.

Products fulfill needs; experiences fulfill desires. Today, it is crucial to do both. As most purchases are driven by price and convenience, the emotional relevance at retail is the most solid strategy to focus on– one that starts and ends up with people at the core. Setting the right stage for the show creates the experience that builds a new, more personal relationship with the product.

But the commitment to a certain ethic and brand vision is paramount for success in this realm. A vision inclusive of the consumer's dream will create an unforgettable emotional experience.

Products and places need to provide an experience that will make the transaction memorable from a holistic perspective. This is where the culture of a brand can truly shine in terms of reaching people directly with the right message. But the commitment to a certain ethic and brand vision is paramount for success in this realm. A vision inclusive of the consumer's dream will create an unforgettable emotional experience.

4

The Fourth Commandment: Evolve from Quality to Preference

Quality for the right price is a given today.
Preference creates the sale.

CHAPTER FOCUS: PRODUCT DEVELOPMENT

This commandment investigates the question of what makes some brands more desirable than others from the very essential point of view of the innovative design of the product offering. The premise here is that quality by itself is no longer enough. With today's ultra-efficient, sophisticated manufacturing techniques, quality is expected. What can really reach people's hearts, what makes a real difference today is innovation and sensory appeal in product development and design. There has been a great deal of talk over the past few years about the importance of fostering innovation in the realm of product development (and indeed throughout the entirety of a corporation). In terms of Emotional Branding and building brand identities that are emotionally potent, this is obviously key. Today, both concept and design have to be relevant to consumer trends. Products must reach beyond the fashionable to respond to those "hidden" human desires and needs that have yet to be realized. This concept implies a sort of visionary and inspirational divining of what could make people's lives better. Through an understanding of *what people really want from a particular brand or product, whether it's comfort, reassurance, ease of use, practical solutions, or excitement in the form of the aesthetic, design innovation must respond to our desire for emotional expression.* What creates preference in a world overcrowded with products in every category is certainly not minor surface only or gimmicky innovations—which may momentarily turn heads and provide an uplift of sales and attention—but the kind of profound, real innovations that break the mold of the expected and create a whole new way of looking at a product category. Citizen Brands understand intuitively and grow their culture around the idea that innovative product design can change people's lives, either by fundamentally changing the way we do things or by creating an entirely new experience. Either way, the choice between an ordinary product–albeit of high quality–and an innovative one is obvious. We prefer things, both large and small, that surprise, delight, and enchant us–whether through their usefulness or their beauty (hopefully, both!)–and we are often willing to pay more for these things. If you are a woman faced with the choice of buying a traditional "razor" or a Gillette's easy to grasp, ergonomically designed Venus razor with its futuristic, womanly, curvy esthetic and its very smooth four-blade shave that can make the chore of shaving more of a pleasure–the choice may be very clear.

This chapter will focus on conceptual innovation, touching on design issues but not addressing them in depth. That will be more the focus of chapter 7, "Evolve from Function to Feel," where I will discuss how to create powerful emotional experiences for people through sensorial and ergonomically sensitive design.

A Technological Wonderland Coming Our Way

Apple's new iPod is a great illustration of the idea of innovative product development from a Citizen Brand perspective, because in creating the iPod, Apple has achieved a technological breakthrough of a magnitude that means it will fundamentally change the way people access and listen to music in the future. As I said in my last book, good design is courageous, and there have certainly been detractors of Apple's courageous leap into the consumer electronics industry, with many people saying early on that the iPod would be an extravagant failure, but I predict this product will succeed and perhaps even change the mindset of the entire industry. Apple has once again proven that it can "think different." More importantly, with the iPod Apple has demonstrated its special gift for creating technological products with a very human touch.

> More importantly, with the iPod Apple has demonstrated its special gift for creating technological products with a very human touch.

The iPod will fundamentally change the way people access and listen to music.

This all white, very sleek, and chic little music playing device, the size of a deck of cards, is, as the *Wall Street Journal*'s Walt Mossberg puts it, a "design home run," and it has generated an incredible buzz among techies, music lovers, journalists, and general consumers alike. First of all, the iPod looks and feels good; it has a shiny, part mirrorlike stainless steel and part white acrylic finish, with laser-rounded edges for handheld comfort. The iPod weighs only 6.5 ounces, fits easily into a shirt pocket, and can hold up to 2,000 CD-quality songs. It has a five-gigabyte hard-drive memory and can use a Firewire port to connect to Mac computers to complete downloads of music so lightning-fast that an entire CD can be downloaded into iPod in five to ten seconds, as opposed to five minutes for most other MP3 players on the market, which work with the much slower USB port. The iPod can be run nonstop for an impressive ten hours (several times longer than most other MP3 players) and has the very clever feature of being able to act like any other small portable hard drive. In addition to music files, any other files from a user's computer can be stored to have handy in this portable package. And, of course, the sound is great. The control interface is incredibly easy to figure out, even for the technically challenged. Wow. This description sounds almost like a spec sheet, but as a *Time* magazine reviewer commented, "When I gave the iPod to my techno-suspicious parents, they figured out how to select and play in under a minute. Why can't all gadgets be like that?"[1] With its highly ergonomic design, the iPod allows the user to easily and quickly scroll through the music listings with one hand. These tasks are awkward on most other MP3 players. The iPod design shows that Apple understood something essential about people's emotional connection to music and what their daily experience and frustrations of trying to find, organize, transport, and listen to their favorite music were like. Music lovers around the world have given it a big thumbs up!

In a nutshell, this device has the potential to change how we think about personal audio-entertainment gadgets, much as Sony's first pocket-size transistor radio did in 1958, and the Sony Walkman portable stereo tape player did twenty years later. The iPod is the result of an eight-month crash-development project, which demonstrates that Apple's engineering and software skills could make it a force to be reckoned with in the consumer electronics business long dominated by companies like Sony.

Many people have even speculated that the iPod will do for MP3 music what the original Palm Pilot did for handheld computing—that is, start a revolution of a whole new, more convenient way of living! As many will recall, the Palm was seen as outrageous and "unworkable" in its time, but the creators of the Palm, Jeff Hawkins and Donna Dubinsky, went ahead despite the criticism leveled at their idea, grabbing the market share from potential competitors.

In terms of innovation, handheld computer maker Palm continues to excel. Its plug-in keyboard for the Palm Pilot, which unfolds from a small, fit-in-your-pocket size all the way out to a full-size keyboard, is a great example of people-solutions product development in the technology category. And so is the SmartPad, which enables the user to write, draw, or type on a pad of paper that downloads directly to a PDA.

Palm and payment-solution provider VeriFone have been working together to create an entirely new way of shopping. If their efforts pan out, consumers with PDAs would simply have to point their device at a specially designed VeriFone point-of-sales terminal in order to transmit credit card information via the infrared light that, as it turns out, all PDAs already are capable of transmitting. This

The Palm Pilot keyboard fits in your pocket and opens all the way out to a full-size keyboard.

means no card swiping and no wayward credit card slips. The system will also support debit and ATM cards and will allow for information transfers for loyalty programs and electronic-receipt captures to the system's "point-and-pay" features. It will mean a big change in receipt tracking, expense management, and tax preparation. Consumers overwhelmed with bill statements and boxes of receipts will have it much easier come tax time.

Indeed, the idea of combining two or more functions into one device—like the iPod's ability to also serve as a portable hard drive that can be used to transport files—seems to be where we are headed in the big picture. We are finally beginning to see a merging of the cell phone and PDAs with phones like the Nokia 9290 Communicator that surf the Web and download streaming video and e-mails. We have the first "view phone," the new 3G DoCoMo Japanese pocket-size video phone; unfortunately, at this writing, it's available only in Asia. When we can actually see the person we are speaking with, it adds a deeper, more intimate, human dimension to the entire experience of a phone call. Surely, everyone speculates the computer and TV will be merging soon. And what about all of these together in one device? It would be so much easier that way!

This ability to combine functions means that the lines between what is considered to be a toy or entertainment device and a practical or work-related device, will continue to blur. For example, Sony's AIBO robot dog has had amazing success with consumers who have fallen in love with the pooch toy that can bark, whine, learn and respond to commands, and so forth. Sony has had the clever idea of making the AIBO more useful to people in a practical sense. They are creating various add-on software programs that teach the old dog new tricks, such as the AIBO Explorer program that works as an alarm system so that people who need a watchdog won't have to get a real one! As our technological abilities become more and more refined and we are increasingly able to make products "smart," I predict that there will be many more clever adaptations like this one. In fact, the wave of the future seems to be indicating that we will all be interacting constantly with many "smart" devices that speak back to us, from cars to vacuum cleaners. And this human-machine interaction will continue to encourage us in our desire to personify these objects as living creatures—a desire that will need to be met through brand/product design and software programs that exude the warmth of a creature or character with personality.

As in the case of the Sony AIBO Robot dog, we will also continue to see many real, practical safety solutions for people. In the future, for example, the danger of getting shipwrecked or lost in a snowstorm on a mountainside may become virtually nil. London Associates has designed an ingenious lifesaving device called the 406 Emergency Position Indicating Radio Beacon (EPIRB) and the Fastfind Personal Location Beacon, which can pinpoint the holder's location to within thirty meters, in the roughest seas. I would bet that in the future we will see the technology of this device develop to include on-land applications, and become part of a watch or piece of jewelry, or a jacket that anyone can wear as needed. Think of the ease of mind this could give parents around the world!

As in the case of the Sony AIBO Robot dog, we will also continue to see many real, practical safety solutions for people.

Another safety breakthrough is on the way from Honda, which is now testing a voice-recognition system due out in early 2003 that will allow drivers to compose and send e-mails orally and have incoming messages read back to them. The program also includes a monitoring system that alerts drivers when upcoming road conditions, such as sharp curves, may temporarily interrupt the connection. But, perhaps, one of the most impressive recent technological feats that will potentially save lives is that of a company called Eclipse Aviation. This innovator is well on its way to developing a new kind of small, fast jet that will be efficient and cheap enough to allow for a totally new kind of air travel for the masses, at least for shorter trips. This twin-engine jet can be flown by one pilot and carry five passengers for 1,600 miles at 400 miles an hour. It will be the cheapest twin-engine jet ever produced, at a cost of just a quarter of current low-price leader, and with less than half the operating cost. The plane can be operated profitably at a cost of $500 an hour, and with three or more passengers, the price per rider will be cheaper than for discount airlines like Southwest. Given a choice between the hassles of a crowded discount-airline flight and hopping on a small private jet for the same fare, the choice will be easy! Their plan is to get enough Eclipse planes in the sky to drive the economics of this system down. This plane, which has been called a "computer with wings" has computer-driven capabilities, such as fingerprint pilot recognition, which ensures that the plane will only fly for designated pilots and which will verify before the engine starts that the pilot's training and insurance are current. They will also have state-of-the-art satellite datacommunication capabilities that will allow the company to keep the black boxes at its company headquarters and to continuously monitor aircraft systems from the ground in order to anticipate and correct possible faults. They will even have a panic button the pilot can push to hand over the flying of the plane to somebody on the ground! The planes will be in the air beginning 2004 and will surely be the first step to a whole new way of travel for many.

When "Old" Becomes New Again

Sometimes product innovations delight us because they offer a new way of experiencing a well-known, loved product or a new twist to an everyday activity we could do in our sleep. In the realm of product development, no idea is too large or too small, and sometimes a "little" idea can be more groundbreaking than a so-called big idea. Simple solutions to everyday problems are not to be underestimated.

Literally thousands of kids and parents contacted Heinz through phone calls, letters, and e-mails asking for another color to squeeze.

One of the best examples of a simple but profound product innovation that has provided people with solutions and revitalized a whole industry is Heinz's introduction of new "color" ketchup products–first green and now purple. These colors, EZ Squirt Funky Purple and Blastin' Green, presented in a fun and ergonomic packaging designed to fit in a kid's hand, brought a very innovative "human solution" to the proverbial problem of getting kids to eat their dinner by making the experience more fun and interactive for kids. The product line has won huge support from kids and parents alike, allowing Heinz to increase their market share by five points, a tremendous increase in a traditional and tired category. When Heinz launched its EZ Squirt Blastin' Green ketchup, more than 10 million bottles were sold in the first seven months, and Heinz factories a year later were working twenty-four hours a day, seven days a week to keep up with demand. Desperate consumers eager to get their hands on Heinz EZ Squirt Blastin' Green have tried everything from impersonating Heinz executives' relatives, to bidding for bottles posted on eBay. Heinz EZ Squirt boosted not only Heinz's share of the ketchup market, but ketchup sales overall! *Literally thousands of kids and parents contacted Heinz through phone calls, letters, and e-mails asking for another color to squeeze* alongside traditional red and the phenomenally popular Heinz EZ Squirt Blastin' Green. To find the new color, Heinz turned to kids for advice and eventually came up with purple.

By focusing on providing a virtual entertainment experience around the daily activity of eating, Heinz ketchup was more concerned with children's pleasure than with the customary obsession with supermarket shelves positioning.

By focusing on providing a virtual entertainment experience around the daily practical activity of eating, Heinz ketchup was more concerned with children's pleasure than the customary obsession with supermarket shelves positioning. Kraft's "Lunchables" was a forerunner to this concept because, with its miniature pizza and sandwich element, it gave kids the ability to interact with their food in a new way and build their own meals. "Kids want to feel like they're in control of everything, including mealtime," says Kelly Stitt, a senior brand manager in charge of EZ Squirt for Heinz. "When they have the ability to change the food, it becomes a more personal experience for them."

Heinz's fun and ergonomic packaging designed to fit in a kid's hand.

Heinz has opened up a whole new way of seeing and developing food products, as interactive "toys" or as educational material, all of which seems to be helping parents with the sometimes difficult task of getting their children to eat. Marion Nestle, the chairman of the Department of Nutrition and Food Studies at New York University and author of the book *Food Politics,* is quoted in the *Wall Street Journal*: "Many parents teach their children to read and count with books about Fruit Loops, Cheerios, M&Ms, and Oreos." Now we are seeing margarines in "electric blue" and "shocking pink," and ConAgra has just launched a margarine called the "Fun Squeeze," with which kids squeeze designs on their food. Quaker Oats has added edible treasures and dinosaurs to their hot cereals, and Cheetos has come out with "Mystery Colorz" chips that are regular orange-colored chips, but color a person's mouth bright blue when eaten. Nabisco's product, Fun Fruits Gamesters, are fruit snacks that can be used as pieces in a game of ticktacktoe. Following this trend, there are now products on the market such as FooDoodlers, special markers that allow children to draw on food!

By understanding that happy children make happy parents Heinz, consciously or not, became part of a lifestyle solution and expanded beyond their boundaries as a manufacturer to become a smart Citizen Brand. Understanding what people want in an emotional and psychological way is key to any success in the marketplace!

By understanding that happy children make happy parents, Heinz, consciously or not, became part of a lifestyle solution and expanded beyond its boundaries as a manufacturer to become a smart Citizen Brand.

Let's take a look at some other product innovations, both recent and classic, from brands that have evolved way beyond quality to create real preference with people:

- A classic product innovation is the PowerBar. Before the PowerBar, trail mix and granola bars were available for a quick healthy snacks. The choice was either that or a candy bar. The PowerBar, initially developed to give athletes an added energy boost, responded to a greater need in our busy lifestyles for healthy, easy-to-transport food on the run.
- Digital pill organizers such as Zelco's Aqua Pill Timer are a great product innovation that can simplify, and possibly save, seniors' lives. Someone realized that there had to be a better solution for people with complex medication rituals for sorting out, transporting, and remembering to take their pills. The Aqua Pill Timer has a programmable alarm that sounds when it's time to take medication, a pill sorter compartment, and even and a compartment that holds two ounces of water!
- Pfizer's new Listerine PocketPaks, portable mouthwash strips that melt on the tongue, are certainly nothing earth-shattering, but their terrific success on the market is surely due to the fact that they are a terrific new solution for our on-the-go lifestyles not only to the problem of bad breath, but, like the mouthwash, they are also effective against germs.
- Alka Seltzer's new product, "Morning Relief," was created as a solution to the age-old problem of hangovers. The humorous tag line of the commercial launching "Morning Relief" says it all: "Feel better than you should." It's hard to imagine no one else thought of this before, and it is a perfect extension for Alka-Seltzer; because of its products addressing heartburn and indigestion, Alka-Seltzer is already known as a brand people can turn to when they have "overindulged."
- Colgate 2in1 Toothpaste and Mouthwash cleverly combines mouthwash with toothpaste in a liquid gel-like formula to simplify the daily ritual.
- Jergens Naturally Smooth is a great new product for women. It is a body moisturizer that makes leg hair finer and less noticeable with daily use so that after eight weeks a consumer will have to

The new Listerine pocket pack designed for our on-the-go lifestyle.

shave half as often. This product has been literally flying off the shelves since it was introduced. Jergens was very smart in realizing that women, who dread the chore of having to shave their legs, would love this product.

- RadioShack has created a "talking picture frame" that can record a ten-second voice greeting. This is, of course a wonderful gift to send to a loved one who is far away. To launch the product, RadioShack had them given to Russian cosmonauts on the International Space Station, whom RadioShack then had filmed for a commercial as they opened their gifts. In the spot, the commanding cosmonaut receives a frame as a Father's Day gift from his daughter at home in Russia. "We felt the first commercial filmed on the International Space Station was an extraordinary way to showcase this cool traveler's gift as an ideal Father's Day present. It's all about helping people stay connected, wherever your travels may take you," said Jim McDonald, senior vice president of marketing and advertising for RadioShack Corporation.
- Dannon has introduced a "Fluoride to Go" spring water for kids, which, if kids will really drink it (!), could make dental visits a little easier for parents and kids. Coca-Cola and Pepsi are also now working on water products that will contain calcium and fluoride.

As these examples aptly illustrate, the innovation ante has definitely been "upped," and companies will be forced to innovate more and more in the future to keep up with the competition. What companies need to understand is that innovation is a "numbers game" and the fear of failure is not a part of this game! People have to have the freedom to try out many different, often wacky ideas before hitting the right creative chord. Innovative product design requires the creative ability to mix and match ideas and forms from observations in different areas of life and import new elements from other disciplines to the project at hand. For example, one of the innovations IDEO, the product design group, came up with for the awkwardness of drinking from bicycle water bottles was a suction valve based on an artificial heart valve made for a medical products company. Inventions like this, which indeed do create consumer preference, do not happen through a results-oriented focus of "trying to come up with a creative breakthrough." They are a natural outcome of a process that has people and their needs as its focus. The best creative strategy is quite simply to keep people in mind–what they love, what they need!

Some of the greatest innovations in product development are also often the result of a very long and serious commitment to R&D, such as in the case where Shiseido's ten-year collaboration with Harvard's Cutaneous Biology Research Center led to the discovery that aromas have revitalizing effects on the skin. This discovery then informed the development of wonderful new cosmetics lines. An effort such as this reinforces the brand mystique enormously–it becomes part of the brand's history and mythology for the consumer and, since the offering is unique, a very strong reason for brand loyalty. The loyalty factor is crucial, because although other brands may follow with similar product innovations, they will never "own" the concept the way the "inventor brand" can. In a similar endeavor Shiseido is now in the process of establishing a research center in China to study ancient Chinese medicine. Shiseido is a company that can make these kinds of commitments successfully because it is not a short-term results-oriented company. This 130-year-old company has a very strong sense of history and longevity, along with a keen sense of what it means to be a Citizen Brand. Shiseido president and CEO Morio Ikeda says, "Money isn't everything, after all. Like most large companies, we have shareholders for whom we must make profits, but that is not our only reason to exist. We also play an important role in society, so we have an obligation to maintain a balance between our financial requirements and our quest for elegance, what you might call 'noblesse oblige.'"[2]

Product development in its highest form of Citizen Brandship means that global companies must use their capacity for innovation to seek ways to match consumers' real needs on a global level. Product innovations that rely on state-of-the-art engineering, such as Toyota and Honda's "hybrid" cars that demonstrate a fuel efficiency that is nothing short of amazing, could truly change the world. In fact, it is estimated that if every U.S. driver was behind the wheel of a hybrid instead of a traditional car we would save 1.6 billion barrels of oil yearly, which is more than we currently import from Middle Eastern countries!

There are, of course, many, many areas where product-development innovation could come to the rescue of the world's ills, especially in the areas of health and safety, by creating products to answer these basic human needs at a price the people of developing countries can afford. Coca-Cola's Vitango is a very good example of the kind of effort needed. This will be extremely important in terms of the new global image America must create to respond to the resentment some feel about the way American brands and culture blanket the globe. Global companies need to think about their product development in new ways for these global markets.

> **There are, of course, many, many areas where product-development innovation could come to the rescue of the world's ills, especially in the areas of health and safety.**

McDonald's has recently shown a new sensitivity toward global perceptions. After observing the growing concern in Europe that consumers have with animal welfare and the very strong feelings in these markets about the use of antibiotics in meats and chicken, they have been actively studying how they can improve the overall quality of their products with wide-reaching policy changes that focus on better control of the use of antibiotics as well as limiting the use of pesticides on fruits and vegetables. As a first step, they have begun to demand that the farmers who supply their eggs change the way they raise their chickens, insisting on less crowded cages and termination of the beak snipping practice. They are beginning to move in the direction of using only free range chickens, a policy already in place in markets like England. As the single largest buyer of eggs in the United States, this kind of initiative can exert major influence on an entire industry and McDonald's competitors are now beginning similar initiatives. McDonald's has shown with this program that it understands the importance of increasing its Citizen Brandship. Research shows pretty consistently that people really do care not only about the quality of food they eat, but also about the treatment of animals–this forward-thinking move by McDonald's will certainly help to build stronger emotional and trust based relationships with people.

McDonald's would be smart to leverage this new direction fully by developing great new menu concepts and a series of products that emphasize freshness and healthy qualities around this concept. McDonald's could, for example, focus on developing children's menus specifically tailored for improving children's diets and developing programs to educate children about nutrition.

5

The Fifth Commandment: Evolve from Notoriety to Aspiration

Being known does not mean you are also loved.

CHAPTER FOCUS: ADVERTISING

Can there be truth in advertising? Can advertising be a tool of Citizen Brandship? Not only can it be, but it must be. Brand communications, truthful or not, can of course be incredibly powerful influencers of people's decisions about which brands to purchase–especially if they go beyond getting people's attention and create brand "notoriety" to tap into people's deeper aspirations. But brand communications can only be truly effective, from an Emotional Branding standpoint, if they strive for honesty, creating an emotional resonance that will lead to a long-term brand relationship based on trust. Honesty will allow a brand to reach people's higher aspirations. The real question then is, what constitutes this honesty? Does it mean not using very young, totally wrinkle-free models to sell a wrinkle cream to older women? Probably, but less because the brand should strive for a "factual" honesty and more because, from an aspirational perspective, the brand should celebrate the beauty of all women. In other words, *there is factual honesty and emotional honesty*–the point is to be real in a way that responds to and encourages people's aspirations. Perhaps older women today no longer find this fantasy of merely *appearing* younger very motivating–today, their aspirations may be largely more about achieving a true state of "youthfulness" that has as much to do with incorporating into their confident matu-

In other words, there is factual honesty and emotional honesty—the point is to be real in a way that responds to and encourages people's aspirations.

rity an overall attitude of mental, physical, and spiritual youth. If that were the case–and according to our research on the resoundingly "age-defiant" Baby Boomers, it certainly seems to be–it is clearly another example of fear versus love and the latter's exerting more influence. A brand must be sensitive to these often subtle differences in ideology. This chapter focuses on brand communications and advertising, but the aim here is more to unearth and examine aspirational trends than to discuss specific ad campaigns and creative strategy in depth. Once a brand's "aspirational angle" is well defined, the creative expression and execution of that concept, which of course needs to be brilliant and breakthrough, is not so difficult. Advertising is an intuitive art because it is about connecting to people's emotions and inspiring people through their dreams. There are no set answers, no dictates–only the need to constantly evolve in response to the changing trends that are reflective of people's changing hearts.

Brand Heroes: Giving the Brand a Human Touch

One of the most effective ways of touching people's aspirations and creating a brand image that people can connect with emotionally is through the human contact of a brand spokesperson, real or not, who conveys a genuine, human dimension of the brand. This simple approach has proven itself to be hugely successful for a number of companies.

CEOs such as Steve Jobs at Apple and Warren Buffet can become representative of a brand's aspirational vision in a very powerful way that lends credibility. In a similar manner, Herb Kelleher, the very warm and lovable former CEO of Southwest Airlines, became the "face of the brand." He won people's hearts by embodying the brand's aspiration: the democratization of the skies. He demonstrated Southwest's idea of being in the Freedom business by showing himself to be free enough of inhibition to even dress up as Elvis for some ads. This personal connection is the reason why Lee Iacocca famously turned around declining sales at Chrysler when he started pitching the company's cars in ads.

Wendy's very personal ad campaign centered on Dave Thomas, the affable owner with a very genuine style, is another case in point. The highly successful ads conveyed much more than just a gratuitous emotional message because of the credibility the owner gave to the value commitment inherent in the brand. Indeed, Mr. Thomas became synonymous with the Wendy's brand. He appeared in over 800 ads since 1989 and holds the Guinness record for the longest TV campaign by a company founder! As Barbara Lippert at *Adweek* said, "He absolutely became the embodiment of the company as sort of the kindly Midwesterner."[1] Mr. Thomas, who named the chain after his daughter, put his wholesome identity behind his fast-food chain, transmitting decency, quality, and earnestness to an adult audience (contrary to the majority of competitors who focus on kids) in his inimitable, self-effacing humorous manner. Consumers liked him because he was laid back and he spoke from the heart; the rougher edges of his own humble beginnings came through in his speech mannerisms, like the use of double negatives. Mr. Thomas, an adopted orphan, was well-known for dedicating his life to helping abandoned children.

This strategy worked because the company backed up these aspirational promises of value and quality with their product offering and overall brand experience. A recent *Forbes* article suggests that Wendy's is winning in the market against McDonald's and Burger King by providing more for less. It is reported that Wendy's refused to join the price war of its rivals and

This strategy worked because the company backed up these aspirational promises of value and quality with their product offering and overall brand experience.

managed to beat them all with a 3.6 percent growth rate in sales throughout the Nineties. "All that through better customer relationship and more focused marketing that does not confuse customers with one-time promotion," the magazine states.[2] Indeed, a cornerstone of Wendy's brand message was inherent in its product; square-shaped hamburger patties, which conveyed in the most visceral way the concept of a company that was "not cutting corners on quality."

It is unclear now exactly how the company will proceed after the unfortunate recent death of Mr. Thomas, but it is said that the firm will likely continue using Thomas's image as an important part of its branding, just as The Walt Disney Company invokes founder Walt Disney and Kentucky Fried Chicken, Col. Harland Sanders. More than a year ago, Thomas agreed to give Wendy's the "entire right, title, interest, and ownership in and to the Thomas Persona." Chairman Jack Schuessler says of the founder, "Dave was our patriarch, a great, big lovable man. He had a passion for great-tasting hamburgers and devoted his life to serving customers great food."[3] As we have seen, this kind of passion can be very contagious! And, this spirit should always be a part of the brand. While everyone wonders about Wendy's after his passing, my feeling is that Mr. Thomas's footprints are there to stay. Personalities that have strongly affected businesses– personalities such as Col. Sanders, Sam Watson, Estée Lauder, or Mary Kay have built too much equity in their vision for their imprint not to remain as long as the brand continues to be well managed with their values in mind.

Star Power: The Brand Superhero

Other brands are even more deeply and intrinsically linked with the personalities and passions of their founders or CEOs, such as Martha Stewart, Oprah, Donna Karan, or Ralph Lauren, who, as the father of lifestyle branding and a very integral part of his brand's aspirational image, taught us all about moving from notoriety to an aspirational relationship with consumers. These brands envelope us in an entire world that feels intimate because it is multi-dimensional and is an unmistakable reflection of the founder's personality, which generates enormous trust and credibility. This trust gives people the freedom to dream. We know that Martha Stewart is not going to sell us something of shoddy quality and that her recipes will work. We know that Oprah's show or magazine or one of the movies she has produced will inspire and heal us. We know that going into a DKNY or Ralph Lauren store will be a total experience of communion with a talented designer where, if we share that designer's vision and taste, we will be able to project ourselves into the brand scenario. And, perhaps most importantly, we can believe that these brands care because the brands themselves are *people*.

And, perhaps most importantly, we can believe that these brands care because the brands themselves are *people*.

Oprah Winfrey is perhaps the best example of all from a Citizen Brand viewpoint. She has made an enormous cultural and social contribution to people's lives by single-handedly starting a huge wave of change in the way that we talk about our problems and issues in America. In short, Oprah has made it OK to be truthful. Oprah's very direct, warm style with a down-to-earth, no-nonsense honesty that

From talk show host to the role of a confidante: big sister or mother for many women.

includes opening up about her own life experiences has revolutionized our conceptions of self-empowerment and given many women (and men) permission to "be themselves." Her show has evolved from the traditional sensationalist talk-show format, where dirty laundry is aired, but problems are not solved, to become more of a "spiritual symposium" where people share their journeys of self-discovery and help one another with their issues. By allowing herself to be vulnerable and human to us, this African-American woman—a member of one of the most disenfranchised demographics in America in the not-too-distant past—has risen to a height of power and influence and become an inspiration to us all.

Her latest venture, *O* magazine, edited by Condé Nast, is a magnificent expression of a brand that is truly connected to its audience. Oprah's personal involvement with each issue, from the cover photo of her to the editor's column to the content choices and editing, is the backbone of this magazine. *What is marvelous and unique about this magazine is that every issue has a very distinct theme—just like an Oprah show*—such as "Family" for their December issue and "Trust" for their January issue, which is explored from many interesting perspectives. The overall brand attitude here is one of generosity–a place women can turn to for practical help with issues in their lives and spiritual inspiration and guidance. Each issue of *O* offers quotes by celebrities, writers, philosophers, and poets, on beautifully printed stock cards that can be torn out of the magazine with the hope that they "bring a measure of inspiration" to the reader.

In the editor's introduction to the December 2001 issue, entitled "Family Now More Than Ever," Oprah crystallizes a concept of family that could fit everyone's situation with the words, "Connection, trust, support, unconditional love is what we yearn for and need to feel complete." This topic obviously

Connection, trust, support, and unconditional love are what we yearn for and need to feel complete.

is appropriate given the holiday season–a family time–but the way it was communicated transcended the concept by bringing a powerful meaning to it and encouraging people to find solace and strength in their own families.

Indeed, Oprah seems willing to step out of the bonds of a particular role, that of a talk show host and editor, to play the universal, emotional role of a confidante and big sister or mother for many women. The tone of the family piece was not preachy but sincere, intimate, and conversational, so that as the reader you could feel as though you were talking to her. In her "What I know For Sure" column editorial she expressed one of the most profound thoughts about September 11 that I have heard so far, saying, "Our responsibility is to create a new standard, a new way of being in the world." Oprah's personality is clearly all over this magazine and she leverages her magazine to express citizen-savvy messages. She accepts her role and her ability to influence society in a major way.

Another woman who had a huge impact on the world and led women to reach levels of increased independence is Mary Kay Ash, who passed away in 2001 at the age of eighty-three. Mary Kay, the founder of one of the most successful direct-selling businesses in the beauty industry, started the business because she had been passed by for a promotion by a younger male associate. She is a case study in building a huge personality for her brand. And what a brand! The company today, with 850,000 sales associates in thirty-seven countries, is showing $1.2 billion in sales. A woman of extraordinary strength and vision, Mary Kay helped thousands of women win financial freedom by giving them the chance to prove their "can-do" aspirations and build their self-esteem. She wanted to be remembered as "someone who helped women understand how great they really are." The Mary Kay charitable trust was established to benefit women's cancer research and to protect women from violence.

Women in business as entrepreneurs have taught us a new corporate model that profoundly contrasts the egocentric, self-centered male-dominated industrial business architecture of the past. We are seeing the emergence of a new paradigm. Not yet totally dominant, but definitely there, *women have a unique, relationship-oriented approach to management that is consensual, participatory, and based on the power of sharing and helping.* To obtain the degree of success they have, women have had to use their strengths as powerful networkers and strong verbal communicators. Women do not generally waste energy in fruitless internal competition–they have a sense of progress being made when one woman makes another successful and they create webs of connections that get to the bottom of issues to find the answers.

The most successful women are the ones that have started their own businesses or been given full responsibility for controlling their destiny within a corporation–sometimes women excel better on their own than when they are forced to adapt to a rigid man's world that does not fit their personality. From Estée Lauder, Mary Kay, Oprah Winfrey, or Martha Stewart we are able to observe the power and humanity women can bring to their enterprises and the personalities of their imprints.

Sometimes women excel better on their own than when they are forced to adapt to a rigid man's world that does not fit their personality.

In the same way that Oprah and Mary Kay have talked to women's aspirations from the personal struggles in their own lives, all brands–whether feminine- or masculine-oriented brands–should seek to make that very powerful emotional connection.

Stonyfield Farm's "Adtivism" Efforts: The Hero Concept Brought to Life

Stonyfield Farm, the organic yogurt company with a corporate mission to promote social and environmental causes, is famous for efforts like its yogurt lid campaign, which carries "call-to-action" messages for everything from organic farming to gun control and its charitable donations, which amount to 10 percent of its profits, went a decidedly different route in its first national ad campaign. The campaign, which took place at the end of year 2000, took on issues about child labor and environmentalism. The campaign centered on celebrities who champion causes, linking their advocacy with Stonyfield's goal to change the world. The campaign, based on CEO Gary Hirshberg's concept, "adtivism," a combination of advertising and activism, was called "I do" and featured celebrity advocates like Trudie Styler, actress and wife of Sting, Kerry Kennedy Cuomo, and filmmaker Ken Burns with a list of the issues each celebrity supports. In the case of the Trudie Styler ad, the description of what she is committed to read, "Protecting the rain forest and the people who live there. A sustainable environment. Healthy living through mind, body, and soul. Organic gardening. Organic Luscious Lemon Yogurt. My family. Businesses run by people who care."

Gary Hirshberg said of the campaign, "What excited me was this possibility of being activists, but using advertising media and also taking advantage of the power of celebrity, which as we know is sort of a dominant force in our culture."[4]

Reversing the Paradigm: Consumer Heroes

It is an undeniable fact that in order to develop our dreams we need the example of "heroes" to give a real, human dimension to our aspirations. Joseph Campbell, the renowned mythographer who studied the meaning of the many hero myths across different cultures, would even say that this need is a profound, basic human need which must always find a new way or form in each culture and age through which to reveal itself, because without heroic expression man loses hope for meaning. In light of this idea and from the point of view of the growing awareness of the importance of community and generosity, our concept of what makes a hero may very well be changing. For quite some time in mainstream culture it has been athletes, musicians, or celebrities of grand stature who have played this role. Now it is evolving to also include the brave, caring individual.

One of the first signs of this was a recurring mention across various media after September 11 about the sudden absence of focus on celebrities. For the first time ever, the Grammy Awards were canceled and the contrast between the day before, when everyone seemed obsessed about the impending Grammys and Gwyneth Paltrow's latest boyfriend or hairstyle, and the day after, when the "ordinary" fireman became our collective superhero, was extreme. A resounding echo of "Gwyneth who?" was in the air. Some even expressed a sense of astonishment with themselves that such trivial things had once mattered.

It seems that perhaps the public is running out of patience with the caprices of hedonistic, self-absorbed, egomaniac celebrities.

Of course, as we move away in time from this event, we return to an ongoing dialogue with celebrities. But something has been altered in our psyches, and it seems that perhaps the public is running out of patience with the caprices of hedonistic, self-absorbed, egomaniac celebrities who seem to hop from marriage to marriage as they do from flashy party to flashy party. We give them their celebrity, I've heard people say, but what do they really do for us? They can embody our fantasies with the fabulous lifestyles we afford them, but what if the fantasy evolves to include more of a sense of reality and humanity and less fluff?

Certainly we will always have celebrities, but the kind of celebrity we choose to revere (as well as the degree of reverence accorded them) may well change. The low-key, very moving celebrity telethon benefit for the Twin Towers Relief Fund where everyday-clad, makeup-free stars answered phones to take pledges from callers and gave huge personal pledges themselves, such as Julia Roberts's pledge for $2 million, was a very interesting and powerful phenomenon. In a sharp contrast to this, a month or so later Winona Ryder was in the media for being brought up on alleged charges of shoplifting and drug use. In the past, the out-of-control, living-on-the-edge celebrities with an over-the-top lifestyle that got them in trouble with the authorities had a certain glamour allure. But that seems to have changed in the public consciousness, and (with all due respect to the wild Winona) I think that the Julia Roberts model is more the one of the future. I think that most people will come to expect this kind of gesture from celebrities. It is no more than an ordinary person would do (especially considering that for Ms. Roberts a $2 million dollar donation, while commendable, will most probably not cripple her finances!). Along these lines, it is interesting to note that one of the highest paid talents on TV, NBC *Today Show*'s Katie Couric, is such a huge star and ratings power wielder precisely because of her human touch factor. She has a very charming, down-to-earth style that allows her to embody the "everywoman."

Of course, as much as we may hear about Katie Couric's basically "frugal lifestyle" and "hectic schedule as a working mother," etc., etc., we know that in fact she is not "everywoman." Neither are Oprah or Martha Stewart, and certainly not Julia Roberts. But they are approachable. They make us dream and admire their accomplishments—in the case of these four women, each has carved out her own undeniable niche in her industry, in many ways redefining the standard of the industry altogether —but we can also clearly see that they are human. The sense of approachability in Martha Stewart may have less to do with the person herself and more with the overall style of the brand. Martha Stewart is a consummate professional—she does not share touchy/feely personal stories with her audience, but what she does share is extremely human—a great sense of excitement in creating beauty and magic in her surroundings and in sharing that magic with others through entertaining. From one point of view the entire Martha Stewart Living brand could be seen as a celebration of womanhood and as such it has been incredibly powerful for women. She has largely democratized style for America by being the first to teach us that "homemade" could also be elegant and then, through her products at Kmart, that the concepts of "style" and "discount" could work wonderfully together.

Dreams and passions—aspirations—have a curious quality of being both highly individual and yet universal. The fact is if you have a dream, you are probably not the only one to have it. If a brand can represent a dream in a very real, unique, and personal way then people will be able to connect with that dream. *It is vital to ask (every day), what is my brand's dream?* And then business becomes about the brand's employees and consumers sharing the excitement of that dream. A great example of this is the Tommy Bahama brand. Like many great, highly successful brands, the essence of the brand comes directly from the hearts of the company founders. In other words, this brand was not created around a conference table where people sit for hours trying to figure out what

It is vital to ask (every day), what is my brand's dream? And then business becomes about the brand's employees and consumers sharing the excitement of that dream.

The "brand child" of two fashion executives fantasizing about what a perfect life would feel like.

kind of products will make a lot of money. It came from an organic, creative, playful process that did not begin with work at all. The cofounders invented the fictional character of Tommy Bahama as a representation of their fantasies. The two men had neighboring beach homes on Florida's Gulf Coast and over the years, as their vacations came to an end, the men and their wives would talk about how great it would be to never have to leave the beach lifestyle and what that life would be like—they'd have a trust fund, an island home, they'd fish all day and play under the stars at night. Together they created the Tommy character and began to tell stories about him. It was only when one day someone asked the question, "What would Tommy wear?" that the founders, both veterans of the apparel industry, realized that they had a fully developed brand on their hands and the line of elegant tropical clothing for men aged thirty-five to sixty-five was created. Today, Tommy Bahama is a $300 million brand that has clearly tapped into the dream of an elegant, romantic island life. The brand has been very carefully and lovingly managed with touches like always using the same model, who perfectly embodies Tommy Bahama. It is one of those brands with such integrity and strength of vision that it can be developed in many different directions, and Tommy's designers employ many different logos for the different product ranges to give texture and different facets of the brand. We can feel all of the facets of Tommy's personality without feeling that he is scattered or disjointed. That is because the founders religiously refer back to their original dream and for each brand decision they ask the question, "What would Tommy do?"

"One of the reasons we've been a success is that we know what came first," says cofounder Bob Emfield, "This guy came first. He has a strong personality and we cater to him."[5]

While Tommy Bahama is a brand hero who was created by the dream of ordinary men, he is not exactly ordinary himself–he is somewhere in between a celebrity and a regular guy. *Today, I think that we are seeing the development of a paradigm of the aspirational hero who is more down to earth.* I think we are seeing a strong emergence of the concept of the individual, ordinary hero based on a longing we have to connect with our own sense of humanity.

Even more important in terms of the "approachable-hero" trend are ads in which the consumer is suddenly the "brand star," such as in a series of print ads for BP, where consumers in the street are photographed and asked their opinions about what oil companies need to do to regain our trust and become better corporate citizens. BP went to nine cities across five continents to interview people on their opinions about oil companies, global warming, and energy. *They asked them what they would say to an oil company executive if they could tell him or her what to do.* Megan McDonald, an event coordinator walking down LaSalle Street in Chicago at 5:30 P.M., says, "The oil companies need to speak frankly and honestly." This young woman, in a very nice full-page color photo, looks very smart, solid, and trustworthy–like someone you know or who could be a friend. The tagline copy of the ad reads, "Responsibility beyond petroleum." And the ad, of course, outlines some of the initiatives BP has undertaken to become a good corporate citizen, which include being one of the largest producers of solar power in the world, developing no-emission hydrogen-powered buses with Daimler Chrysler, and vowing to reduce its greenhouse gas emissions to 10 percent below 1990 levels by 2010–the equivalent of taking almost three million cars off the road. The ad goes on to say, "We are in the oil business. But we are also in the natural gas business, the technology business, the yet-to-be-discovered-energy business." Now that's aspirational!

In light of the dynamic between individual aspiration as expressed by the consumer brand hero versus a more celebrity-oriented brand hero, it is very interesting to look at Revlon's recent switching back to the celebrity format. After ten years of working with Cindy Crawford as the "Revlon face," last year Revlon decided to change to an advertising strategy that does not use celebrities, but to appeal more to the "everywoman," with the "It's fabulous being a woman" campaign. However, after seven months it has now reverted to a more celebrity-oriented strategy. The "everywoman" strategy did not work, perhaps less because of the lack of a celebrity and more because of the lack of a clearly identifiable hero. The ads, which featured glamorous models who were certainly not representative of the "everywoman" and tag lines like, "On a bad day, there's always lipstick," were vague and nonspecific in terms of an aspirational message. For their new campaign, Revlon plans to use the actress Julianne Moore, who, although certainly glamorous, is also a celebrity with a certain amount of substance as an award-winning stage and film actress. The tag line, "Be Yourself: Be Fabulous," is interesting because it attempts to create a relationship between the world of the consumer and the beauty and glamour of the "brand star." What is evident in all of this to me is simply that a brand needs a clearly defined hero, whether it's a celebrity or not, whom people can connect to emotionally!

6

The Sixth Commandment: Evolve from Identity to Personality

Identity is recognition. **Personality is about character and charisma!**

Today, to make people love your vision, you need to show them how much you care. From a Citizen Brand perspective, emotional identities, or "personalities," have a huge role to play beyond the traditional visual expression of a corporation through typography and symbols by extending the entire corporate program to become one of insight, personality, and humanity. An emotional identity, or "E.I.," can express a rich voice from a company's management and an overall message of intent. Corporate identities of the future will need to evolve to become more expressive and deliver strong personalities in a humanistic way. That is what E.I. is all about.

In this chapter we will observe how emotional identities have been managed in an innovative way both in profit-driven and in nonprofit organizations. We will also look at the work of Paul Rand, the most incisive graphic designer of the last century, who will show us today how a logo can become a warmhearted, long-lasting message.

Moving from C.I. to E.I. Means Creating a Thoughtful and Purposeful Enterprise

Great corporations or institutions with a sense of leadership and ethics are extremely assertive in defining business visions that put people at the center of everything they do. They are open, transparent, and reach out to connect with their audiences. And they give us the strong sense that somehow they will leave a positive imprint on history. But others don't. Enron was a company that certainly had a well-communicated, highly recognizable corporate identity, C.I., but no emotional identity, E.I., or personality. We knew about its size but little about its vision. It was a kind of money machine without soul or emotional reach. The name was even scary—evocative of some kind of weird Industrial Age equipment or the name of a frightening, not well-identified planet . . . a dark hole in the universe. When associated with Arthur Andersen, you had the two so-called brands that most represent arrogance, secretiveness, and the darkest practices of business underbellies.

The real question here is, was Enron really a brand? The concept of branding and what it means forces us to reassess the old idea of the concept as one limited only to "corporate identity," which is corporate driven and dictated; brands today hold new criteria that are people driven or emotional. We should differentiate between branding that is based solely on awareness and financial performance, and branding that incorporates other criteria, such as community involvement and ethics. If Enron existed in a world where corporate identities are sometimes used as a smoke screen for bad practices, it is time for that world to evolve into one where people are the center of every organization's philosophy.

In a certain ironic way, at about the same time as the Enron scandal erupted, George Harrison's death moved the world in the most personal way imaginable. Being part of the Beatles, the rock group with the most impact on music in the last century was certainly a reason, but, as one of the numerous people interviewed about how they felt about this tragedy stated in the *New York Times*, "For me, being in my mid-forties, they were integral to my life." There is a huge sense of indebtedness to artists like the Beatles because they surpassed their role as musicians and entertainers to play the much larger culturally important role of a conduit for expressing people's rebellious and passionate ideals of the times.

Of course, the objective of a rock band is to sell records, millions of them, in order to get endorsement and to be able to finance tours and overhead, and the Beatles were also a business—and an incredibly successful one at that. The music industry sometimes sets a great example for the traditional corporate sector, capturing our emotions in the most powerful way. I don't mean to suggest that Enron should have sent its management on a tour to convince its shareholders of its good intentions, but the lesson for corporations here is that the old, cold way of doing business is a thing of the past. There are other avenues to follow that create positive response with people. The music industry is more geared to reach us emotionally with its products, but

George Harrison became renowned for leveraging his popularity to build support for causes or movements whether political or spiritual in nature.

the commitment that industry has to leveraging its enormous power as an industry to raise consciousness and money in support of causes is also very strong. George Harrison actually was the first to organize these kinds of events and he became renowned for leveraging his popularity in order to build support for causes or movements either political or spiritual in nature. He was, in fact, the forerunner of an entirely new mindset–with others, such as Sting and U2's Bono, to follow powerfully in his footsteps. The Beatles, often characterized as "the biggest British export of all time," were not only a financial success, but a national success and a "people's success story." What do we remember of the Beatles' enterprise even after they dissolved? What has staying power is their connection with us through music, the songs that are part of our lives. They won our hearts in so many ways. And having understood how important they were to us, they took on their roles with grace. Witness George Harrison's statement to the media a year or so before he passed away, when he asked his fans to please not worry about his health–he wanted to reassure everyone that he was fine.

In the corporate arena some businesses have built this kind of trust between themselves and the public through building a strong emotional identity and personality based on the power of a founder or CEO's personality. *The idea that CEOs of corporations need to be "rock and roll leaders" is not so farfetched when you think about the humanizing effect of leaders showing their passion and talent in a unique way*–think of the positive response people had to former President Clinton playing the saxophone. This is a very real way to humanize a leader and strike a chord with an audience. I once saw Bernard Arnault, head of LVMH, who has had some training as a concert pianist, do a duet with his wife (a well-known concert pianist herself) at a business function, and it was touching and impressive. Having a corporation be perceived for what its leaders stand for; the quality and integrity of their own personal, human vision, is a much better plan for success than setting up offshore funds on the backs of stockholders and employees' 401k plans. It may be obvious at this point, but in a nutshell, greed is clearly not "in" anymore! To have the wrong personality even if you have a strong identity will not work in a global world. The McDonald's ubiquitous arch and self-congratulating corporate statement that celebrates its having served "over 1 billion burgers" make the restaurants easy targets for activists and, in the long run, alienates people. The proof of corporate success is not only about bragging around your business performance but about sharing your company commitment to enhance people's quality of life.

Warren Buffet has, through his own personal reputation, changed the corporate perception of owning a jet from being one of frivolity and vanity to one of necessity.

E.I. is the experience of that unique emotional connection successful brands have with people. Warren Buffet understands this; he has redefined a business category by practicing this theory and he has built enormous credibility. For example, in promoting his company, Net Jets, Warren Buffet has, through his own personal reputation, changed the corporate perception of owning a jet from being one of frivolity and vanity to one of necessity. Only Warren Buffet could have done this. His image as a disciplined, thrifty, and responsible manager brought to his proposition the necessary credibility. As the most admired businessman in America and a role model for other CEOs, Warren Buffet is convincing corporate America and their boards that this kind of expense is legitimate, necessary, and smart. In this case, the emotions associated with the owner of the company are the most potent asset in selling the company . . . stronger than the product positioning or the technical offering. The trust and respect business people have for Warren Buffet has helped corporations to make guilt-free decisions and served as a foundation for the success of Net Jets. That's the true E.I. of that brand.

Good Citizenship Means Culture!

You may think that nothing much happens in the cash-poor, not-for-profit organizations, and that their limitations in getting funding cripple their opportunities to shine. Well, think again. It is actually the reverse in many ways. Precisely because of the scarcity of funds and

The emotions associated with the owner of this company are its most potent asset.

the need these organizations have to rely on others to survive, *non-profit organizations have to be extremely imaginative and creative in order to stand out among their peers and all other forms of entertainment.* The fact is that *it is only through creating an identity that conveys a strong personality that their operations have survived and prospered.* Only by generating passion will their programs be seen. Only by standing for what they believe can they assure their survival. And only by understanding, enticing, and ultimately respecting their audiences can they motivate people to come. Their activities are at the heart of the Citizen Brand concept. Culture, you might think, is an activity that naturally leads to a strong Citizen Brand . . . not! Culture, when it loses its contact with the people can become very elitist and off-putting. Culture can continue to live in the past without considering the future and culture can very easily become obsolete if it loses its relevancy. A not-for-profit cultural organization questions its reality everyday. If you think Wall Street is tough try your hand at this one!

Let's see what inspirational and innovative ideas we can glean about how to move people through an emotional brand personality from two of the greatest cultural institutions in the United States: the Guggenheim and the Brooklyn Academy of Music.

THE GUGGENHEIM: THE MAKING OF A MECCA

A great deal has been written about the Guggenheim and its mission, often with a good measure of criticism heaped on Thomas Krens, the controversial director of the Solomon R. Guggenheim Foundation, who has been called a "cultural bulldozer," and "the businessman of museums," for his highly pragmatic, sometimes commercially flavored approach to art and culture. But what Thomas Krens has done in crafting a new brand vision of the museum as not only a cultural, but also a sociological institution will remain forever as a monument to our civilization, well beyond our children and great-grandchildren. I am convinced it is an example of personality at its best, elevating the world of culture to a new height. Thomas Krens, through his intelligent "licensing" of the Guggenheim concept on a global level–with the Bilbao museum in Spain and the new one that was opened in Las Vegas, with further plans for . . . who knows where else!–is certainly a great example of the power of personality. Thomas Krens is a visionary in how he has enticed people into a world of culture through emotional branding! The core of the Guggenheim's brand personality could be expressed with the words: "contemporary, risk-taking, American." The Guggenheim continues to chart new territory in the world of culture, taking risks that no one else is willing to take. In my opinion, we can only thank them for it!

I recently had a terrific and very inspiring meeting with Ben Hartley, the Guggenheim's former director of corporate communications and sponsorship and now owner of Ben Hartley Consulting, a company that helps corporations assess and leverage their opportunities in the cultural field. My conversation with him elucidated for me new ways of looking at the enormous role culture has to play in our society today–and even more importantly, how that role is changing and how companies can be a part of this exciting transformation.

The first point Ben wanted me to understand about museums is that, in his opinion, they should be viewed today not just as an educational institution, but also as an entertainment institution. He explained to me that there is a lot of resistance to this idea in the "old guard" of the museum world, but the fact is, museums now have so much competition for peoples' time—television, shopping, movies, the Internet, amusement parks, and a myriad of tourist destinations. To spend one's time pursuing culture is just one of the many choices out there. In order to become a choice, museums must reinvent themselves according to a new, twenty-first-century format. The concept of the museum needs to transcend the antiquated eighteenth-century idea of collecting artwork in order to show it off in the "boxes" of exhibit cases or rooms. As Ben put it, "the box is no longer big enough," and the Guggenheim is striving to find a new definition for the museum in the twenty-first century, a definition that will include cutting edge architecture, new multi-media formats, and entirely different kinds of art both in form and content.

When I asked Ben what it was like to work at the Guggenheim, his response was that it was very challenging, that often they operate under a "siege mentality" because of the controversy they generate, but he had been thrilled to be a part of this dynamic organization because he feels that it is "an essential element in the conversation about culture." He went on to explain that what the Guggenheim does, without fail, is to create passionate debates—people tend to **People will tend to be more passionate and care more about the corporate world if they are investing in things that we as consumers care about.** either love or hate the place, the exhibits, and so on. But, there is little indifference—everyone seems to have an opinion—because the Guggenheim has cultural relevance. The Guggenheim clearly operates under the idea that a cultural institution must recognize and comment on key phenomena of our culture, whether it is done through a show like *Motorcycle*, which investigated motorcycles from every aspect, from industrial design, to historical/sociological, to image/cinematic, or through shows like the Armani show, which some felt was only about luxury consumer goods and a money-making device. But fashion can reveal a great deal to us from a sociological, historical, and artistic perspective!

The fact is that Thomas Krens was one of the first to recognize and leverage the enormous equity cultural institutions can have. Why are more brands not recognizing this? Businesses don't seem to really understand the impact culture can have on a community nor how culture can be used as a vehicle of goodwill. As Ben put it, *"People will tend to be more passionate and care more about the corporate*

133

world if they are investing in things that we, as consumers, care about." Like culture. When I asked Ben what companies should do to help bring a positive perception of their brand through cultural endeavors, he responded that it is crucial for corporations to engage with culture on multiple levels, not just with a "PR/sales-driver" approach. He believes in trying to find a way for corporations to support museums in a manner that clearly helps people to enjoy that experience further. When he works with corporations, he looks for new ways to give them benefits on many levels beyond the traditional "name on the wall" at an exhibit. For example, in a program he developed with Deutsche Bank, which unfortunately did not come to pass, he came up with a very interactive, people-oriented new idea. In an effort to reach Deutsche Bank's desired target group of young, affluent people, the Guggenheim proposed ideas for helping them learn about art. For example, this group of people is just starting to collect art, and photography is the art of choice for the majority of them due to its accessibility, but many of these young collectors have questions regarding the purchase of photography, such as the difference between buying a "1 of 1000," or a "1 of 100" print, whether it is a good thing to buy a recent print of a work done in 1930, or whether it makes sense to buy from sources like eBay. The Guggenheim's idea was to give seminars about how to build a photography collection to Deutsche Bank's clients and potential clients. This is a good example of how to think about bringing culture to people.

During the last five years, we have witnessed a rising awareness of the powerful role culture can play in strengthening and leading a community so that it becomes a "hot spot" people are attracted to; a place where they can find a valuable exchange of ideas. In the case of the Guggenheim in Bilbao, the museum was built to become the cultural "jewel in the crown" of the Basque region's $1 billion initiative to revitalize their culture and move from a semi-autonomous region to a fully autonomous region. They knew that if they were able to bring people to their region for the museum, they would stay for the hotels, shops, and other attractions—and they were right. The Basques very consciously went after a brand-name cultural institution and for a $20 million licensing fee they bought into the Guggenheim brand and collection. As Ben put it, if the Basques had spent the money on an ad campaign instead, they would have never reaped the same benefits. According to a McKinsey & Co. report, the region recouped $300 million in positive economic impact in the museum's first year! And, unlike an ad campaign, the museum is, of course, a permanent cultural mecca, there for all to enjoy for centuries. "Great cultures," Ben said aptly, "are not remembered by their financial institutions but by their cultural institutions."

BAM: A Flexible Expression of Creativity

The Brooklyn Academy of Music, or "BAM," as we New Yorkers know it, is another fantastic cultural destination. BAM, founded in 1859, virtually emerged from the ashes in the Eighties, a time when Brooklyn was not considered "safe" by most bourgeois New Yorkers. The theater knew that, unless it broke the ceiling of innovation, it would not be able to attract many people, but it did manage to accomplish this seemingly impossible task. In spades!

BAM 2001 Next Wave Festival
Sponsored by Philip Morris Companies Inc.

BAM Next Wave's innovative program cover.

First of all, BAM's vision/objective does not read anything like a tra-ditional corporate or cultural mantra: *"Since its inception in 1983, the BAM Next Wave Festival has constantly questioned, redefined, discov-ered and explored new forms of artistic expression."* Now this is per-sonality! And they constantly deliver on this promise with the best innovations in theater, dance, music, film, and new media from around the world. Their communication materials, done in house, are among the best I have seen, using typography and visuals in the most innovative and challenging ways. If you want to experience cul-ture in New York, BAM is the place. I recently had the pleasure of speaking with both BAM's vice president for marketing and commu-nications, Jeffery Levine, and director of design, Eric Olson, and found our conversation very enlightening.

Eric Olson is responsible for a four-person design department that builds communication with attitude and relevance. The inspiration for their unique visual approach was created by Michael Bierut of Pentagram. Michael's recommendation, according to Eric, came from minimizing the role of the logo and play up a typographic approach that would stand out through its unique style. The designer recom-mended also that an internal department be created to carry out an ongoing flexible expression of the communication for the constant change of the programs. It really works; the typography expresses the innovative attitude of the theater with letters coming out of the pages or running off across the cover. To emphasize the concept of emerging global talent performing at BAM, the design system con-nects to an audience with "emerging" typographic treatments. The imagery of the different shows, even though they are provided in varying states of quality by the different artistic groups, always come out as innovative, vibrant, and intriguing in the context of this new layout.

According to Eric, the creative positioning, the overall feel and look for a season, is always impressionist in approach, with the focus more on bringing out the creative spirit of a production than provid-ing hard "information." Unusual cropping and layouts such as the series for Next Wave Down Under of the 2001 festival are eye-catch-ing and unusual, reinforcing the innovative aspect of the program and redefining Australia's vibrant art scape. According to Jeffrey Levine, the entire personality of this program emerged through the type treatment that was designed for the public to appreciate BAM's emotional identity through the flexibility of the approach. Mr. Levine says, "The logo was the last thing we wanted to use and in our case [it was] not appropriate." This emotional, people-driven solution of a design program shows that in order to express one's personality, a visual vocabulary could, at times, be more relevant than just a logo treatment. "With twenty-five productions annually, the performance is the star," emphasizes Jeffrey Levine. "We are not FedEx, not a one-product operation; we are more like a high-end department store." This very intelligent and multifaceted graphic program also reflects the innovative spirit of BAM as a community leader. The successful artistic and urban renewal of Brooklyn, as well as the new passion for some to rediscover the roots of the city, is attributed to the work of Harvey Lichtenstein, BAM's leader from 1967 to 1999. Through culture and with a mandate to either succeed or see his beloved theater turned into something like a parking lot, Harvey Lichtenstein's artistic vision led the renewal of his community.

> **"We are not FedEx, not a one-product operation; we are more like a high-end department store."**

The neighborhood has attracted a core of artists and designers. Mark Morris, for instance, has located his dance company across the street from the BAM. They have brought with them a diverse and talented group of young artists who have created a new community in a non-alienating fashion. *I was impressed that Eric Olson, who worked with major branding companies, left the world of Manhattan branding firms run now by strategic consultants to work at BAM.* What is most interesting is Eric's description of his environment. "I found camaraderie here; an organization not a company . . . the spirit of volunteering reigns here and affects our presentation." I would add as a personal fan of The Brooklyn Academy of Music that the feeling is shared!

Bringing Culture "Inside" the Brand

Corporations love to associate themselves with cultural organizations. It gives them a good conscience and the perception that the public will respond positively to their investment. But the public doesn't really think about it this way. The public *expects* corporations to do these kinds of things, and this does not necessarily give a clear advantage to sponsors unless they prove their sincerity.

There are many other, far more interactive ways to bring culture to a brand's constituency, both inside and outside the corporation. One big idea today is to partner with nonprofit cultural organizations in new ways that allow businesses to learn their spirit and drive—to have them teach corporate executives about the value of innovation and to bring this culture of innovation inside your organization. Culture should be used by business as an agent of change!

How do you accomplish this? There are no clear-cut answers to this question, but think about the impact of enrolling a corporation's executives in the Sackler Center for Arts Education, the Guggenheim's new "dynamic twenty-first century educational hub and learning laboratory," in order for them to experience new cultures or discover new media arts or collectively build a work of art. *To me, it would definitely win out over some of those boring retreat ideas, like sack races and war games, where your employees run after each other with toy guns to build team spirit!* Or, what about companies lending some of their top executives to help find funds for those institutions always looking for talent in management and marketing? A few months of this kind of "learn-and-teach" training could be a great eye-opener.

There are many ways, as yet unexplored, to use culture to strengthen a brand's emotional bond to the people. The most important thing is to recognize how powerful it can be and then experiment with ways of contributing to a community's culture and bringing that culture inside the company. With the renowned Wexner Center for the Arts at Ohio State University, Les Wexner, CEO of The Limited, Inc., has created an entire cultural universe near his corporation's headquarter city, Columbus, Ohio. He had the brilliant foresight to know that this cultural institution would provide a nexus of artistic creativity in a community that does not have a strong cultural diversity and that it would infiltrate his company, affecting his employees' lives in a myriad of ways—perhaps even helping in the recruitment process by enticing management to Columbus from other, more culturally active cities in the United States.

Personality Is Not about Perfection, It's about . . . Personality!

Just as people are not perfect, a brand cannot be either. And just as sometimes it is people's imperfections–their undeniable "humanness"–that we love the most, brands should avoid creating identities that are so slick and polished that they obliterate the essential truth of the humanity behind the brand. This is a brand's most valuable asset from an emotional perspective and it is diametrically opposed to the creation of the "dictated" identity format! I will take a look at the creation of the Zagat Guide to illustrate this point.

ZAGAT: THE LITTLE GUIDE THAT CONQUERED THE WORLD

This restaurant guide, created by a couple literally on a handful of napkins in the beginning, is one of the most successful guides in the world. Zagat does not present itself in a slick way—no shiny paper, no sexy photographs, just great, well-presented, well-written information. Interestingly enough, it has managed to beat any "guru" driven editions on the market, such as the Michelin Guide in France, that rely only on professionals and specialists to give or take away the forever sought-after Michelin "stars." You have them and you get instant recognition, you lose them and you are headed for a grueling and gut-wrenching uphill battle to win them back. The Michelin judges are feared and loathed. They don't have to answer to any higher authority.

But Zagat is different. The rating of the restaurant is made by people. The vote of people in aggregate leads to the overall rating. The process is fair and trusted, giving the guide a unique place in the hearts of food aficionados everywhere. The owners, Mr. and Mrs. Zagat, had started their guide as a tool to be used by their food-loving friends. They came up with the idea of gathering everyone's impressions on the restaurants they went to and then

But Zagat is different. The rating of the restaurant is made by people. The vote of people in aggregate leads to the overall rating.

tabulated the results and sent ratings to those who participated. This collection of information was too good to be kept between just a few friends and eventually they saw a much bigger business proposition in their idea, one that has supported their passion for culinary pleasure. And so a democratic, people-driven manual that reflected the most interesting, salient pieces of information on places we are considering for dining was born.

The look of their book is slim and vertical in shape, fitting easily in a bag, a briefcase, or the inside pocket of a suit and taking just enough space to be presented on counters in book stores. The format is smart. The color is a unique, appetizing burgundy shade that stands out and makes a very proprietary, unique statement.

There is something valuable here for any brand to learn. First, that being voted on by the people as a relevant product is a real key to success. Second, and even more important, is that to make people part of your business by asking them to bring you the right information is smart. Zagat can only survive if it is relevant, insightful, and sensitive to the needs of its readers. In order to achieve this goal, it needs to rely on its audience to bring the best information.

Zagat is unique because of its credibility and is a standout because of its anti-brand positioning, which makes a sincere statement to the public. *Brands sometimes try too hard to ring true or impress, and as a result, they can't connect with people. They lack the sincerity and plain old common-sense approach of building communities around their brands.* I wonder how this concept would have tested with traditional market research given the lack of slickness and perceived amateurism of the presentation? Sometimes the imperfection associated with a brand is part of the image and personality of that brand. The perception of a food product as being overly sweet does not mean that it is not also loved. Sometimes the defect of a product is quite appealing for people. Harley-Davidson solved what they thought was a flaw in their motorcycles–the strong vibrations of the handle–with a new, improved model only to discover to their surprise that customers loved the arm-numbing sensation as an integral part of the experience of riding their Harley; this forced Harley to spend several years balancing the engine on its Fat Boy to reduce the vibration (for comfort's sake) without eliminating it altogether! The strength of Zagat is the personal experience people bring to the process. In the French edition, for instance, people have selected a restaurant which is quite good but totally unfriendly. People liked it in part because they saw in the attitude a certain Gallic charm and authenticity! People had voted for a place that had personality and in Zagat it fit quite well, since the place is described as being for the adventurous culinary types.

They lack the sincerity and plain old common-sense approach of building communities around their brands.

Personality is not about reaching a level of perfection that pleases everyone. It is about taking a stand and showing a human side. The Abercrombie & Fitch catalog is not liked by everyone but stands for certain flavor of youth culture that challenges established values. When Dior, the couturier, launched his first collection right after

World War II, some of the women who wore his fashions were attacked in the street by conservative men who resisted change. Personality means a rich commitment to lead—a brave approach to impacting the world around you in a positive way.

ROLLING STONE MAGAZINE: A UNIQUE CREATIVE VOICE

Another great example of the expression of brand personality that gained its success from striving for a flexible, organic creative chemistry as opposed to a rigid expression of "perfection" is *Rolling Stone* magazine. *Rolling Stone* has succeeded for many years, and continues to succeed, by appealing to youth. This magazine has survived the passing of several young generations by providing them with current information concerning the world of rock and roll in an exciting, relevant format. No other magazine has been able to project such a sustained and long-term personality. This magazine has kept rock and roll relevant and accessible to generations of fans. The secret is in the content but also in its design.

Rolling Stone has a complete, highly recognizable look. For fourteen years as the creative director of the magazine, Fred Woodward, has pushed the limit of the creative logic of the magazine's layout, making it the most innovative in its field. Renowned as the best magazine art director in the United States and known for pushing photographers and illustrators constantly to reinvent their work, Fred Woodward is the recipient of numerous awards. He has said that he always wanted photographers to think "this is a magazine that will print the best thing you can do; not put it in a drawer or pick the wrong picture."[1] He challenges the photographers and illustrators in a way that allows the magazine to evolve and live. Not all the covers of *Rolling Stone* are the same, a strategy that has kept the magazine always fresh. The typography is never the same twice and the look evolves from issue to issue. The editor and publisher, Jann Wenner, is known for trusting designers to do their best work. Woodward was recently hired by *GQ* to help it transcend its slick, generic look and win back its circulation numbers, which have been slipping away to the competition. Throughout all of the years he was at *Rolling Stone,* Woodward was courted by *Vogue* and countless other magazines, and he stayed at *Rolling Stone* because he was allowed a wide range of freedom to play with the magazine—the kind of creative license that smart companies give to talented people.

Personality here is in evolving with a revolving demography through innovation. Personality means showing the rich character and vitality of the brand. It is about challenging the reader himself in an engagement that is real and profound.

Emotional Shorthand: Capturing the Spirit of the Brand in a Single Iconic Character

In the last century very few identities were truly emotionally driven, in my opinion. Powerful symbols with significance were the Nike swoosh, the Apple logo, the Ralph Lauren polo symbol, and the IBM logo, as defined originally by Paul Rand, and the Coca-Cola dynamic ribbon, which has been mistreated at times and yet remains a powerful symbol–the first "swoosh" created as a way to communicate visually in a global world. But, unfortunately, most other brand images or corporate identities have been managed around logo creations and sophisticated, rigorous brand architecture systems with little flexibility. This approach, what I call the "Mao jacket" syndrome of corporate identity, leads to symbols or word marks that offer no personality beyond just being "brand markers."

From a Citizen Brand perspective, emotional identities have a huge role to play beyond the traditional visual expression of a corporation through typography and symbols by extending the program to become one of insight, personality, and humanity. An emotional identity can express a rich voice from a company's management and an overall message of intent. Emotional identities will need to become more expressive in a humanistic way. We have the example of pioneers like

From a Citizen Brand perspective, emotional identities have a huge role to play beyond the traditional visual expression of a corporation through typography and symbols by extending the program to become one of insight, personality, and humanity.

Paul Rand, who in designing the original IBM identity brought tremendous intellect and personality to a brand by giving it life. Through a very rich logo he evolved the industrial look of IBM to an emotional identity.

Indeed, Paul Rand, the illustrious creator of the ABC, Westinghouse, and UPS logos, and many others in addition to the IBM logo, offers the last word in emotional identity and a very useful refresher course for us all. He was a professor at Yale University and considered to be the most influential graphic designer of the twentieth century. When Paul Rand passed away at the end of the twentieth century, he left his legacy in the hearts and minds of hundreds of students. Two of them, Peter Levine and Phyllis Aragaki, are partners in my firm and are two of the most brilliant graphic thinkers I have ever met. They have taught me how to bring a story, an emotion, and personality into an emotional identity program.

Paul Rand explained better than anyone the mission and role of a graphic designer as "one who creates ideas that are expressed in words and/or pictures, and generally solves problems of communication."[2] Myths and symbols, whether commercial or religious, have always connected with an audience and they are the most powerful communicators between a brand and a spectator. When creating symbols, Paul Rand knew how to bring a humanistic story to his designs and personality to the message in the simplest way.

Reading the books published by Paul Rand on graphic design and listening to his former students, one begins to understand the magnitude of the intellect this designer brought to his work. A logo's effectiveness in Paul Rand's vocabulary is based on six important factors: (1) Distinctiveness, (2) Visibility, (3) Adaptability, (4) Memorability, (5) Universality, and (6) Timelessness, and three essential questions: (1) Who is the audience? (2) How is it marketed? and (3) What is the media?

These parameters are crucial in a world where the graphic image of a corporation has largely been relegated to the abyss of the "unimportant" compared to the so-called enlightenment offered by strategic corporate brand valuations. The vision piece of the puzzle in creating corporate identities is that an identity is first and foremost the reflection of the soul of a business and the brand value only mirrors the company's ethics. You can spend time and money on strategic brand valuations, but a corporation's true worth is only as good as its social ethics and that is a very challenging task.

The vision piece of the puzzle in creating corporate identities is that an identity is first and foremost the reflection of the sould of a business and the brand value only mirrors the company's ethics.

In designing a logo, it is, above all, important to realize that the representation of the logo does not necessarily need to represent the business you are in; the Apple logo is not about computers, neither is the alligator or polo player about fashion; and the Mercedes star is not about cars. What is important is how committed you are to supporting a brand identification system that will represent your corporate values in a way that is distinctive, visible, adaptable, memorable, universal, and timeless.

I have seen in numerous meetings how clients or consultants with minimal understanding of visual logic could relegate the better designs to never-never land. For better or for worse, everyone is an expert when judging a logo! When the new IBM logo was presented to the company, one executive quipped that it reminded him of "a Georgia chain gang," and another commented on the Westinghouse logo, when it was first presented by Paul Rand, that it looked "like a pawnbroker's sign." This very important decision needs to be led by the true experts. The role of the designer is key for the success of such a process. Let's not forget that, as I once heard a designer say, "good design goes to heaven and bad design goes . . . everywhere!" Unfortunately. Let's be careful.

Another misconception is that a logo is just a marker to be managed in the most disciplined way, what I called earlier the Mao Jacket approach. Emotional identities with personality are not based on rigid identity manuals or intensely dictated corporate nomenclature systems. A brand with personality has a life of its own that is about imagination, beauty, and fun. The original logo for IBM as designed by Paul Rand was so much more fun then than it is in its current expression, which has been too rigidly controlled through brand "jail keepers," and their corporate manuals. A logo like this was not meant to be so limited in its execution. There is a great deal of creative expressiveness that has been lost by this overpolicing of the corporate identity!

Another misconception is that a logo is just a marker to be managed in the most disciplined way.

Paul Rand saw it differently. He compared the stripes of the new logo to images of Romanesque architecture, African ornament, and Parisian fashions. He saw IBM as being in the innovation business, which for him meant communicating intuition, imagination, and

Paul Rand's expression of the IBM logo.

invention—the essence of originality. He saw such programs as serving the dual purpose of identifying a business and dramatizing an idea that triggers moods and brings seasonal themes, patriotic celebration, or just plain fun. The brand's expression of "we care," as stated in the beginning of this chapter, meant, for Paul Rand, caring to show the beauty of a brand. It meant creating attractive, memorable, and adaptable expressions of the brand for an infinite number of applications. As he said, *"At no time is the integrity of a logo altered by variety and surprise which can be achieved by color alternation."* His design of the three posters "eye," "bee," and "M" are testimony to the personality a brand can and needs to express in order to connect emotionally with an audience.

Paul Rand's belief that a logo is a symbol of goodwill cannot be overestimated. Logos for him were not simply passive decorations on a nameplate or letterhead. A brand has a life. The Nike swoosh, the Mercedes star, the ABC round logo, the IBM logotype, the UPS shield, the Ralph Lauren polo player, and the Coca-Cola dynamic ribbon all have a story to tell and a meaning for our hearts. They are distinctive, visible, adaptable, memorable, universal, and timeless.

Air France: Making the Sky the Best Place on Earth

Our company was privileged to redesign the emotional identity for Air France, including the interior of the airplanes, the lounges, and the Web site. I still remember as a child living in Brittany how I would make a point to go out and watch the Concorde on its way to New York. The trail the plane left behind in the sky and the spark created by the reflection of the sun on the plane was so beautiful and inspiring to me that I compared it in my mind to the shooting star in Antoine de St. Euxpery's book *The Little Prince*. I could not help but imagine adventures and future travels toward unknown countries around the globe.

When our creative team, led by Alain Doré, one of my partners in Paris, proposed to use the trail left behind a plane as the foundation of the creative concept and visual vocabulary I was surprised and thrilled. The trail for him, even though I had not shared my personal experience with him, signaled a feeling of connection to new worlds and crystallized our human desire to explore and connect with others. He gathered a team of designers from the fields of architecture, graphics, and ergonomics, as well as stage directors and stylists, to think about the expression of this idea at all points of contact of the brand with the travelers.

I still remember, as a child living in Brittany, how I would make a point to go out and watch the Concorde on its way to New York.

The concept was subsequently executed to influence every minute detail of the emotional personality of the airline, including the inside of the plane where new floor carpeting design with horizontal lines visually increased the size of the cabin. All of the printed materials and the choice and color of fabrics for the seats in the cabins were influenced by this creative approach. The concept was

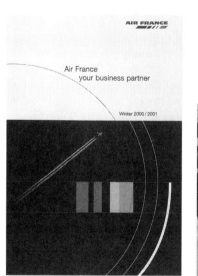

The Air France identity challenges travelers by appealing to their imagination.

executed to be cohesive and yet flexible in its use in order to convey a different experience in the airline's three service classes. First-class expression is more subdued and elegant, the business class is corporate looking and comfortable, and the economy class, which is preferred by tourists, has been designed with a more dynamic use of color to induce a sense of relaxation and vacation.

This solution reinforced the identity of an already well-known brand and challenged the company and the travelers by appealing to their imagination. The theme of the program, in this case, was "from identity to imagination"—through our exploration of imagination we found a new personality for the brand to own. Our aim was to create an extensive visual language and vocabulary around this design philosophy based on people's emotional experience. We focused on making the emotional and sensory brand experience more compelling, responding to the brief to "make the sky the best place on earth."

The Colors of Our Emotions: What Color is Your E.I.?

Color is a very powerful emotional signifier for people and one that I believe is vastly underused by corporations in developing their identities. Sometimes even when a brand has a great proprietary color, the company does not fully capitalize on the potential equity it represents from a human perspective. A great example of how to do this is how Home Depot refers to itself internally as being "orange-blooded." Home Depot manages their color identity by humanizing it and making it part of the link that brings people and values together, as if the brand and its color were the liquid that fuels the passion of associates and customers alike.

Orange is a perfect color for this brand, which encapsulates, as we saw in chapter 2, a neighborly "can-do" attitude. The color is at the core of the brand's personality. The color orange—the most optimistic in the color alphabet—is the color of the sunrise, the color of warmth and beginnings. It is a color that conveys perfectly the concept of "home." As CMO Richard Sullivan said to me, "We have an identity that spells 'welcome.'" In this case, the color is not just the ubiquitous "face" of this brand's identity. It is the core of its personality. A one-color statement of confidence that is a lot more than just background on a sign or a statement on the wall. Being orange blooded means endorsing and practicing the emotional values of the company, and from what I saw during my visit to Home Depot, the color of the brand truly lives in the associates' hearts and lives.

> **We have an identity that spells "welcome." In this case, the color is not just the ubiquitous "face" of this brand's identity. It is the core of its personality.**

The Color of the Future

In 1969 man lands on the moon, the Baby Boomers are in their twenties, and a decade of endless opportunities inspired by science, social progress, and modernism seems to be ahead. Courrèges, the French designer who was one of the most influential of his generation, invents a new futuristic, minimalist fashion based on innovative, synthetic textiles. The fashion color is white. White is indeed the color of a fresh, unspoiled canvas—the stage on which all creations can happen. It is the color of light, relationships, new beginnings, wedding dresses, the color of birth, and, above all, spirituality. Courrèges's first perfume is named "empreinte," or "imprint" in English—as if this generation's dream were to change their world with a new message. The emotion is hope.

In 2002, the millennium has barely started and is tainted by the September 11 tragedy, a horrendous moment that erupts suddenly in our lives. Gen Y is barely twenty years old. Already confronted with one of the most dramatic moments in our recent history, this generation must begin to reckon with their inheritance and carve out their future in a world of unprecedented uncertainty. In this time of change, the world seems to be shrinking around them, bringing close to home critical challenges. Gucci's Tom Ford is one of the most influential designers of our time. His fashion color is black. His first fragrance is called "Envy." Black is sexy, black is hip, but black is the color that closes the door. Black is elitist. Exclusive. Conservative. Black also means the end. The emotion is fear. Color always reflects the emotional mood of the time and defines personalities. And for the past ten years you could not go wrong wearing black. It has been a fashionista favorite. "Black is as good as gold," says Marianne Rohlich in a recent *New York Times* fashion article. For quite a long time now black has been back—is it fade to black forever? Perhaps not. I am very intrigued by what seems to be the return of white as a predominant color in fashion. The Gap brand, interestingly, used to own white as a powerful expression of its identity (remember the white T-shirt, the ultimate statement of one's creative personality?) and they lost it. But today white seems once again to be in vogue. The new Apple iBook is white and a new Dior men's fragrance named "Higher" is presented in white packaging to convey the concept of spirituality. *Figaro Madame*, the French fashion magazine, titled its January 2002, predominantly white cover, "Desire for White"; the same month *O*, Oprah Winfrey's magazine, had a white cover, showing Oprah dressed head to toe in white with "truth" as the magazine's theme for the month. And of course, the Spring 2002 runways (and now the streets) were swimming with white. The resurgence of white seems to be sending a new message of change and hope. Will black entirely disappear? I don't think so (if only for the reason that the fashion and communications industry might never be able to handle such a change—just kidding!). But the emergence of the color white indicates clearly the beginning of a new era. New generations need to start with a clean slate to express their vision of the future; white, therefore, must be inspiring and motivating that vision in our time of introspection. What is the feel of the future? This is the question for brands to answer—in a colorful way.

The Euro: Creating a Cultural Identity of Unity

I would like to conclude this chapter with the example of what, in my opinion, was one of the new century's most interesting emotional identity programs: the design and launch of the Euro. The context itself is very interesting from the point of view of Citizen Branding. In order to have a common currency reflect a new economic reality, the European union needed to create a simplified tool to trade and protect itself in terms of the fluctuations of currencies during changing economic cycles. Most members of the union and their central banks were in approval of the process, and from a political perspective, national governments were motivated to make the changes.

But what about the people? Three hundred million citizens attached to century-old, familiar currencies like the Franc, the Lira, or the Deutsche mark. How would they feel about such a change? And how could the people be persuaded to embrace this change? In order for this initiative to happen, each country had to have a majority vote for it. The Euro initiative indeed brought painful national debates around the issues of loss of identity, cultural dilution, and national pride. The concept barely passed in many countries and was even defeated in Britain, Sweden, and Denmark. But despite these difficulties, when the new currency was offered on January 1, 2002, everyone in the world was in agreement that the launch was a success and an unprecedented positive initiative. Several factors are interesting to study here from an Emotional Branding and citizenship perspective, and a lot could be learned from this launch about how to create excitement around a concept that is initially only mildly supported.

Several factors are interesting to study here from an Emotional Branding and citizenship perspective and a lot could be learned from this launch about how to create excitement around a concept that is initially only mildly supported.

From an emotional perspective, love and fear once again did battle. Fear of losing control, fear of change, fear of the future, fear of giving up one's national identity were very evident during the political debate. The goal was to transform those fearful sentiments into a love-based sentiment of hope for a future changed by the positive aspects of a partnership between different nations. This was a goal that had been talked about in Europe for over 150 years, ever since Victor Hugo first proposed the notion as a way of alleviating the people's poverty and leveraging Europe's common strength.

Much ink has been devoted to the subject and many originally predicted a backlash to what they saw as a process that was being "forced" on people. Many of the older citizens of Italy and France, for instance, were still calculating in terms of old currencies. My father was calculating in "old Francs" that were in use forty years ago. In my conversations with him, if he told me that he paid 10,000 francs for a shirt, he meant 100 francs. When I asked him how he thought he would adapt to this change, his response was, "Well, I will understand the dollar better now, since both currencies are close to parity." But young people in many emerging nations, such as Finland, Spain, and Greece, saw the future in this new currency. They saw the possibilities of a new world in motion and were ready to leave behind them the sometimes-negative burden of the legacy of an older political and cultural system. The Euro symbolized for the young a positive change and a bigger world in which to play. *The big emotional ideas here were to focus on the younger generation's desire for change and to provide people with a design of the currency that includes a taste of every country's cultural heritage.*

Design played a key role in this program in terms of creating excitement around the look of the currency. How different, beautiful, and practical this new currency could be! Actually, for a while design was the only physical expression of the new initiative. It crystallized the intent and the content and served as the symbolic link that communicated to everyone the new reality of the change. The design of **The challenge was to unite the population of Europe behind not only a financial program, but a new vision.** the currency was fundamental to the success of the Euro because it was the first emotional signal that was expressed. European governments realized the importance of that design and looked for visual solutions that would be an expression of the heart and soul of the European population and not only an expression of its banking system. *The challenge was to unite the population of Europe behind not only a financial program, but a new vision.*

The design of the Euro is stunning in both its look and concept. The winning design from a large group of entries from European designers expresses in a realistic, but nondenominational way the architectural heritage of Europe. What Austrian banknote designer Robert Kalina wanted to convey is the Greco-Roman and Gothic influences that permeate the physical landscape of Europe through the architecture of churches, bridges, and government buildings that link all these nations around the same cultural history. From Athens to Helsinki, the influence of these heritages is evident as Europe's history of shared artistic influences. The use of the metaphor of those styles to illustrate the currency gave every citizen a sense of grounding that was reassuring. The seven bills have different sizes, indicating the nominal value of the bill based on the size of the currency, and they also can be recognized by touch, a great concept for helping people avoid errors when they are in a rush or exchanging currency in poorly lit places, or for those who have vision impairment. Different pastel colors identify each bill and link the currency to the national flags.

Great ideas need great launches in order to become a rallying point for enthusiasm and support. What could have been more appropriate than creating celebrations for the

Great ideas need great launches in order to become a rallying point for enthusiasm and support.

launch of the currency around a New Year's celebration! That's what most countries did; from Paris to Madrid, celebrations around the launch of the currency were organized and hundreds of thousands of people showed up to celebrate their local tribe's becoming part of a bigger tribe. Maastricht, the Dutch town where the monetary treaty was signed ten years ago, held an extravaganza with a huge "Euro tree" on which acrobats performed to the music from the national anthems of the twelve member countries. In Madrid, at the Puerta del Sol, under a huge laser-designed Euro five meters in diameter, thousands of enthusiastic Spaniards witnessed pyrotechnic creativity, the launching of blue balloons, and the video projections retracing the end of the 133-year-old history of the peseta. Paris illuminated its oldest bridge in blue, and Greece sent hundreds of balloons into the sky of Athens while showcasing a 21,000-watt blue neon sculpture in honor of the new currency.

The launch of the Euro was indeed a physical initiative that created the type of enthusiasm only great moments in history can conjure. In the end, the launch of the Euro conveyed a message of hope for some Europeans that entirely transcended the idea of money. A true Citizen Brand initiative!

The design of the Euro conveys a message of hope that entirely transcends the idea of money.

7

The Seventh Commandment: Evolve from Function to Feel

*The functionality of a product is about practical qualities only. **Sensorial design is about experiences.***

Design is quite simply the most tangible, far-reaching, and potent conduit through which corporations show their true colors. Environmental communications, products, and the places where people work send powerful signals that can make a lasting impact on people by showing that a corporation cares.

The Rise of Meaningful Aestheticism: Deep Beauty

Today we are experiencing the very exciting time of an age of rediscovery and celebration of aestheticism in the art, design, and fashion worlds. These previously separate disciplines are now all fusing to create an entirely new kind of culture. For a while now, we have seen a movement toward people becoming more and more sensitized to aestheticism, but most recently, it seems that we are collectively seeking a whole new kind of "beauty." It is beauty with dimension, beauty that is sensorial in nature, and, above all, beauty that is real. It is what I would call "deep beauty" because it transcends skin-deep notions of surface aestheticism to become beauty with purpose and soul. Sensory design is all about going beyond the surface of how things merely look to create "human solutions" to very real problems and give people a more emotionalized, immediate experience of a brand. As I've said before in this book, I define design as "ideas you can see," because, to me, this describes the life-enhancing magic that happens when a good concept can be brought into being through the efforts of a talented designer. Oscar Wilde perhaps said it best when he declared, "One does not see anything until one sees its beauty."[1]

In the art world we are seeing this "return to beauty," after a long period of Modernism. Modernism began in Paris in the 1860s, as a sort of revolt against empty, academic prettiness, with the mission of challenging our traditional ideas of beauty. The book *Venus in Exile* talks about the current trend toward a return to beauty. The author, Wendy Steiner, suggests that "Invoking beauty has become a way of registering the end of modernism and the opening of a new period in culture . . . but this is not a return to pre-modernist prettiness."[2] *This trend is about reinventing aestheticism to fit more closely with our society's evolving emotional needs.* Making the world a better place is an "aesthetic responsibility" and definitely a very important part of creating a Citizen Brand culture. For example, one of the major aspects of this trend is evidenced in technological design, where we are seeing the need to explore how much we can possibly humanize and "soften" the technology that is increasingly a part of our lives. Later in this chapter, I will talk about the new Apple iMac in light of this idea. Along these lines, it is interesting to note that Richard Linklater's new computer animation film, *Waking Life*, in which the characters have an ongoing discussion of the nature of beauty, is itself an exploration of the potential beauty in the animation form. The film is a synergistic expression of color and form that is almost painterly. An article in a recent *New York Times Magazine* opinioned, "The rediscovery of beauty is not a sign that artists are retreating form the world; it is, rather, the evidence of a renewed engagement. Aestheticism can lift up ideas to transcend not only banality, but many other limitations. A willingness to embrace aestheticism is a sign of strength and hopefulness."

This trend is about reinventing aestheticism to fit more closely with our society's evolving needs.

Design for the People, People for Design

One thing is clear in today's aesthetic rebirthing period: People from all walks of life and all social levels are hungry for great design. We have seen the democratization of design, which includes, of course, the "innovative design for a great price" revolution begun by companies like Ikea, Target, and Martha Stewart. But, at this point, the "idea of design for the people" has gone beyond the price revolution. Today, design at every level—whether it's "affordable" or "refined and sophisticated (and, of course, more expensive)—is more an expression of individual taste and aesthetic point of view, than an expression of social status.

On top of this sincerity of expression, there is a growing sense that good design must also make sense from a practical point of view—it should marry form and function. Otherwise, it may be seen as frivolous and shallow. In the car industry, we have seen this form-meets-function revolution taking place at lightning speed with virtually every carmaker now developing highly creative new car concepts to reflect this new demand. GM's Robert A. Lutz states: "I see us as being in the art business—art, entertainment and mobile sculpture which coincidentally, also happens to provide transportation."[3] This is a significant statement about the shift from a primary focus on the functional to a dedication to providing products that are also beautiful objects.

I see us as being in the art business—art, entertainment and mobile sculpture which coincidentally, also happens to provide transportation.

In this new realm of a "people culture," imagination will fuel our growing desire to be surprised constantly. Another great example of this change in perspective was found in another recent *New York Times* article, where Herbert Muschamp challenged the coalition formed to rebuild the World Trade Towers several weeks after the tragedy. Mr. Muschamp calls this coalition between three private professional organizations—the New York City partnership, the Real Estate Board of New York, and the New York Chapter of the American Institute of Architects—a group of "corporate developers and their architectural mercenaries," meaning a disaster in the making from a creative point of view. "There is a growing public appetite for work with the energy to lead popular taste, not meekly follow it," claims Mr. Muschamp, clearly uncomfortable with developers, politicians, and corporate architects dictating culture regardless of people's aspirations. This statement is very profound and relevant to how our society thinks today—how much people want to be part of creating an environment that matches our emotional needs.

We are looking for dreams from both the environments and the products in our lives. Design is a powerful way to give people the luxury and personal rewards—whether large or small—that they are looking for today. Most importantly, design brings a sense of humanity in a changing world where we are losing our grounding.

Citizen Brands Are "Artists"

Corporations have, through the billions of dollars spent in research, gained an in-depth understanding of our habits and lifestyles that matches or even exceeds the knowledge base our government has accumulated on us. The corporate research is even more potent, in fact, since it has focused more on better understanding our emotions and the underlying motives for our actions. The sad thing is that these huge amounts of data are rarely analyzed beyond tactical and marketing initiatives to encompass how a corporation could use this knowledge to provide proactive thinking and creativity for human solutions. *If, as people, we want to surround ourselves with beautiful things, is it not the new role of corporations to take the lead in developing the objects, products, buildings, and communications that would enhance our environment in a manner that is sensitive to our own values?* If branding attempts to reach an expression that reflects, responds to, and even at times leads the formation of the popular psyche, then perhaps branding is art, after all. If a brand wants to play the role of an "artist" to society, however, it must do so with a mixture of passion and responsibility. And with a realistic acknowledgement of the potential risk—that risk which every artist takes when reaching beyond the ordinary to express something more profound, which can, of course, end in either success or failure. In taking the leap to position traditional, once stodgy General Motors as a producer of artwork, Robert Lutz symbolizes this merger of corporate culture and artistic sensibility which is one of the most fundamental recent events in our emotional society. *It is setting the stage for a new form of relationship around human factors and for the way our society is progressing.*

Imagination indeed becomes part of the recipe for creating a culturally relevant atmosphere of sensitivity and openness. *If we are defined and judged by the creations we leave behind us for other generations, we all have a responsibility to evolve and challenge our resolve to bring an expression of new, refined values to the world.* Corporations need to be citizen corporations that motivate and bring environmentally relevant solutions for all of us. Today they are being challenged to do this, and I am convinced that they have the means and the knowledge to meet this new vision. The opportunities are endless when we consider how greatly innovative design solutions can help people's lives. Design can transform people's lives through highly underdeveloped realms like ergonomic design or through addressing the needs of third-world countries–for example, by aiding those affected by traumatic war consequences. This could be a powerful initiative if taken on by a corporation. Creating better prostheses for children and adults victimized by land mines could, for example, be a first step.

Shortly after the tragedy in New York, the *New York Times* published an article entitled "With the World Redesigned, What Role for Designers?"[4] This article captures a very interesting point of view on design as it relates to humanity. The writer's first major statement, that "designers' talents could give design a role in leading the national recovery emotionally and economically," crystallizes the criteria used in selecting the featured seven designers. The designers featured in the article were all influential talents from the worlds of architecture, landscape architecture, interactive, new media, and graphic design,[5] who were nominated for the 2001 Chrysler Design Award. In this article's interview of those selected for the award, the focus was clearly on the role designers have in being more socially responsible and how they are now looking at their work in order to bring a deeper meaning to it. Susan Kare, the graphic designer responsible for the Apple desktop icons, was probably the most incisive of all in

People will not accept another layer of confusion in an already confused world. People will, above all, seek and respond to direct messages that inspire a sense of genuineness, trust, and personal touch.

making the statement that "in times of stress people are reassured by what's familiar" and that in our out-of-control confused world "design needs to be about clarity and simplicity." Her statements signify one of the most potent trends in today's design world: that the messages of design need to be humanistic and direct. *People will not accept another layer of confusion in an already confused world.* People will, above all, seek and respond to direct messages that inspire a sense of genuineness, trust, and personal touch. The dot.com explosive graphics reflective of a multitasking generation challenging a world order will evolve to a more disciplined expression of individual vision and imagination. As Stefan Sagmeister, a laureate and graphic designer well known for his rock music packaging for clients such as the Rolling Stones, states in the article, "I know for myself that I am much less cynical."

And this new attitude is a huge statement about the way corporations will need to interface with people—as friends, solutions providers, and, when necessary, as provocateurs. Because the best of our friends are all of these, aren't they?

Can a Corporate Environment Become a Brand's Home Sweet Home?
Citizen branding starts at home by creating environments in which people working for corporations experience the emotional support and connection that give them the freedom to explore creative thoughts. *Most corporate headquarters are not designed to reflect the brand from a big-picture perspective that has at its center the consumers' understanding, but instead express an egotistic corporate ethos.* Offices very often are plain and oppressive—designed to encourage productivity and save costs, regardless of the well-being of the most important asset of a business: its people. Series of larger and smaller offices acknowledge ranks and status based on past achievement, while, generally speaking, the real thinkers, and certainly the future of the brand, are cramped into small, sterile cubicles. But some are beginning to realize the importance of changing this paradigm. After extensive research collaboration with the research and consulting firm Cheskin, Herman Miller came up with a revolutionary new design to replace the infamous cubicle. The aim of this design is to inspire creativity, communication, and freedom of expression. The workstation system, called "Resolve," is based on a beehivelike rounded hexagon structure with individual workstations that are angled at an open 120 degrees instead of the closed and hard 90 degrees of the traditional cubical. This design allows people much more flexibility in how they personalize and arrange their own spaces, plus more opportunity for interaction with other workers, and with less of a sense of restriction while maintaining a measure of privacy.

In commenting on *Business Week*'s Architectural Record Awards, Gerry Khermouch stated that the selected entries share "a common understanding that a grand architectural gesture can say as much about a group's value or brand as any written mission statement, advertising campaign, or lobbying effort."[6] Inspiring employees is the most important priority a corporation can focus on. Offices selected for this award include the SAP offices, which are described as offices created to attract and retain talent, the LVMH New York headquarters that serve the corporation's "cultural manifesto," and the Wieden and Kennedy advertising agency's headquarters in Portland, Oregon, which is designed to encourage creativity.

Our client Coca-Cola has invested in such initiatives to create in some of its offices the type of environmental design that reflects the buyer's lifestyle–including some hip interior design for the Sprite brand–putting to shame even my own company's New York offices, which I thought were pretty cool until I visited Coca-Cola's Atlanta offices! **Bath & Body Works in Columbus, Ohio, has a cafeteria that serves the hearty comfort food that is consistent with its heartland imagery.** Bath & Body Works in Columbus, Ohio, has a cafeteria that serves the hearty comfort food that is consistent with its heartland imagery. Bringing the brand culture "inside" is a sure way to create a better understanding of that culture as well as a deeper understanding of the market. It creates an opportunity for employees to respond to the brand culture in a relevant way and become its best ambassadors.

Abercrombie & Fitch's new headquarters outside Columbus, Ohio, is a case in point in the art of creating a brand-reflective corporate space. The new A&F "campus," which was built on a 300-acre, rural compound, cost $131 million and took two years to complete, was conceived to foster innovation and communication. This hip, relaxed corporate headquarters conveys a fun, social environment and feels like a true campus. The staff, composed mostly of recent college grads who are the brand's target, sit in democratic work spaces on workbenches arranged in library style. No one has a set office space, not even the company's CEO, Mike Jeffries. A mix of the latest music plays all day throughout the buildings. As architect Ross Anderson of Anderson Architects says, "Mike Jeffries, the company's CEO, was very clear about ending up with something that was not like other places to work. He wanted the employees to really feel this was a cool place to work."[7] He goes on to say, "We started by asking ourselves, 'If Abercrombie & Fitch were a place, what would it be?'"[8] The answer to that question is expressed through a real dynamic fusion of a laid-back outdoors attitude with a more energetic urban feeling that is totally reflective of A&F's brand essence and a great conceptual approach to brand architecture.

The open-plan offices are housed in barn-style, neo-industrial buildings made from robust materials like stucco, corrugated cement board, galvanized metal, and plywood. The buildings are set against each other around a winding street along which kids ride scooters to get around, thus creating an urban environment in the midst of this very rural site. There are plenty of nonspecific spaces that are unprogrammed, so that employees themselves can determine their use. There is a great emphasis on the outdoors. To reach the main buildings from the parking lot, employees must walk through the forest along trails that are lighted by torches in the winter. There are open fire pits outside and an open-air assembly hall with an oversized fireplace. "There's a very up attitude here, and it has to do with the community in the new buildings: the kids passing each other on their scooters, yelling out the windows. This generation is into hanging out with their friends and family, and that's what we do here. We all feel very much at home." [9]

This sense of community is very important, and is more and more at the forefront of corporate architectural design. Barry Ludwig, an architect renowned for designing cutting-edge office parks, focuses on trying to create a sense of community and connection. He takes much of his inspiration from studying the design principles of ancient cities where people needed to interact and work very closely together. He incorporates these concepts into distinct "neighborhoods;" quiet side streets and plazas or thoroughfares where people can walk or meet and talk about their work. He is designing the Cisco Systems' new office park in Coyote Valley, California, to be in harmony with its beautiful surroundings of orchards and farms through a design that incorporates parking lots that look like plowed fields, nature trails, and barnlike buildings with minimalist silos. Similar to the idea conveyed at Abercrombie & Fitch's headquarters, he tries to design lots of ways to get people out of their offices to interact with one another or have new experiences of working in different places in the park.

The question of creating corporate environments that celebrate and respect their surroundings is an important one.

The question of creating corporate environments that celebrate and respect their surroundings is an important one. What could be more inspiring to employees? Through the simple idea of bringing the outdoors inside through windows, the redesign of a Phillips Plastic plant has boosted employee morale at one of its factories and increased on-time deliveries by nearly 10 percent. Phillips created an open structure which, in turn, helped to create an open culture. The 85,000-square-foot structure of glass, steel, and native sandstone has floor to ceiling windows to give employees views of the wooded site, and its lake and is separated from the offices only by a seventeen-foot high acoustic glass wall, which has facilitated contact between managers and workers. There is also a great deal corporations can learn from architectural solutions in other areas, such as hospitals. For example, in Brazil, architect Joao Filgueiras Lima has repeatedly shown how large health and research "institutions" can be warm and inviting instead of cold, austere, frightening places. What is so incredible is that he has done this through imaginative design at very low costs. Using one of the lowest-cost forms of construction, pre-molded concrete, Lima, known for elaborate structural solutions to schools, bus shelters, and city infrastructures, has a sophisticated aesthetic. "Post modern architecture wants to be science fiction, but without harmony, rhythm, and pause, architecture is nothing,"[10] Lima says. The Sarah Foundation, which treats more than one million disabled people a year, provides a great example of how to be a public institution with a social conscience and a human face. To create a clean, soothing, regenerative atmosphere, Lima removed the air-conditioning in favor of natural ventilation and designed patient rooms that opened up onto internal patios and sundecks, integrating natural elements such as light and water. Lima's use of bold colors and futuristic forms that are informed first and foremost by function is inspiring. If you thought wheelchair ramps could never be beautiful, think again!

Feng Shui: Ancient Recipes for Achieving Spatial Harmony

Certainly, in many of these corporate headquarters' designs a recurring theme seems to be an attempt to create a sense of harmony with the buildings' natural surroundings and to bring nature inside to the people, and the people outside to nature. In many ways these ideas are very reflective of feng shui, the ancient Chinese practice of spatial design that seeks to create harmony within the natural environment so that the surrounding energy, or life force (*chi*), can flow freely through a space and be used productively.

Feng shui, which has been around for thousands of years, enjoyed its first golden era in the fourth century and has been popularized in America since the 1980s. Feng Shui is neither a science nor a religion. To the Chinese, the principles of feng shui are merely based on environmental observations, like the weather reports are for us. I can only offer here a very simplified explanation of feng shui that cannot do this complex practice justice. *Many feng shui ideas are another way of thinking about or emphasizing the importance of something that could be seen as common sense from a Western point of view.* For example, in feng shui negative chi emanates from sharp corners; therefore it is best to create tables with rounded edges, which encourages a positive force of unity for people sitting together—and, of course, it is better for avoiding potential bruises from those sharp corners, too!

Many feng shui ideas are another way of thinking about or emphasizing the importance of something that could be seen as common sense from a Western point of view.

Regardless of what you may think of the ideas behind feng shui, the underlying, principal aim of creating buildings and interior designs that are in harmony with the landscape, the planetary positioning (i.e., north, south, east, west), and nature's basic elements—wood, fire, earth, metal, and water—is clearly a interesting idea to pursue, since it is about helping people to connect with nature. When all is said and done, the fact that the practice *seeks to bring conscious intention to people's experience of a space makes it, in my opinion, a fascinating and very worthwhile study.* For example, in certain forms of feng shui (there are several different schools) much emphasis is placed on entrances, and an attempt is made to help people crossing a threshold into a space recognize and appreciate this transitional moment, so that emotionally and psychically they can recognize and appreciate the difference of the space they are entering. Wouldn't this be a smart idea for most retail spaces?

Ergonomics: Design for Real Living

Ergonomic solutions can help us all—from aging Baby Boomers to young children, from office workers to construction workers to drivers, and so on—by bringing enhanced safety, efficiency, and pleasure to our daily experiences. As Baby Boomers redefine what old age means for their generation, they are still beginning to experience the inevitable drawbacks of aging, such as decline of eyesight and encroaching arthritis. Brands must develop new approaches to help this generation, which craves activity and fun, enjoy life better. The "OXO" cooking line, which was designed for people with arthritis, has become a huge hit with the general consumer population. This is because of its excellent design. OXO, based on the concept of Universal Design, seeks to create high performance products with problem-solving features that are easy to use by the largest spectrum of people. Now the company is beginning to develop other product lines, such as the "Good Grips Automotive Care Tools," as well as yard and workshop tools.

Another company, Gold Violin, has created a Universal Remote Control with big buttons for those with vision problems. Gold Violin also produces a package gift intended for seniors called "The Best Everyday Arthritis Gadgets," which consists of six ergonomic tools—from a potato peeler to doorknob/faucet turners.

As the enormous population of Baby Boomers continues to age, we will most likely see more mainstream development of ergonomic products and tools created for the ease of use not just by seniors, but by any hand. The difference in using these tools is sometimes dramatic. If you compare, for example, working on a construction or repair project with a Stanley ergonomic screwdriver, which has a handle that fits the grip of a human hand snugly and very comfortably, to working with any traditional round-ridged, hard plastic-handled screwdriver, you will soon see that not only is the Stanley screwdriver more comfortable, it also allows you to work much more efficiently and finish a job more quickly with less strain—and there's a lot to be said for that!

Another great ergonomic solution for a younger crowd is the rolling backpack being produced by Land's End and REI, which take their design cues from luggage with wheels and solve the very real problem of kids carrying too much weight in their book bags. Some studies have shown that kids carry as much as one-fourth their body weight on a daily basis because of busier after-school schedules, more homework, and the widespread elimination of school lockers after tragic events like Columbine. The problem is beginning to be so serious and widespread that doctors are launching studies; orthopedists at A.I. DuPont Hospital, for example, are conducting a yearlong study of 1,000 people to evaluate the potential long-term damage to the spine. REI's ergonomic backpack with padded shoulder harness, sternum straps, compression straps, and a T-shaped handle to pull the pack on wheels is a great looking design answer to this problem. Another example of an everyday problem that could be solved through ergonomics is our use of the computer mouse, which uses the large muscles of the shoulder and arm to make precise movements and creates a constant tension. Swedish medical doctor and ergonomics expert Dr. Johan Ullman has created a solution called the "Pen Mouse," which resembles a gear stick shift and allows the user to grip in a more natural way, apparently without the same muscular tension of the conventional mouse.

In the automobile industry, people-oriented, ergonomic design is becoming the "expected." Bill Fluharty, vice president for industrial design at Johnson Controls, which creates interiors, complete dashboards, seats, and doors for carmakers like Daimler Chrysler, Ford, GM, and others, has specialized in studying how people use cars through video ethnography. He has discovered how to make people both happier and safer in their cars. A system Johnson Controls designed for the Volvo Advanced Safety

He has discovered how to make people both happier and safer in their cars.

Concept car can actually "read" the position of the driver's eyes and places the eyes where they'll have the best visibility by adjusting the seat height, the steering wheel, and the position of the pedals. One of their interiors, the InMotion interior, has carpeting in areas for adults and washable rubberlike flooring in the back and includes an electronic table called the "Go Pad," which combines a DVD player with a digital camera and an Internet connection so that kids can download games and send electronic postcards of scenes along the way to their friends. With all this, one would think the kids would be happily occupied until they reach their destination, but if they do get too rowdy, adults up front will know about it via the KidCam video system for backseat surveillance, which comes equipped with a Travelcom intercom so that parents will be able to tell their kids to cool it! This interior even has Comfort Massage seats embedded with vibrating motors for the adults.

Since not everyone can afford these high-tech, fancy solutions, it is important to remember that there are often inexpensive ways to make customers happy (no matter what the industry!) by demonstrating a real understanding of the "user experience." In the car industry, features such as small plastic coin holders for tolls and efficient food management compartments and trays are classic examples of this concept.

Making "People Ideas" Real in Product and Packaging Design

Product design is the ultimate brand voice. Product design helps create a sensory connection between a product and people. In a world where we feel most insecure, products can bring us a sense of human touch, humanity, and a message of hope that sometimes makes our lives better. Surrounding ourselves with products that help create beauty and solutions is a reason why good design solutions are always based on an articulated thought process that people put first in the experience.

PRODUCT DESIGN

Most computer design does not consider touch, or sensory experiences of any kind, but Apple's new iMac does. Through its design, it actually invites touch and responds. This is a smart move for Apple because touch is very reassuring–it sends to our brain stimuli that in this case enliven an otherwise cold office product. We want to touch paintings in a museum and play with the objects we care about in our lives!

Instead of taking up precious desk space like a typical flat monitor, the iMac's fifteen-inch screen floats in the air, attached to a jointed, chrome-pipe neck. The screen is framed in a glowing translucent plastic that makes you want to pull it towards you. Jonathan Ive, chief of Apple's ID lab, who also designed the original iMac, the iPod music player, the lightweight but heavy-duty titanium PowerBook, and the ice-cube-inspired **This machine appears to fit you, rather than the traditional dynamic of people fitting themselves to the machine.** Cube desktop, says he designed it so that you would want to touch it, want to "violate the sacred plane of the monitor."[11] The chrome connects to the computer, which is an improbably small hemisphere at 10.4 inches in diameter. This new design means that people can now regain a huge portion of their desk space, adjust their monitors however they need to best see and feel comfortable, and even easily swing the monitor over to show someone something on their screen. Once again, Apple has created a computer design that appeals to our senses and our humanity. *This machine appears to fit you, rather than the traditional dynamic of people fitting themselves to the machine.* Bringing the element of flexible movement to the desktop computer contributes to the computer's sense of being approachable and even lifelike–the overall design has tremendous personality.

Ive talks about industrial design "as product narrative. My view is that surfaces and materials and finishes and product architecture are about telling a bigger story." The story the new iMac wanted to tell, he says, was about "a flat display so light, fluid, and free that it could almost fly away." The underlying visual blueprint of the design is that of a sunflower, an inspiration that suddenly came to Steve Jobs and Jonathan Ive as they strolled in Job's garden discussing next steps after Jobs sent the "final" concept back to the drawing board to ask that it be completely redone! Engineering the machine–squeezing all the gear into the little box that Jobs wanted–took nearly two years. Jobs, known to be a perfectionist, tends to get his ideas from his gut rather than relying on extensive research and focus groups.

While the computer industry suffers and other computer makers are vying to be the cheapest on the block, Apple has been holding its ground in terms of prices and betting that innovation, and not price cutting, is the answer. "The way we're going to survive is to innovate our way out of this." Apple's "build-it-and-they-will-come" approach has paid off in the past. The original iMac, which launched in May 1998, sparked a 400 percent Apple-stock surge during the next two years, and has sold more than 6 million units. Furthermore, the robust sales of the new iMac sent Apple's revenue for the second quarter of 2002 well above most analysts' estimates.

The way we're going to survive is to innovate our way out of this.

But beyond innovative design from an aesthetic point of view, the new iMac, just like the original iMac, which offered "power to the people" in terms of facility of connecting to the Internet, has another mission: to simplify people's lives. Jobs believes that what consumers most want from technology is control of their digital lives, which have become incredibly cluttered with digital cameras, camcorders,

Palms, cell phones, and MP3 and DVD players that seem to get harder to use, not easier. The new iMac was designed to connect us to our gadgets as a digital hub. Jobs claims that we are now entering the third phase of personal computing. The first was about utility–people using their thinking machines to do word processing, run spreadsheets, create desktop graphics, etc. The second was about wiring all those machines together on the Internet, and the next, or the third, is about people using computers to orchestrate all the new digital gear that has steadily crept into their lives. Besides editing, managing, and storing work from these various devices, a personal computer can enhance the value of these devices. Apple's core programs, iTunes, iMovie, iDVD, and the new iPhoto, are all designed to do this and to give people more control over their creative lives in easy-to-use formats. These programs have been lauded in the industry as superior in terms of user-friendliness and the ability to organize data over other programs. Apple's secret, which doubtless comes from Jobs's early flirtation with Zen Buddhism, is knowing what to leave out, understanding that in the complex world of computers, less is way more. The ease with which people can make a short film, develop and edit and store their photographs, or create music can make an artist out of any talented amateur!

Another great example of the unexpected ways product design can enhance our lives is seen in a new golf ball design by Callaway. Talk about harnessing the power of design to solve problems and give people pleasure–what about a better golf game? Only golf enthusiasts such as myself would understand the true euphoria that could bring! The challenge of creating a better golf ball has always been to reduce the drag so that the ball will fly farther. Callaway golf researcher Steven Ogg, a former Boeing engineer who first invented the traditional "dimples" of the original golf ball, now has replaced the dimples with a tubular lattice network that is a series of ridges, interlocking hexagons, and pentagons, similar to chicken wire. Apparently, through this groundbreaking design he has achieved what has long been considered to be the holy grail of ball design: 100 percent surface coverage. The ball, the Callaway HX, released in March 2002, has no flat spots, and in test after test, it apparently flies farther than any other ball. PGA Tour players and golfers around the world are already begging to play it. So, apparently, Steve Jobs could be right; build it and they will come!

Reinventing the Wheel

As I mentioned in the beginning of this chapter, the car industry has been leading a dramatic design revolution to reinvigorate people's enthusiasm for cars. Part of the reason for this is that as all carmakers have increasingly been able to provide the same standards at similar price ranges in terms of reliability, safety, and good mileage; design has become the only way for one company to stand out from another in the market. They must differentiate through emotion and sensory experiences now, through tapping into America's growing love affair with beautifully designed, highly efficient objects. VW, with its new beetle, was, of course, one of the first to understand this—and Chrysler was not far behind with its 1920s "gangster style" fun family roadster that replaces more boring, traditional family cars.

In the 1950s, design was big in the car industry, but when gas prices went up, design took a backseat to a focus on practical engineering. In today's user-driven world, designers have become virtual stars—but more importantly, they have served as the humanizing factor in a previously "cold" industry. These star designers are now even featured in car commercials as an essential element in promoting the brand. Car companies from Nissan to Mitsubishi to Chrysler to GM are all investing in "star designers" like Bryan Nesbitt at GM, and their cutting-edge car concepts. Nissan's devotion to this approach has promoted its star designer, Shiro Nakamura, to the larger role of a corporate strategist. He oversees the overall corporate aesthetic from the corporate logo to the look of the showrooms. In this new world we are relying on the visionary executions of designers to inspire us rather than on the cautious executions based on the lowest common denominators. As a designer, I would say there is really no conflict here because great designers always have an intrinsic feeling for what will make people happy. They have their finger on the pulse of the "popular vote." The difference is that they can translate the desires of people into designs that are truly innovative. "Over-reliance on research is like trying to drive by looking in the rearview mirror,"[12] says Robert Lutz, head of product development at GM. As I mentioned before, this move by GM at such a stressful time for American carmakers, when they are faced with intensifying pressure from foreign automakers and recession at home, is very significant. Mr. Lutz exemplifies this new, right-brained approach to solving business problems through innovative design with his conviction that "the way to compete in a market where every niche has been filled and demand is expected to drop next year is to create risky 'love them or hate them' designs."[13]

PACKAGING DESIGN

Packaging design can help solve some very important problems for people and bring a heightened sense of caring to a brand. The Tylenol cap, designed in response to the Tylenol episode in which people were poisoned, is a great example of how design can help make people feel safe and comfortable and win back a consumer's trust in a brand. In addition to practical solutions to problems, packaging can provide visual cues that serve as a kind of "public service announcement" for consumers. Sutter Winery produces a selection of wines with pink corks and bottle necks that serve as reminders to women to get mammograms and provide information on how they can join in the fight against breast cancer. The pain reliever brand Aleve has recently launched an "educational packaging" initiative, the mission of which is to teach people about arthritis, stressing the fact that it is not just an "old person's disease," as well as to promote benefit events

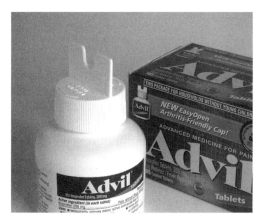

such as the Arthritis Walk. Advil, for its part, has developed an "arthritis-friendly" package, which incorporates a flange design on the cap to make it easy to twist open. This is one of those "small" innovations that can really mean a lot to people when faced with the sometimes daunting task of opening a pain reliever bottle while in pain!

In terms of practical everyday hassles, Prada's new line of skin care gives some very original and effective answers for women on the go. The products are not presented in the prototypical jars, but rather in disposable and easy-to-carry plastic containers. The plight women face when traveling of carrying cumbersome skin care packaging was clearly taken into consideration.

The plight women face when traveling of carrying cumbersome skin care packaging was clearly taken into consideration.

Men, I was told at Prada, were also in favor of the disposable presentation. Men are comfortable with the disposable concept, from condoms to shavers, and skittish about the "feminine" presentation of most beauty products, so I was not surprised to hear that 40 percent of Prada's beauty business customers are men. Prada has also used ingenious packaging to offer a new level of freshness and scientific efficacy with their new anti-aging skincare product, Lightening Concentrate/Face. The product has a high concentration of freeze-dried vitamin C that normalizes dark melanin cells, reduces inflammation, and encourages collagen production. But vitamin C needs to be protected from light, air, heat, and bacteria to maintain its potency and it is a highly volatile compound. The team spent a

The plight women face when traveling and having to carry cumbersome skin care packaging was clearly taken into consideration in this clever Prada design.

year developing the package by exploring the food, motor, dental, and pharmaceutical industries to find a container that would keep the product stable until it was ready to be mixed with the other active ingredients. They came up with two mini-canisters that snap into a tiny tube so the vitamins and the liquid ingredients can be shaken into a fresh and potent skin treatment. The finished product, totally portable, practical, and very appealing, is wrapped in a very attractive purple sachet.

The Prada beauty products packaging is evidence of Prada's commitment to a balance of substance and style, or form and function. Miuccia Prada says, with regards to the practicality of the packaging, "I am personally obsessed with not pretending things are better than they are."[14] While many designers merely lend their name to beauty products that they do not make, Miuccia Prada became personally involved with the development of the products and their packaging. When Prada Beauty products first came out over a year ago, people were saying "They look great . . . but that isn't enough," says Jill Scalamandre, general manager of Prada Beauty, "for Prada, function always comes first."[15]

A New Synergistic World of Artistic Collaboration

In today's design-savvy environment, there is a whole new generation of consumers that doesn't recognize the boundaries between fashion and art or design and style. These boundaries will continue to blur as we move more and more into a world where our computers, cars, homes, and housewares are designed *objets d'art*. Armani has been one of several designers to smartly make the move into the world of furniture and houseware design, and, as we saw in chapter 3, other fashion brands such as Diane Von Furstenberg have been steadily connecting with the art world. *We have reached a very exciting age of striving for total cultural synergy that will continue to expand in ways we cannot possibility imagine.* We will see the merging of influences, more borrowing of cues and lots of cross-inspiration. Get ready! A fun example of this that I saw recently was when *Women's Wear Daily* asked fashion designers to create costumes for women to wear on the Segway Human Transporter (aka "Ginger"), the super-high-tech, battery-powered, self-balancing scooters which are supposed to revolutionize urban transportation. These scooters are not just another transportation vehicle but also a very comfortable escape—a rolling device that puts the personality of the driver first. This creative personal expression of freedom was immediately understood by the designers who were asked to show us all how a woman can look chic while scooting about town. Ideas such as James Coviello's "Retro Aviator Babe," Nicole Miller's evening-gowned "Glam Goddess," Vera Wang's short wedding dress, or Josie Natori's sexy leggings (a strategic design solution to the problem of wind updrafts when wearing a skirt) were testimony of the meeting of product and fashion designers to create a holistic and imaginative lifestyle story around a product launch. The concept is phenomenal because it brings together a team of imaginative designers to create a new perspective in bringing a product to market. The past model of designers working in separate bubbles—when their combined talent can bring such a fantastic new world of solutions—clearly needs to change. *The collaborative process is interesting precisely because it puts the common goal of determining the overall human experience first in the equation.* Whether the Ginger will have a successful life and will continue to inspire our frivolous and imaginative side is to be determined, but this kind of endeavor can certainly make us feel better about the capacity for humans to expand certain creative boundaries—and to take us with them for the ride.

What does all of this mean from a Citizen Brand perspective? It means that corporations have a role to play in bringing the human

The collaborative process is interesting precisely because it puts the common goal of determining the overall human experience first in the equation.

The It Kit

NEW YORK — It's time to find out who has what it takes. It, of course, is the latest trend in gadgetry, the Segway Human Transporter, aka Ginger. WWD asked designers how a woman can look chic while scooting about town, and they came up with solutions for all kinds. Here, from left, Nicole Miller's glam goddess, Peter Som's flirt and James Coviello's retro aviator babe. For more on Scooter Chic, see pages 4 and 5.

The Ginger scooter's design makes us feel better about the capacity for humans to expand certain creative boundaries and takes us with them for the ride.

aspect to design. Corporations impact the work environment and our daily environment in profound ways–physically, psychically, and spiritually. Their messages to the world are constantly being decoded by people in the context of the question, "how much do they care about us?" Brands that are sensitive to their profound impact on people's lives make it their responsibility to create beauty to enhance people's lives. These are the brands that will be perceived most positively and will assume their role in the world as far reaching organizations. There are always good practical reasons for design initiatives, but by associating the power of emotions to this rational thinking, a bridge between the business world and the world of humanity will be created to build powerful and successful partnerships.

8

The Eighth Commandment: Evolve from Ubiquity to Presence

*Ubiquity is seen. **Emotional presence is felt.***

Transcending mere ubiquity to create an emotionally powerful brand presence in the market requires developing an uncanny sensitivity to people's states, in terms of both being in sync with overall collective moods and having an in-depth emotional understanding of people's day-to-day lives. To create real emotional presence in a world crowded with brand messages, brand presence initiatives must be extremely creative, flexible, and must always seek a humanistic point of contact. A great example of finding that humanistic point of contact is a Sprite bus shelter ad that taps into the emotions of people waiting for a bus through thoughtful humor. The ad reads, "A soft drink will not save you from this ordeal of public transportation. It will not save you a seat on a crowded bus or keep the bus from getting caught in traffic. It cannot give you exact change. It will not make you popular with other riders, unless you buy enough for everyone. But used correctly, it can quench your thirst. . . ." In this chapter we will focus on the emotional relevance of messages and the question of ubiquity, as well as on the issue of privacy in a ubiquitous commercial world. Part of the emotional relevance of Citizen Brands will indeed be a growing sensitivity to this oversaturated commercial world.

> From a Citizen Brand perspective, any marketing effort that smacks of self-congratulation or taking advantage of a terrible situation for profit is, of course, totally counterproductive.

In terms of sensitivity to collective moods, September 11 once again offers us a very valuable perspective on this commandment. In the weeks after the tragedy marketers scrambled to find the right note to sound with a vulnerable, grieving public. Some were successful in doing this while others missed the moment, either by ignoring it or through overzealous marketing that seemed to be taking advantage of people's very sensitive feelings. One thing was immediately clear to almost everyone: It was important to be positive. Communications that were edgy, gloomy, or violent in tone were quickly weeded out of marketing plans and replaced with imagery that was more optimistic. Diesel USA removed the words "Save Yourself" from their outdoor ads, replacing them with "Stay Young"; the company also removed images that showed models wearing oxygen masks. An industry debate raged over whether a brand should continue using patriotic imagery after an initial solidarity/condolence message, as did the debate over whether companies should advertise their charitable contributions to the Twin Towers Relief Fund, with some people feeling that corporations were capitalizing on the tragedy. From a Citizen Brand perspective, any marketing effort that smacks of self-congratulation or taking advantage of a terrible situation for profit is, of course, totally counterproductive. This can be a very fine line and the real determining factor for staying on the "right side" of that line is the degree of sincerity in any effort to maintain a strong brand relevance. There is nothing wrong with advertising contributions to a cause such as this, particularly since such announcements encourage other companies to do the same, but it should not be overemphasized, since it is absolutely the natural, expected thing for a Citizen Brand to do in these circumstances. These initial, short-lived messages of solidarity and encouragement from corporations were important as a reflection of the public consciousness and as a way of simply acknowledging (instead of ignoring) what was happening in our world.

Perhaps the best way to play a Citizen Brand role in times like these is to create a foundation, or system, that customers can contribute to along with the brand's contribution. In that way, people themselves are participating in the brand's effort firsthand. Many brands did this through a special product or line of products, donating the profits to a relief fund. It makes sense in a situation such as this to use the inherent power of the brand to rally people around a cause and convey solidarity. A great example of this was the way the more than one

The fashion community came together to design and produce the "Fashion for America" T-Shirts with the heart-shaped flag to raise money for the relief fund.

hundred designers in the fashion community came together to design and produce the Fashion for America T-shirts with the heart-shaped flag to raise money for the relief fund–a totally not-for-profit operation. However, too much emphasis on patriotism also seemed to some to be insincere, a superficial "jumping on the bandwagon," and in order to avoid that, it is best to keep these communications simple, heartfelt, and short-lived. It was a moment for companies to mark and tell people that they understood what people were going through. The best communications attempted to do nothing more than "mirror the mood" of the people. For example, Miller produced a commercial that simply showed a myriad of signs like those that we all saw posted on people's houses, cars, and in shops across America expressing sentiments like, "America the Beautiful," "Go USA," and "We Are All New Yorkers." Brands that have a very strong "America" image, such as Ralph Lauren and Tommy Hilfiger, could go further with an expression of patriotism and emphasize this concept for a longer period of time, since it is an organic part of their brand concept. In the same way, DKNY created a campaign that emphasized the great qualities, strength, and sexiness of New York City. This made a lot of sense because New York is an intrinsic part of the DKNY brand.

There were brands that rose admirably to the unprecedented challenge of September 11. Ogilvy & Mather created a wonderful commercial for American Express that sounded just the right Citizen Brand note. The commercial gave a retail tour of lower Manhattan, showing how businesses there had reopened and encouraged consumers to return to support these ailing businesses. As an *Advertising Age* journalist put it, ". . . Even with its clear self-interest in retail commerce, the focus here is on the primary beneficiaries and the message is proportionate to the circumstances."[1] In other words, American Express was using its money and brand power to not only to promote itself, but also to help other businesses in a very practical, neighborly kind of way.

Cultural Sensitivity

Similar to the struggle to sound the right note in the face of tragedy, global brands are now facing a new, unprecedented challenge: presenting their brands to the world with much greater cultural sensitivity, in different countries where their presence may or may not be appreciated. The most successful approach for global brands seems to be along the lines of the model of Kentucky Fried Chicken, owned by Tricon Global Restaurants, which also owns Pizza Hut and Taco Bell, with five thousand restaurants in the United States and six thousand abroad. KFC is an example of a multinational brand that has managed to sustain a strong brand presence in global markets that is simultaneously true to the original, all-American brand concept and highly adaptive to local markets. Both its menu and how it conducts business changes according to local tastes. For example, in England KFC stresses gravy and potatoes, in Japan it sells tempura crispy strips, in Thailand it offers rice with soy or sweet chili sauce, in France it sells pastries, and in China the chicken gets spicier and spicier the farther inland you travel. In some countries, like China, KFC wisely uses its restaurants to host various community outreach programs, such as inviting local low-income senior citizens for free food and cultural performances.

The Mental Environment Movement

In my last book, I talked about how sometimes a whisper is much more powerful than a shout, and how consumers today are so incredibly inundated with marketing messages that appear now even on public bathroom walls and stall doors. When a communication is truly emotionally resonant, less can be more. Certainly this applies to brand presence. Several very powerful, well-placed ads are much more effective than embarking on a "logo war" and plastering your message everywhere. This is actually highly ineffective–the more people are inundated, the more they develop the capability to tune things out. If communication is not emotionally arresting, it will probably not even be noticed. Not only is the logo-war approach ineffective, it is actually dangerous because it risks annoying people, not unlike person at a party who wants so badly to be liked and follows you around all night and becomes, eventually, a bore. As an example, think about how, during the Major League Baseball divisional playoffs, when an AT&T logo appeared on the screen each time a team changed a pitcher, accompanied by the irritating loud ring of a phone, fans unanimously complained.

And I would venture to say that people today are more annoyed by rampant commercialism than ever before. As I mentioned in the chapter 1 section on Gen Y, there is a new underground movement, particularly strong with this generation, that the *Adbusters* magazine has labeled the "Mental Environment Movement," which reflects a growing anger among people about the extent of commercialism in our society and the need to clear away the clutter of advertising from our daily lives. This is a real cultural revolution that is taking root in, but not limited to, this very powerful, influential generation and that often takes the form of the "Culture Jamming" activities we talked about in that chapter. When you think of it, it makes perfect sense that this would be the generation to begin such an anti-marketing revolution. Why wouldn't they rebel against this infringement on their mental space? They crave authenticity and are seeking to create their own culture and, as we have seen in the past with movements like the hippies of the Sixties, a new culture is almost always, at first, a counterculture. The fact that some of their ideology and rhetoric is skewed toward extremism does not take away from the seriousness of their movement; in fact, it shows just how angry they are. Of course, calling out for a "no brand world"–something we have only seen in communist countries and which, even there, was not truly adhered to–is not practical, since

The *Adbusters* magazine has labeled the "Mental Environment Movement," which reflects a growing anger among people about the extent of commercialism in our society.

people have proven time and time again that they want brands in
order to be able to at least differentiate qualities of products. But it
shows how people's love affair with brands can truly come to an
untimely demise if brands are not respectful of people's needs–with
physical, mental, and spiritual "space" being one of these needs.

If brands do not learn to demonstrate this respect, there will surely
be increased backlash, with more and more activist events such as
"Buy Nothing Day"–and just like all cultural movements, what may
start out as a completely underground, fringe movement may eventually filter down into the mainstream culture in ways we may not
expect. What if brands and anything that vaguely smacks of commercialism suddenly become "uncool," not just to a select group of
Gen Y kids, but to aspiring hipsters in all demographics? It may be
hard to imagine, but it is surely not entirely impossible!

The dramatic acceleration of marketing to kids over the last several
years is a good example of brands pushing too far into people's lives
without enough sensitivity. Many advertising and marketing professionals themselves have begun to agree that we have gone too far
with, for instance, advertisements and television in public schools.

Jelly Helm, professor at the Virginia Commonwealth University's graduate school of advertising and a former ad executive himself, is pushing for a ban in the United States similar to those that exist in other countries and claims to have had an incredible response from parents. He says, "The process of seeing children as a target market commoditizes childhood. Everything children are geared toward is tied to a profiting corporation."[2] In countries like Sweden and in the province of Quebec there already are bans on ads aimed at kids under twelve, and a similar ban is currently under consideration by the entire European Union. Sometimes the best approach may be to show people that you understand their need for this "space," as Benetton did several years ago when, as part of a national ad campaign in North America, it bought up all of the billboard ad space on several particularly cluttered highways and left them blank to give people respite from the constant barrage of ads.

The dramatic acceleration of marketing to kids over the last several years is a good example of brands pushing too far.

As brands rapidly move into new territories, these issues will continually surface while we weigh the benefits against the potential downside and test people's tolerance. What is certain is that something of value must be given to people in exchange for their time. Movie theaters, once a relatively ad-free environment, are now increasingly marketing to people. Exit polls have shown that nearly 80 percent of theatergoers can recall the advertisement they saw in the cinema–four to six times the number who can recall television commercials. However many people are adamantly against advertisements in the cinema, which is a place that people go to relax, "escape," and experience culture. While movie theaters offer a great opportunity because the audience is captive, brands should be careful to be sensitive to this precisely because people are in a "captive" situation and taking excessive advantage of this could result in a backlash. This is actually the reason advertisements have not been allowed before any films distributed by Disney Studio Entertainment Films since the early 1990s. When Disney allowed advertisements, it received angry letters and phone calls from parents. Any brand-presence initiative in a movie theater should take into consideration the reasons why people go to the cinema and appeal to them from a more artistic sensibility. One thing is for certain: People don't want to see television commercials on the big screen–they will respond best to ads with a cinematic feel.

Technology: Friend or Foe?

There is a great ad for the Internet service Earthlink that says it all. It shows a harried, befuddled young man hurrying to work in the morning, confronted by strangers every two steps who "know" the intimate details of his life and are trying to hawk wares or services of some type that correspond to his lifestyle . . . He runs from them all to the refuge of a park bench only to have the man next to him ask from behind his newspaper, "Love life not what it should be, Harry?" Earthlink has smartly positioned itself as the Internet provider that understands how we feel about our privacy. Kenneth Cole also developed a great print ad along these lines, which shows a man looking into a bathroom mirror where someone has written, "Think you have no privacy? You're not alone." This hot, much-debated issue of our times is far from being solved and needs constant attention. Not only do people want to have choices about levels of privacy afforded them, they also want to have choices about when and how they will be contacted with marketing messages. Of course, we all know that when free services are being offered, people are sometimes willing to sacrifice some level of privacy and tolerate certain marketing messages. The point is to maintain communication with people in order to find out what level of privacy a person wants and to respond accordingly.

This hot, much debated issue of our times is far from being solved and needs constant attention. Not only do people want to have choices about levels of privacy afforded them, they also want to have choices about when and how they will be contacted with marketing messages.

The best way to use technology as a brand presence/marketing tool is to offer people handy, fun, everyday solutions. The ads inside elevators that Captivate Network displays via their wireless Internet monitors are successful because they are paired with useful content such as news, weather, or stock quotes. The Miller Brewing Company has found a fun way to use technology both to advertise its brand and to be of use to people. Miller is offering a unique tool for people to send high-tech drink invitations: the Miller Lite Beer Pager. The free Miller-branded pager software is downloaded onto a computer and allows the person to create, coordinate, and customize a rendez-vous with friends at their favorite local bar. A person inputs his friends' e-mail addresses and the locations of favorite bars; he can then instruct the pager to invite a selected group of friends for a drink at the chosen bar at a specific time and date. The receivers' pagers will flash a green light when they get the invitation and they can then send an RSVP to the sender. The invitation also includes a message area concerning the invitation–the default message is, of course, "for Miller Time."

The infrared broadcasts of useful information and discount coupons from telephone kiosks are based on the same idea. Advertisers can send information from outdoor media like telephone kiosks and bus shelters directly onto Palm PDAs (personal digital assistants) and wireless phones. A blinking red light on the outdoor media lets consumers know that information can be downloaded onto their device and a small infrared broadcasting device within the media display sends information to all compatible devices within its range. When users point their device at the light, they receive a message asking whether they want to download the information. If they do, the information will be stored on their handheld device. Users can get news updates from a news media advertisement, or show times for a movie at a nearby theater (and maybe a coupon for free popcorn). Some advertisers hold trivia contests with prizes and I even saw one clever content-oriented ad for a book that allowed people to download a portion of the book to be read as an enticement for buying the book. Another clever "ad gadget" that also serves a useful purpose is the FunPad, which is the first wireless device designed to entertain customers while they wait for a table or for their meal, which can certainly feel like an eternity when people are hungry. It features ads and branding within games, movie previews, promotions, and videos. It has an eight-inch touch-navigation screen and rubberized handgrips that vibrate for a sensory effect. It also has two high-fidelity speakers, a joystick, and game buttons, a video/still camera, a monochrome printer, and a credit card reader to make purchases. Each FunPad displays company logos on the edges of the screen. When a customer touches a logo, the screen displays that advertiser's content, which could be a TV spot, a game, a promotion, or a chance to buy the advertiser's product. Advertisers pay on a cost-per-click basis, at 20 cents per click, with revenue divided between the company and the restaurant. Some people may find this gadget overly commercial for a restaurant experience and a turn-off for that reason, but the great thing about them is that they are not collectively viewed–a customer can choose to play with them or not.

In Asia, wireless campaigns using text messages via a "short mes-saging system" (SMS)–text messages limited to 160 characters–are becoming common. Coca-Cola launched an SMS campaign in Singapore to promote its new fruit juice, Qoo, with tremendous suc-cess. The company sent a picture message of the blue-skinned, bal-loon-headed Qoo animated character to 500 teenage role models, encouraging them to pass it on to their friends. About half a million mobile users in Singapore received the message and within nine weeks Qoo became the number one juice drink in Singapore. June Kong, Coca-Cola's spokesperson in Singapore, says, "I think SMS speaks to this group of people, especially when traditional methods like TV campaigns are less effective."[5]

One thing is for certain–these high-tech "gadgets" will keep coming and marketers will be faced with more and more decisions about the overall presence of their brand in the market. With the objective of being a true Citizen Brand that contributes to people's lives in valu-able ways, those choices will be much easier to make. The big idea is choice–do you or don't you want the intrusion? In empowering people to access commercial messages when they want to, you cre-ate a most effective way to communicate–to a willing audience.

Attention Please! The Art of Seduction
Brand presence initiatives need to continually surprise us with cre-ative solutions to the problem of capturing our attention. It is an invisible dance, a silent dialogue between the brand and the people. Absolut, a master of the art of seducing our attention through cre-ative brand expressions, once again demonstrated its emotional understanding of people during the California energy crisis. During the worst part of the crisis in the summer of 2001, when there were many electricity blackouts, Absolut created a solar-powered bill-board and placed it on Sunset Boulevard in Los Angeles. The solar panels powered 210 light bulbs that spelled out the headline "Absolut Alternative." This was a very special way for a brand to show its sol-idarity with people during a very trying time.

What is also so great about the Absolut ads overall, is that they never cease to surprise us. It is like an ongoing conceptual game that involves consumers more each time they see a new portrayal of the Absolut brand. The great use of the element of surprise in these ads

Absolut ads overall never cease to surprise us.

is not to be underestimated in importance. People love to be surprised. Potentially mundane promotions can become something very different if they make use of the element of surprise. For example, in order to advertise a promotion, Starwood Hotels and Resorts had terrific success with a promotional ploy when it placed 300,000 false passports around airports and taxi stands in Chicago, New York, and San Francisco. Inside each faux passport was an invitation to play the "Win the World" game from Starwood Hotels and Resorts. The "passports" were actually a four-page booklet explaining how to play the game, the prizes that could be won, and the rules of the game.

A well-loved, ubiquitous brand can also gain a great deal through the element of surprise by suddenly showing us a new face. Nike, an incredibly ubiquitous brand, understands that it now needs to "work backwards," in a sense, in order to continually create new and deepening emotional connections with people. One clever, highly unorthodox brand presence campaign Nike developed to help push its image toward a more fashion-oriented concept was to create an "art show" around their product! Nike rented a high-profile gallery in Manhattan's trendy meatpacking district where 182 Nike shoes were displayed on a wall in front

As a Citizen Brand, Nike could sponsor shows for up-and-coming artists or curate brand-relevant shows about product design that makes a real contribution to the art world.

of squares of different colors. Nike hosted an invitation-only opening party that included art critics and then proceeded to attract a wider audience, focusing on the art community and trendsetters. It was a risky move, which could have been perceived as silly or pretentious, but it went over well and was largely successful. Nike's creative director, Stanley Hainsworth, said of the campaign, "One thing I liked about it was the audacity. It was an irreverent thing for Nike to do: put our product in a gallery and call it art. But it was amazing to look at, and it generated buzz in a nontraditional community."[4] Nike could take this initiative much further beyond just asking us to see its product as art by truly becoming involved in the artistic community it wants to infiltrate as a Citizen Brand. As a Citizen Brand, Nike could sponsor shows for up-and-coming artists or curate brand-relevant shows about product design that makes a real contribution to the art world.

A crucial part of the art of seduction is also, of course, appealing to people through the senses. The Nike art-gallery show certainly appealed to the sense of sight by offering an entirely new visual experience of the brand. Coca-Cola is taking the sensory brand-presence approach much further to envelop several of the senses at once with fully branded entertainment pavilions in the Las Vegas Monorail system. The Coca-Cola station is to be built in the shape of a Coke bottle. Then, when a train goes into the pavilion's bottleneck, passengers will hear the sound of cracking ice and fizzing Coke and smell the scent of Coca-Cola.

The Content Craze

As our world of media continues to rapidly change, the effects on the process of the merging of entertainment/cultural content and branding messages are numerous. With the advent of Replay TV, TiVo, and the new generation of computers that can download television programming, all of which allow viewers to zap through or skip commercials, the trend that Jack Feuer at *Adweek* has called "entertising," and others have called "advertainment," has become a new reality. Brands such as Coca-Cola and Victoria's Secret are making forays into prime-time TV. Ad agencies are quickly developing news ways of working with the entertainment industry, such as the joint venture deal WPP has just made with the U.K. production company Shine Entertainment to create TV shows. The more traditional marketing strategy of product placement has become much more commonplace on television and in films.

As brands move into these new ways of connecting with people, the important thing to remember is to find ways to connect to people emotionally. Product placement has worked incredibly well for some brands, like Oakely sunglasses, which saw its sales soar after appearing on Tom Cruise's face in *Mission Impossible 2*. Because product placement does not interrupt the flow of the program or film, some people feel it is less obtrusive than other forms of advertising, but here again, brands have to be careful not to inundate people with brand messages when they are not expecting it. I personally despised the movie *Cast Away* because the overt commercialism caught me unawares. I thought I was going to see a movie–not a two-hour-long commercial for Federal Express!

But initiatives such as Interpublic's purchasing of two of the most powerful publicity firms in America (PMK and Huvane Baum Halls) with the goal of making deals with all of the major Hollywood celebrities in order to pair them up in commercial endeavors with their major corporate clients can only mean that more movies like *Cast Away* are on their way to us very soon. As the "entertising" movement picks up more and more momentum, I expect we will increasingly see an opposing movement of underground or elitist works of art created by those who are striving for a more "pure" creative expression, which it is important to recognize the need for and respect. One needed only to log on to the fan bulletin board for Talking Head's David Byrne (*www.davidbyrne.com*) after the announcement was made that his song "Like Humans Do" would be used as the promotional song for Microsoft's Windows XP operating system to understand the intensity of feeling people have on this subject. Fans overwhelmingly felt betrayed that this icon of artistic independence (and anti-commercialism) had "sold out." The monumental painter Julian Schnabel, who recently completed his second film, *Before Night Falls*, about the life of the Cuban writer Reinaldo Arenas, also takes a stand on this subject. In a recent interview in the *New York Times*, he is quoted as saying, "I watch a movie like *Cast Away* and I want to commit hara-kiri. The dumb lobby, the money lobby–there are companies that would rather make one dumb movie for $200 million than twenty $10 million movies that might have some meaning."[5] While statements like this clearly show that the tension between art and commerce is alive and well, other artists will certainly embrace the "entertising" movement on their own terms and show just how it is possible to wed the two worlds without compromising the quality of content. BMW USA adopted this strategy and got amazing results. It hired some of the hottest directors, such as Ang Lee (*Crouching Tiger, Hidden Dragon*) and Guy Ritchie (*Snatch*), to make five short films (not TV commercials) promoting the BMW brand with actors like Madonna and Mickey Rourke. BMW allowed each director to shape the films according to his own vision, and, although the films certainly promote the qualities of the cars (speed, agility, etc.) and they are, of course, the cars driven by the "good guys," there are no other overt marketing messages in the storylines. This was a very smart choice because it means that the films have a certain artistic integrity. The viewers certainly know that they are being marketed to, but they are being offered something of value in exchange for their precious time and attention. Content as entertaining and well done as this can only enhance the brand image immeasurably. The six-minute, streaming media films can be seen on the Website *www.BMWfilms.com*, which is a wonderful Web site full of interesting content about independent film. In addition to the BMW Web site, the films were promoted through previews in theatres and on TV, in print ads and in magazine articles. Later this year, they will also be made available as a compilation DVD, along with extra information and images. This is a great example of how to combine culture and commercialism and it has been a huge success story for the brand. Since the launch in April, the films have been downloaded 6 million times and BMW's U.S. sales are up 32 percent from a year ago.

Of course, the difference between the BMW short films and a movie like *Cast Away* is that people know beforehand that the entertainment offered conveys a brand message. This is often a better approach than product placement by sheer virtue of honesty. Victoria's Secret prime-time one-hour ABC special was clearly all about promoting the brand and people loved it. The appearance of VS supermodels on shows such as *Spin City* and *Who Wants to Be a Millionaire* prior to the special was also as a huge success. At a reported cost of $6 million, the lin-

Of course, the difference between the BMW short films and a movie like *Cast Away* is that people know beforehand that the entertainment offered conveys a brand message.

gerie retailer's show drew extensive publicity as well as 12.4 million views and a robust Nielsen Media Research 4.4 rating and 10-share among adults aged eighteen to forty-nine. Victoria's Secret's sales for the four following weeks were up 9 percent.

Coca-Cola, for its part, is spending $6 million to be seen everywhere within and around a new teen TV show called *Young Americans.* Coke will have numerous product placements within the show, at least three Coke commercials per episode, and the brand will be mentioned in every ad for the show itself. This broad-ranging sponsorship demonstrates Coca-Cola's new intense advertising philosophy. The company wanted to really push the limits in order to stand out from all the other advertising noise on television. The first episode was heavily saturated with images of Coke (the show's stars were shown in slow motion while drinking Coke), among other product placements. When asked if he is not afraid that teens will reject the in-show commercialization, Coke executive Jeff Dunn says, "No. Teens actually expect it; as long as the content is real and authentic, they're cool. They've moved from cynical to savvy." Whether or not Cola-Cola is right in its analysis (and it may be right in terms of the specific population of teens it is trying to reach via TV), it could explore also an emotionally impactful way of reaching this group and creating excitement around its product. Coke could develop its own films, like BMW, or create a music-video awards show, or even create a film school for kids to learn about the art of independent filmmaking.

Apart from TV, the Internet, and film, more traditional forms of entertainment are also joining the "entertising" movement. Bulgari is one of the first brands to attempt a branding campaign through a book. Its much talked about initiative of hiring author Fay Weldon to write the book *The Bulgari Connection* was certainly original and seems to have been successful in terms of creating a buzz around the brand. Bulgari gave the author free rein in terms of creative license, and the story line follows its own path, with, naturally, Bulgari jewels as a main element of the plot. Now, advertisements are being placed inside books as well. One of the best examples of this is a series of short novels written for young urban kids—eight pages of advertising are inserted in each compact-disk-size paperback. As a marketing tie-in, the first 50,000 copies of each book will also be packaged with an original hip-hop compilation CD from Def Jam records. The retail strategy is also innovative: The novels will be sold mainly in music stores like Tower Records and Virgin Megastores, hip-hop clothing shops, and some independent bookstores aimed at a hip hop audience—all of them places where the kids hang out. The cost to advertise on one page is $5,000, and the book will be sold for $16.99.

Guerrilla Marketing Mania

Guerrilla marketing methods are gaining even more favor as marketers seek to garner attention by any means necessary in an increasingly difficult economic climate. However, as these methods become more and more prevalent, we are again faced with the "privacy issue." The power of guerrilla marketing lies in its ability to reach people on intimate levels in their everyday lives and surprise them. However, this can truly backfire if the surprise is an unwelcome one and perceived as an intrusion. A Citizen Brand must make it its business to differentiate between what will be perceived as a delightful, fun, or interesting brand experience and what will come across as obnoxious. In the interest of creating that all-important buzz and test creative limits with outrageous promotional stunts, emotional sensitivity is sometimes left out of the picture.

The recently growing initiatives within this "viral marketing" movement where undercover marketers are placed in everyday situations to promote products in a word-of-mouth fashion is inherently flawed from an Emotional Branding/Citizen Brand perspective because it is dishonest and manip-

The recently growing initiatives within this "viral marketing" movement, where undercover marketers are placed in everyday situations to promote products in a word-of-mouth fashion is inherently flawed from an Emotional Branding/Citizen Brand perspective because it is dishonest.

ulative and risks doing more damage than good if people realize they've been unwittingly "hit on" by a brand. This marketing technique is especially popular with brands targeting Generation Y trendsetters. Big Fat Inc., a buzz marketer with fifty "operatives" in thirty cities, has seen its billings increase fivefold since last year. Big Fat Inc. handles marketing projects of this kind, such as promoting a particular vodka brand by sending trendy twenty-somethings out into bars to buy people drinks and slip a brand message into the conversation. John Palumbo, the CEO, says, "In order for a product to really succeed right now, the product has to have credibility, people have to see it, they have to understand in a real way, and the only way for them to understand it . . . is for it to be in their world. That's what we do. We put it in their life." However, Generation Y (or perhaps any other generation for that matter) is not so slow to sense the "marketing vibe" in these situations and when they do, they often find it creepy. I recently read a description of one such encounter where a young man in a bar was approached by another hip-looking young man who seemed to want to make friends and gave him a CD of some new music that he claimed would be the "next big thing"– then left to pursue other potential targets. The young man realized that this person was not a new friend, but a marketer and was annoyed with this subterranean approach. Perhaps the idea is that the target person will be so thrilled with the free product sample that he will not even care why or how it was given to him. But I think this is a mistake. It would be better to have hip, trendy people who resemble the consumer target group for a CD, for example, go to a bar and say honestly that they are promoting a CD for their client and offer a free sample copy. If the marketer is truly hip and possesses an interesting or charming personality, it can only enhance the brand image, and it doesn't risk offending people through trickery or falseness. In fact, one of the greatest advantages of guerrilla marketing is the opportunity for a person-to-person interaction based on the brand. A now very popular and effective initiative (and therefore, by definition, no longer truly a "guerrilla" tactic . . .) is ad-wrapping the vehicle of a trendsetter or "brand-appropriate" person who then hands out product samples throughout the daily course of his life.

Peapod, a company that sells and delivers food, produce, and other merchandise sold by supermarkets owned by the Dutch food retailing giant Royal Ahold, has been using the New York agency Stain, which specializes in buzz branding through ideas that create conversation to market their services. Mike Brennan, senior vice president for product management and marketing for Peapod says, "More than 20 percent of our customers come from word-of-mouth programs, so to grow buzz is key to us to grow the business." For Peapod, Stain is creating a twist on the promotional ploy known as door hangers, which typically consist of literature or product samples placed inside plastic bags that are left on the doorknobs of the front doors of apartments or homes. The Peapod door hangers are full-size grocery bags, printed not with the names of supermarkets but with messages like, "Five minutes in front of your computer last night and this would be full," and, "This is a test to see if it's easy to deliver groceries to your door, and it is."

The Stain agency often invents its own media forms to get people's attention. For instance, Stain "sprinkled New York City with quarters" for its client Basics Furniture. The quarters, "left on the streets and in coin-return slots" of pay telephones, he adds, were plastered with stickers reading, "Hi, Thrifty, we've got your furniture," along with the Basics phone number. Other examples of what the agency calls "invented media" are thin sheets of plastic that use static to cling to train windows, and another idea that Stain submitted to Peapod, which they have yet to sign off on, is to print on sticky message pads, "Honey, don't stop for milk on your way home," then affix the notes to windows of commuter trains that run from downtown Chicago to the adjacent suburbs so that people would see them on trains as they're heading home.

If done right, guerrilla marketing can be the very best way to reach Generation Y. For example, the American Legacy Foundation's 2001 "Truth" anti-smoking campaign, which specifically targeted teenagers, has been a real guerrilla marketing success. The campaign had teenagers themselves filmed participating in various activist events, all of which were extremely imaginative and well executed. To address the little known truth about the toxic ingredients in cigarettes, for example, the teens walked around the executive halls of a major cigarette company (until they were asked to leave) with pitchers of what they called "Amonia-aide," offering glasses of their concoction to passersby, explaining that since ammonia is added to cigarettes, it seemed like a fine thing to put in Lemonade . . . Another spot showed teens putting signs in dog poop in the street that said "Ammonia is found in dog poop. Tobacco companies add it to cigarettes."

CASE STUDY: RED BULL

Since its entrance into the U.S. market in 1997, Red Bull has shown itself to be a champion of guerrilla marketing techniques, which have brought it the incredible success of a virtual cult-like following. Red Bull commands 65 percent of the energy drink category with sales of $130 million wholesale in 2000, up from $12 million in 1997. First of all, the company had decided that instead of relying on existing infrastructure for distribution, it would create its own channels. Small distributors dedicate themselves to the product, set up their own warehouses, and deliver the drinks in Red-Bull branded vans. They managed to sell the company's product in nontraditional venues, such as nightclubs, bars, record stores, and hair salons. Red Bull's sales and marketing units are decentralized and operate in an entrepreneurial manner, with the goal of staying relevant to its market always the top priority. Teams scout out the popular venues of the trendy crowd in an area and then infiltrate them. Alternative sports venues and events like snowboarding contests have been one of the biggest focal points. Red Bull also hires hip locals in an area to drive around in a Red Bull–logoed car and hand out samples. The company intuitively demonstrates an understanding of the fact that a tactic that might work in New York may not work in Florida, so each market receives a very different treatment.

One of Red Bull's recent creative programs was to begin the "Red Bull Music Academy," a school for aspiring deejays with idolized "master spinners" as teachers. The Academy has hosted classes for the past four years in Berlin, Dublin, and New York. This is unique because instead of approaching deejays and asking them to push their product or hand out T-shirts, Red Bull is actually helping music lovers fulfill a dream and contributing something tangible to the culture of this scene. The result of this kind of brand experience is that the emotional connection is more organic and when the participants talk about their experience, it is likely they will mention Red Bull in a very positive light.

The elements of surprise and humor are also important aspects of guerrilla marketing campaigns. The BooneOakley ad agency made such intelligent use of the element of surprise in a billboard ad for a job-search Web site in the fall of 2000 that it became a media coup. They put up a billboard promoting "Gore 2000" that showed instead a photograph of Republican candidate George W. Bush. The national news media picked up the story, assuming it was a real error on the part of the Gore campaign and the amusing visual was shown on *CNN* and *Good Morning America*. The agency pretended to have made the mistake in earnest, but a week later a second ad for job-search site 123hire.com was put up that read "Today's job opening: Proofreader." The correction also made national news media.

As a final note on brand presence, I want to emphasize that the greatest challenge today for brand-presence programs is to present a cohesive brand identity across all of the various media, which conveys a consistent message while maintaining enough flexibility to reach different groups of people in different environments. The intelligence and sensitivity required to do this successfully will be cultivated on an ongoing basis by the true Citizen Brands.

9

The Ninth Commandment: Evolve from Communication to Dialogue

Communication is telling. ***Dialogue is sharing.***

What are some of the evolving ways to create a real, meaningful dialogue with consumers? Innovative initiatives include customization and other ways of involving consumers in various levels of the product development and marketing process. The Internet, with its powerful ability to break down the old brand/consumer walls is creating a new forum for this dialogue. Interesting progress is being made in the field of ethnography to get inside consumers' day-to-day lives, talk to and, above all, listen to them, to learn the truth of how they really feel about things.

In a tough economy where competition is more fierce, desperation sets in and the hunt for "consumers" gets going. "Smoking them out of their hiding places" (those consumers) is a mild way to describe the actions that some corporations will take as they pursue any and every technique to find their target audience. So, it seems there is a war happening on the branding battlefield between armies of marketers and their consultants and a new breed of consumers whose agility in escaping the media guns and sapping the juice from any communication strategy is notorious. The ironic part of all this is that so-called consumers are really a bunch of smart people who are watching in awe as desperate corporations push harder and harder even when confronted with rejection and failure.

Corporations today spend fortunes inventing and employing a myriad of weapons to avoid cannibalization, competitor shelf dominance, or the loss of market share. And weapons there are: from promotions to ambush marketing, enhanced media coverage, advertising to individual households, demographic profiling, and wide-scale deployment of broadband services or multiple-channel deployment. Viral marketing is the new term for what should be the fatal blow.

The worst enemies are those, god forbid, "ad-skipping types"–these men and women of different nationalities, gender, cultures, races, and sexual preference who are trying to escape the dreams given to them by commercialization. This enemy is hiding, difficult to recognize, and terrifying when determined to fight a brand back.

But marketers have plenty of determination and imagination to boot. For one thing, as I emphasized in chapter 8, there is not one iota of space in the world that will not soon be covered by some sort of brand message. Not one moving vehicle including buses, individual, personal automobiles, bicycles and skateboards, or items of clothing will be spared. Perhaps people's nails will soon become the latest idea for creating a brand's visibility and the backs of our heads will be shaved or tattooed to display a trademark. The Internet, television, and cinemas will be commercial minefields from which no costumer will escape. Commercial messages will pop up, ambushing you wherever you go, including ads in bathrooms–such as the ones I found promoting hamburgers in the men's room at the Smithsonian museum!

Perhaps people's nails will soon become the latest idea for creating a brand's visibility and the backs of our heads will be shaved or tattooed to display a trademark.

If this continues the Grand Canyon will soon be renamed "deep Sony," and the state of Connecticut after Pepperidge Farms! It seems that the accepted solution for marketers today is "more" when in this world the objective should be "smarter." People love brands and want to interact with them. We want brands that bring solutions to our lives. If this madness continues, we will have a rejection phenomenon or, worse, a jaded attitude that will defeat the partnership that needs to exist between people and brands. Brands are not at war and people don't want to be ambushed. In the United States, the sensitivity toward consumers might not be as high as in other countries where media is more regulated and people are more protective about their space, but still, brands will not be able to ignore customers' responses to this siege, nor will they be able to ignore customers' true needs.

The focus on creating brand awareness is so strong that, in presenting the 2001 U.S. Open trophy, the president of Lincoln praised the runner up and hugely popular sports figure Pete Sampras and could not avoid comparing Pete and Lincoln with the statement, ". . . from an icon like Lincoln to an icon like Pete Sampras. . . ." That was so pathetic and lame that it bordered on the ridiculous; and the public smiled politely. Not one iota of emotion was expressed.

There is always a defining moment in any endeavor we make in life and the same applies to brands.

There is always a defining moment in any endeavor we make in life and the same applies to brands; in this case, the split-second opportunity that existed to link the brand's emotional values to people's emotional mood on television in front of a worldwide audience was botched by this overtly commercial statement.

Pete Sampras had given the world one of the best tennis matches of his career, where he beat Agassi in what everyone considered to be one of the most moving semifinals of the U.S. Open. Two aging giants fighting for what would be one of their final shots for glory in these sought-after finals. A few days later Pete Sampras's defeat for the title to Lleyton Hewitt signaled the passing of the baton to a younger player. In a very moving speech Sampras, the leader of the tennis world acknowledged the talent and promising future of the winner, by identifying him as his successor.

Lincoln, as the sponsor, could have been in this moment a part of history. This defining moment could have given the brand a huge lift. The only word that should have been uttered was "legendary." Instead of attempting to compare a car not on the charts as one of the ultimate driving machines to the ultimate tennis machine, Lincoln could have acknowledged in a more subtle manner its pride in being associated with this moment. Lincoln is no icon and certainly no Sampras but they are both legends, part of the American dream. The press would have made the connection, the public would have made the emotional connection between the two, and Lincoln would have been with Pete on the podium. The communication was made, but people were not engaged in a more meaningful dialogue of ideas. The speech fell flat.

From the Outside In

People want to embrace and vibrate emotionally with a brand. People want to learn, want to have fun, share information, and be part of the process. The best ideas are the ones that intrigue people and excite their sense of adventure and discovery. People love interactive relationships. People love to be part of the creative process. The tribe is key here—people are gravitating toward communities of like-minded citizens. Truly convincing one person is convincing many, as groups will endorse each others' recommendations. The power of word of mouth is alive and well and people are very willing to participate in a process if they really believe in something. The problem is that corporations want to box people in when people want to define their relationships with corporations on their own terms. Corporations want to cram messages down customers' throats when people just want a little treat out of life. Corporations are obsessed with getting their message across when people need a little therapy and, above all, to be stress free once in a while. Corporations are invasive, but people want more privacy. What is wrong with today's marketing model? Why can't people seek ads and review them when they want? Ads of the future may well look like *Cast Away* with its promotion of Federal Express, but people will have the foreknowledge that it is a "commercial." In a true citizen sense a new relationship needs to be built through more effective studies and messages. People are starting to say: Instead of being bombarded, why not be supported?

In order to create this kind of added value and supportive relationship, the brand has to first find a powerful emotional link with the consumer. Finding a brand's emotional links requires interacting with its customers, then integrating marketing and sales efforts. *It is primarily an outside-in process—based on what customers tell us about their needs, interests, and desires—rather than the traditional inside-out or product-sell model.* Outside-in is about inspiring people emo-

The tribe is key here—people are gravitating toward communities of like-minded citizens. Truly convincing one person is convincing many, as groups will endorse each others' recommendations.

tionally to become involved in a dialogue with the brand to the degree that they become a brand advocate. It is about igniting the passion of consumers so that they want to talk to the brand and to their friends about the brand. Once this passion is ignited, all the brand has to do is listen and act on what it learns from people! This model makes so much more sense because it means finding people who are really and truly interested in what the brand has to offer–it is a win-win situation.

The People's Forum: What We Can Learn from the Web

Clearly, in order to create an "outside-in" marketing model that will result in a people/brand dialogue, there must be a forum for people to talk to the brand. The Web, a powerful interactive medium that puts people in charge, is the perfect forum for this dialogue. Because it presents layered access to information, it allows people to choose and empowers them to find whatever information they wish in whatever depth and amount they wish. It uses people's smarts and can satisfy their intellectual curiosity, and bring visual- and sound-oriented sensory experiences to them. The key is in making the communication an interactive game where the people participate willingly. The investment necessary in dictated media is more expensive, less effective, and more polluting for the environment and the mind. The most exciting thing about the Internet as a medium, however, is that it has not yet reached its full potential and opportunities are unlimited as far as how corporations can partner with people through this vehicle.

Seth Godin, author of *Permission Marketing,* recommends that marketers "turn their ideas into epidemics by helping their customers to do the marketing for them." He goes on to explain that this can be done through creating powerful consumer networks. The fact is that the Web can do this quicker and more efficiently than any other medium. Take, for example, the case of Tamim Ansary. This Afghan-American sent a letter to twenty people, revealing the plight of the Afghan people and begging America not to bomb right after September 11. The letter ended up spreading like wildfire around America; it was posted on major Web sites, printed in newspapers, and eventually landed Tamim Ansary a spot on *Charlie Rose, Nightline,* and *Oprah.* According to the *New York Times Magazine,* millions might have seen the letter. Many others have leveraged the

Web to accomplish significant things in the realm of politics, health, and so on. In fact, a study by Cone/Roper indicates that there are over 50 million social activists on the Web who use it to pool information about their concerns and create like-minded communities.

The strange fact is that while the people are tapping into the power of the Web, companies are not! Just think what this transformative power could mean for brands. But it is not being used that way. Companies send boring e-mails that are just another version of direct mail or print ads. Companies post annoying, uninventive banner ads. But what

The strange fact is that while the people are tapping into the power of the Web, companies are not!

about creating a community and letting the people come to the brand? What about creating a marketing program that is so enticing, interactive, and inventive that people could not help but become involved? This is how a very smart group of marketers went about promoting the movie *A. I.: Artificial Intelligence.* A Web address was listed on the movie's promotional posters to create a highly interactive game where people who went to the Web site were lead through a series of intriguing clues, from Web site to Web site (over 1,000 were created), from e-mail to e-mail, to solve a mystery–which they did not know was set up to be a game! In some cases the people "playing" this game even received phone calls, from someone playing a role in the game, containing a piece of information or clue to lead them further into the game. Anyone observing this could see how much the Web feeds our curiosity and desire to get to the bottom of things! Eventually, the different people playing the game were led to one another to communicate and share their pieces of information, furthering the story bit by bit. In fact, the game was intentionally designed to be too complex for a single player to solve–in this way a virtual community was created and 7,000 of the players created a Web site of their own to crack the mystery. This ingenious, well-orchestrated promotion worked so well that I am sure we will see much more use of this kind of communications maze approach in the future.

The formulas that seem to work the best on the Web are based on this concept of community where people can talk to one another and share information, thoughts, and feelings. It is no mistake that iVillage, the women's content and community Web site, is one of the most heavily trafficked Web destinations since it has mastered this idea in the architecture and content of the site. iVillage and its sister site, Women.com, provide women with a quality, in-depth experience of community. The site is replete with content that addresses all aspects of a woman's life from health care to relationships to careers to parenting to finances to food to entertainment, and,

The formulas that seem to work the best on the Web are based on this concept of community where people can talk to one another and share information, thoughts, and feelings.

above all, it provides plenty of opportunities for women to communicate with one another and bond. Because the site has built a strong trust factor with women, it is very successful in integrating interactive branding programs. For example, iVillage launched a health-content link, in partnership with Coca-Cola's Dansani, that is very well executed and gives women a very different kind of brand experience than a mere pop-up or banner ad would because it addresses in a holistic manner a woman's health concerns. Another recent ad on iVillage for Pantene hair products takes the pop-up format further by offering a questionnaire for women to fill out about their hair type, color, questions, etc., which when submitted responds with recommendations not only for products, but also for styling and general

iVillage. Results.

iVillage is one of the women's content and community Web sites that is the most heavily visited.

hair-care suggestions. This value-added approach is so much more interesting for people because it gives them something useful! Weight Watchers' new Web site has also become a forum where women can share their concerns about weight loss, ask questions, and get support or take online classes in total privacy. This site is hugely successful because it has become a true interactive community.

A retail Web site that promises to be excellent in terms of exploring the interactive, dialogue-oriented potential of the Web is the site for the Remo store, the terrific "general store" with quality eclectic merchandise. This site is built on the philosophy of "B *equals* C" (as opposed to B *to* C), where the customer becomes an integral part of the business process by voting on products for their inclusion in the site and making merchandising recommendations. The site is based on a membership approach with people "sponsoring" friends and family to become new members in the site so that they can have access to the great products and prices.

Another great example of how to use the Web to foster a brand relationship with people is how Elle Girl used its own Web site and the highly popular Web site "alloy.com" to create a new concept for its magazine in partnership with its readers, teenage girls. In this highly creative initiative, Elle Girl asked teenage girls to help it pick from nine contestants a boy the magazine would hire to be "Dr. Boy," a love advice columnist. The Web site featured videos of the boys from which the girls could determine which guy was the nicest and best candidate for helping girls with any issues

Another great example of how to use the Web to foster a brand relationship with people is how *Elle Girl* used its own Web site and the highly popular Web site "alloy.com" to create a new concept for its magazine in partnership with its readers.

concerning the opposite sex. I spoke to Francois Vincens, the SVP group editorial director about this program, and he told me the initiative was a great success. He emphasized that with teenagers the Web has a great deal of potential when used as a community/dialogue-oriented device, as opposed to using it purely as a commerce interface. He confirmed to me that teens do not really like to shop on the Internet—only 1 percent of their purchases are made there! This generation promises to have a huge influence on the Web and the new formats developing there. While Gen Y could eventually begin to shop more on the Web as they grow older, their primary percep-

Elle Girl official advice guy, Dr. Boy, was voted into his job by visitors to the Elle Web who chose him from several other candidates.

tion of the Web will always be that of an empowering tool that can add dimension to their lives from a social, informational, and entertainment perspective.

Customization: The Power of Choice

Of course, the whole concept of customization relies on the existence of a real dialogue between the consumer and the brand. One of the greatest advantages of customizing products for people is that it can lead to a fierce brand loyalty since the product has been customized just for them. Why switch brands when you've managed to co-create a product that perfectly suits your needs? Another great advantage to mass customization is that it creates a constant feedback loop with customers, which enables a company to react quickly to changing demand, allowing the brand to see and react swiftly to constantly changing cultural trends.

This is part of why Gen Y is one of the groups most interested in customization, which is used by this group less for practical purposes than it is as a great, inexpensive way to achieve self-expression. For years they have been retooling their inexpensive compact cars to make them faster, flashier, and cooler with new racing

wheels and blasting stereos through a process called "slamming."
Now automakers are beginning to release economy cars in different
"preslammed" versions to make these kids happy. Mitsubishi Motor
rolled out a $14,000 Lancer sedan and at the same time released
modified versions with spoilers and bright colors like "lightning yel-
low." Mazda is upgrading its Protegé sedan with a faster engine,
lowered suspension, and a 280-watt sound system that plays MP3
music files. General Motors is expected to launch an affordable, all-
inclusive model that reflects young car buyers' aspiration for a
hotrod, racer look. And Pontiac's new Vibe hatchback, which has
been "preslammed" with a more powerful engine, racy alloy wheels,
and flashy interior features, is set to be launched in 2002. In Europe,
the Smart car, an eight-feet-long and five-feet-wide joint venture
between the German Daimler Chrysler and Swiss watchmaker
Swatch, is a big hit. This bubble-shaped car, easy to park and eco-
friendly, comes in nine different psychedelic neon colors that are
easily and cheaply changeable—people "wear" them almost as a
fashion statement.

Another company, Visteon, is currently developing technology
that allows people to design their own car dashboard, including the
color and size of their car's dials, gauges, and speedometer. The
dashboards will include an optional baby-watch feature, which lets
you view the back seat via a video camera feed, as well as displays
of traffic updates and compass readings.

Of course, one of the best, most efficient ways to implement a
customization process is through the interactive medium of the
Web. The Web allows customization opportunities impossible to
deliver a few years ago and this option will only continue to grow as the process becomes ever more streamlined and refined from an operational standpoint.

The Web allows customization opportunities impossible to deliver a few years ago and this option will only continue to grow as the process becomes ever more streamlined and refined from an operational standpoint.

Nike has been offering online customers the option of configuring their own shoes since 1999. Customers can choose between twenty models, customize the colors, and add a name ID to the shoes. Now Nike is also
offering customized cushioning for running shoes. Land's End has
had a very successful online customization business for quite some
time as well, which it is currently expanding with more products.
The appeal of made-to-order clothing is about convenience and fit,

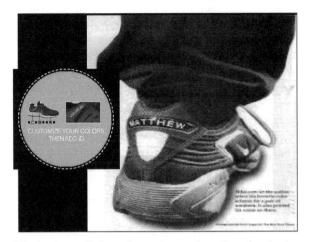

Nike has been offering online customers the option of customizing their own shoes since 1999.

and in some instances it can be particularly useful since some generations with changing weight problems may find it somewhat traumatic to try on products that do not work in front of sales people and fellow customers. The best mass-customization initiatives come from observing people's needs on both a practical and emotional level and recognizing a real opportunity to make people's lives better. Sometimes mass customization can serve as a true Citizen Brand solution to a problem in people's lives in a very humanistic way. When Bradford Oberwager, president of Acumin Corp. in Philadelphia, saw firsthand the vitamin industry's lack of empathy for its customers when his sister had to swallow dozens of pills each day following radiation treatments for cancer, it gave him the idea to found Acumin, which offers customized multivitamins that can be taken in fewer swallows. Acumin can put all the vitamins a customer wants in dosages tailored to the individual's needs, age, and lifestyle-and then fits them in two or three pills instead of the customary seven or eight. For people who take a lot of vitamins, customization also makes Acumin's products a better bargain than vitamins found at the corner drugstore.

Customization, no matter what form it takes, is all about giving the power over manufacturing back to the people.

The Web is–slowly but surely–empowering other media to reach consumers in new, more interactive ways. As broadband service grows, the rollout of "interactive-TV" services is expected to accelerate. UBS analysts forecast that "the interactive-applications industry, as characterized by VOD (video on demand), t-commerce (shopping), and interactive advertising will grow at a combined compound annual rate of approximately 100% between 2001 and 2004."[1]

The growing medium of interactive TV promises to substantially change the way companies market to people by transforming what is now a passive medium into an active way of building stronger ties with individuals who actually ask to be marketed to rather than being forced to evade intrusive pitches. It quite simply creates the possibility of an "opt-in" relationship.

TiVo and other marketers of iTV applications, which allow consumers a great deal of control in how they are marketed to, have caused marketers today to experiment with many solutions to the "ad-skipping" phenomenon. These include picture-in-picture formats to deliver ads that are reduced in size but reside in the larger frame when consumers fast forward, text-over-video, where the marketer's brand, logo, or copy is placed over the fast-forwarded image; and telescoping ads that enable viewers to click onto a longer form of video similar to an infomercial. The most interesting of these solutions, and the ones that will work because they will empower the people, are the formats that allow people to enter into a dialogue with the brand in a natural, noninvasive manner–in other words, following the consumer's initiative. This will bring more content/commerce partnerships, as we discussed in chapter 8. As long as these "opt-in" commercials are done in a way that does not spoil the content but enhances the experience for the viewer, they will be successful. For example, when watching a show on TV, if the viewer is able to find further information about an actor, such as his bio, and this includes information about the clothing brands the actor is wearing in a scene, with links to commercials and shopping sites, both the brand and the content could be dimensionalized, thereby creating a rich emotional experience for the viewer.

This interactive revolution is in the process of creating advertising that is "targetable" by network, by individual household, and by demographic profile–and really, in the end, by individual.

Another form of Interactive marketing that is growing has people downloading specific informational screens to their computers that will enable them to receive certain information (via e-mail) about certain products or services that interest them. This concept will be incredibly important in the future of iTV as well. The way this is working for now is that a wireless application lets a customer request information about what he is looking at or reading at that moment by a "Power DOT," which is a new type of bar code that is scanned by a Personal Information Assistant (PIA). Once the Power DOT is scanned, an e-mail is sent to the customer, which contains specific information associated with the Power DOT he tapped. For example, a person looking at the event listings in a newspaper can receive concert schedules or a list of bands playing at a local club; a Power DOT in a catalog can provide instant product/purchasing information, and detailed company information can be requested by scanning the DOT on, for instance, a business card. After the scanned Power DOTS are uploaded into the PC, the PC uses its existing Internet connection to contact Power DOT's server, which delivers the requested content immediately by e-mail.

This interactive revolution is in the process of creating advertising that is "targetable" by network, by individual household, and by demographic profile— and really, in the end, by individual.

What is really interesting about this is that once the customer registers, the upload process becomes completely automatic. The PC needs only to be turned on. The company providing the service tracks each scan from every ad so that advertisers receive real-time demographics on how many people respond to each ad, what time of the day the publication was read and in what order, how long people read it at one sitting, and so on. This technology is not tied to the PIA device, so in the future, any existing piece of equipment—a cell phone, a computer mouse, a PDA, a pager—could have a Power DOT reader built into it. This system is another way for brands to connect in a real and even helpful or useful way to what people want to know or want to buy—getting desired information and the best products effortlessly and without haste. For people it can mean a quick and simple way to receive tailored information about their interests without having to pick up the phone, tear out pages, or hunt for a Web page.

Democratic Communications: You Oughta Be in Branding

A new, and so far pretty successful wave in branding has been recruiting consumers' help, opinions, and, yes, even creative thinking in designing a brand's commercials, new products, and marketing plans. It makes sense, after all. If you want to win someone's heart, it's a good idea to ask him what he or she wants! Today, it is fast becoming the new expectation, and it can even be detrimental for a well-loved brand to leave its consumers out of the brand-development and marketing process. The car company Mazda was surprised to discover Miata consumers cared a great deal about every little detail in their cars. In 1998, Mazda had the audacity to redesign the cup holder and customers complained vehemently! Now Mazda tests modifications with customers first.

People love to be a part of the process—the potential for emotional involvement is huge here, not to mention the "fun factor." Giant advertisers in competitive categories like beer have been trying to develop closer ties to consumers by involving them more directly in the marketing process. This approach is especially effective with those marketing- and tech-savvy consumers in their twenties and thirties who have demonstrated that they are increasingly interested in the strategies used to sell them goods and services, as evidenced by the attention paid each year to Super Bowl commercials; the ratings for TV specials on funny, foreign, and unusual commercials; and, well, the readership for e-mail newsletters about branding.

People love to be a part of the process— the potential for emotional involvement is huge here, not to mention the "fun factor."

There have been some very clever executions of this concept, which, because of its great potential for creating a real dialogue, will more than likely become a growing trend. Let's take a look at several of the most interesting "democratic" branding executions.

FORD

To launch their Focus model (aimed at entry-level drivers), Ford recently produced live TV ads that gave consumers the possibility to determine which character would appear in the ads as well as make dialogue suggestions. Thirty minutes before each live spot, consumers could go to the Focus Web site (*www.focus247.com*) to determine which of five actors would play and which scene would be used in the next commercial, and a network representative was present on the live set until the very last minute to approve dialogue suggestions submitted by consumers. For the first spot, the site received 15,000 visits!

ICEHOUSE BEER

Plank Road Brewery, a division of the Miller Brewing unit of the Philip Morris Companies, is asking consumers to submit ideas for campaigns for Icehouse, a premium-priced brand of ice beer that is popular primarily in the Southeast. The company's agency, Square One, held a contest and picked the best ideas. The campaign, called "Your Idea Here," was aimed at beer drinkers aged twenty-one to twenty-seven and carried the theme "We'll make the Icehouse, you make the ads." The campaign used television commercials and outdoor ads to entice would-be advertising geniuses to submit ideas by calling a toll-free telephone number (1-800-ICEHOUSE) or visiting the brand's Web site. The rules were simple and presented in a humorous way, "Keep it clean, and stick Icehouse in there somewhere." Jesse Bayer, account director for Plank Road at Square One says, "The idea for the campaign grew from a request from the Icehouse brand team at Plank Road to 're-engage and reconnect with the consumer on an emotional level and go back to the roots of the brand,' which are all about participatory advertising. The campaign to introduce Icehouse in 1994 asked consumers to phone in suggestions for slogans; many commercials based on those ideas were produced, in that instance by the brand's previous agency, Young & Rubicam. Mr. Bayer, says, "The brand has always been very participatory, having a dialog with its consumers," as part of its persona as "a very approachable brand" and "a beer for the regular guy, a very laid-back guy with a sense of humor." The campaign promises to be successful, with close to a dozen of the thousand ideas submitted in production. In each commercial will be a slide showing a photograph of the consumer who came up with the concept of his or her name and city.

BUDWEISER

While Budweiser has not actually produced consumers' ideas about their "Whassup" campaign, they have created a forum in which consumers can participate and share their creative ideas on the company's Web site. After the phenomenal success of the "Whassup?" campaign for Budweiser, DDB Chicago managed to go even further with the concept by launching the hilarious "BCBG" version "What are youuu doing?" which is just like the first one except this time the four black friends are replaced by "snobbish" white guys. Realizing how much people loved the playful stereotyping, Budweiser went on to produce seventeen more ads, including the "How ya doin?" New Jersey Sopranos version. The Web site has now collected new parodies from consumers from around the world, such as the "Whassup" grandmas, or Beavis & Butthead. This has spawned a plethora of "Whassup" Web sites around the globe, as different cultures try their hand at interpreting the "Whassup" concept (my personal favorite is the British "Tea & News" version someone put together!). Since the beginning of this award-winning campaign, Budweiser's sales have grown by 2.4 million barrels, to 99.2 million barrels. Bob Scarpelli, DDB's chief creative officer, says the campaign has "talk value" . . . which creates an emotional reaction and "captures something so true that it ultimately becomes a shorthand for a feeling or a state of mind."

COCA-COLA

Coca-Cola, SC Johnson, and others have agreed to pay consumers for ideas about new products, services, and business processes through a new Web site called Ideas.com. The way it works is that companies post an "idea quest," which is an explanation of the idea they want to receive. Any visitor can then leave an idea on the Web site for the company to see. Some idea quests offer money for the best submissions. The site also allows inventors to propose any idea they have, on an unsolicited basis.

Coca-Cola, SC Johnson, and others have agreed to pay consumers for ideas about new products, services, and business processes through a new Web site called Ideas.com.

Coke has so far requested ideas for beverage packaging, water marketing, and a healthy new drink for kids. The company received eighty-eight idea submissions for the new kids' drink in the first seven days! Coca-Cola solicited consumers' ideas about how to encourage people to drink more water, either through the marketing of Coke's brand Dasani, or through creating a new brand or product, encouraging people to come up with ideas for new devices for the home, office, school, or person on the go. The contest winner was awarded $5,000.

Ethnography: Love Is in the Details

As I've said before, there is an amazing increase in the demographic diversity of America today, which is resulting in a constant evolution of tribes from an ethnic, cultural, and social standpoint. Of course all of these small groups of people–each tribe with its own varying rituals and habits that define it as a group–present a great new challenge for marketers who must find more intimate ways to study their needs and desires.

Focus groups have certainly gotten a very bad rap in this atmosphere and are now looked at as being very passé with new, cutting-edge approaches to uncover the consumers' hearts–from the creative to the just, well, bizarre. One such method even attempts to use hypnosis to reach a level of honesty and discovery of people's innermost thoughts and feelings about the brands in their lives. In some "Focus Group Hypnosis" sessions participants are "age-regressed" so that marketers can find out what their earliest experiences and memories are of particular events, issues, or products! Well, if it works . . . but, c'mon folks, there must be a better way!

The better way, for the moment at least, seems to be in gleaning what we can from the discipline of anthropology by bringing researchers trained in ethnography face-to-face with people in the course of their daily lives to observe what really goes on. We know that the traditional focus-group format faces real limitations for giving accurate data–what people say and what people really do is often very different! Often, ethnographic studies are able to uncover what other types of studies cannot. According to Hy Mariampolski, president of QualiData Research Inc., a firm specializing in ethnographic studies for marketers, ethnography "permits a more holistic and better-nuanced view of consumer satisfactions, frustrations, and limitations than many other research approaches, offering insights into consumer language, myths, and aspirations."[2] One of the most exciting claims of ethnographers is that they can, through their keen observations and interviewing techniques, uncover unarticulated needs–those needs or desires that cannot be divulged by asking questions because the consumers themselves haven't consciously registered them or because in focus groups they may not be honest about it (a big, well-known problem of focus groups). QualiData discovered a serious safety risk and comfort-factor problem with a plumbing fixture made by their client Moen, for instance. *By videotaping consumers, they realized that women were shaving their legs by holding on with their free hand to the unit's temperature control.* Many of us have particular unconscious habits such as this that we may not even mention if questioned. Housecalls, another New York ethnographic consultancy, specializing in visiting people in their homes to observe and talk to them about their daily rituals and relationships with products and brands, provided one client with a new understanding of middle-aged women with chronic acid indigestion. In this study, the researchers spent time with people as they went through the entire process of eating spicy foods, feeling poorly, taking a product and beginning to feel better, asking them questions about their physical and emotional experience all along the way. They saw that these people have very strong, intimate emotional bonds of trust with their anti-acid brand of choice as a true friend and "helper," and realized that they are very unlikely to experiment with other brands and switch camps. Obviously, this kind of information is extremely valuable for any brand. Most product-design firms today employ anthropologists and conduct extensive fieldwork, observing how people actually act in consumption situations and how they use products. This is how the firm, IDEO, discovered that children's small hands tend to grasp their toothbrushes in a fistlike grip, and it was the first to conceive of and develop fatter, easier to hold toothbrush handles for kids–a great idea and a big help for parents and children alike in the perennial task of getting kids to brush! At Desgrippes Gobé, we have partnered on such projects with the research and consulting firm Cheskin, which has a great track record for conducting cutting-edge research that gets to the true heart of the matter with consumers. In one of our branding programs with Cheskin, we helped Weight Watchers to understand new ways to talk to women. I asked Steve Diller, a Cheskin Partner, to comment on our approach to this branding program for Weight Watchers.

What Women Want *by Steve Diller, Cheskin Partner*

Traditionally, market research has been about force-fitting customers into a demographic category that can be easily explained with charts, graphs, and clinical definitions of characteristics and desires. This approach is not only distant from and disrespectful of the true functional and emotional desires of the individual, it is also alienating to the designers who must communicate the client's value in a meaningful way. We must understand that one cannot serve consumers without truly understanding who they are as people—their purpose, values, aspirations, and the context of their lives.This is the new focus of research and design, and the reason that research cannot be separated from the design process.

Weight Watchers had found itself at a strategic crossroads. Increasingly, a range of competitive options, from other food companies and workout facilities, to new medications and "anti-diet" activists, suggested that their traditional standing for "weight management" alone might not resonate with their customers in the future. To address the issue, Cheskin and Desgrippes Gobé initiated a worldwide collaborative study to understand the underlying benefits people sought from a full range of health and weight management options. The goal was to redefine the category and to reposition Weight Watchers so it could embody the new definition.

Cheskin and Desgrippes Gobé first conducted extensive interviews with Weight Watchers management to better understand what issues were driving their concerns. Then, Cheskin utilized a combination of innovative and traditional methods to explore the true motivations of a wide variety of individuals, and to understand what's relevant in the context of their daily lives.

Based on Cheskin's work, Desgrippes Gobé and Weight Watchers were able to develop a unique understanding of the evolving perspective of customers worldwide on what it means to be energized, healthy, and looking good. This perspective provided Desgrippes Gobé with a customer-centered basis for repositioning the company's identity to communicate Weight Watcher's ability to deliver the benefits customer seek.

In another very interesting program, Cheskin tackled the challenge of creating a computer game for pre-adolescent girls, despite the conclusion reached by many after half a dozen failures on the market that girls just don't like computer games. Cheskin's client, Interval Research, decided to find out if perhaps all girls needed was a different kind of computer game and so Cheskin set about delving into the hearts and minds of young girls. The first thing Cheskin discovered was that girls were not adverse to computer games at all, they just felt that there was nothing on the market that really interested or inspired them personally. As part of the extensive multiphase project, Cheskin researchers had girls take photos of their toys and play spaces and spent hours talking to them about their favorite games, their dreams, and their worries—fears such as losing your best friend to some other girl, which loom large for an eight-year-old but are easy to undervalue as an adult. They determined that although girls' play patterns were similar to those of boys, their motivations were different; girls preferred more dialogue, less action, and less structure. In developing two games—one focused on social play and one on fantasy play—Cheskin consulted extensively with the girls to determine the characters, plot, scenery, navigation, and rules. The games were eventually introduced to the market under the brand name "Purple Moon" with great success—girls gave the games a big thumbs up. Clearly, the dialogue created doing your ethnographic homework has great rewards for consumers and brands alike!

10

The Tenth Commandment: Evolve from Service to Relationship

Service is selling. ***Relationship is acknowledgement.***

Remember the ultra-charming scene in *Breakfast at Tiffany's* when Audrey Hepburn takes her handsome neighbor to the famed store—the place where she always goes to cheer herself up when she feels down? The pair of struggling New Yorkers, on a lark to spend the day doing only things they have never done before, are determined to have the experience of buying something at Tiffany's—but then they realize that they have only $10 to spend! The salesman doesn't miss a beat when they inform him of their spending limit; he graciously shows them the one or two items in their price range and when these are deemed "unromantic" by the couple, he suggests that they have something engraved—an idea that meets their enthusiastic approval. But they have nothing to engrave and Audrey Hepburn sweetly asks the salesman if an exception can be made to the Tiffany's policy to only engrave their own merchandise and have a sentimental object, a tin ring she got as a prize from a box of Cracker Jacks, engraved. "You don't think they will think it beneath them, do you?" she asks the salesman. "Oh no, Madame," the salesman replies, "I think that you will find that we are very understanding at Tiffany's" "You see," Audrey tells her beau, "I told you this was a wonderful place!" This scene, crafted in gorgeous techni-color in the best tradition of Hollywood, certainly represents the quintessential great customer service experience. The customer is not only

A true Citizen Brand must establish this humanistic, emotionally sensitive relationship with people.

well-served by a charming, patient, and knowledgeable person with the authority to make decisions (and bend a rule or two) in order to give a customer great individualized service, but is also treated with the kind of emotional sensitivity that ensures that Audrey Hepburn's character, if she were real, would become a life- long devotee of the brand. What's important about this scene is that it is not just about commerce. It is about building a relationship that is, yes, based on commerce, but that extends far beyond mere commerce to encompass a more holistic perspective of the consumer's emotional needs and a deep understanding of the very important role a brand can play in a person's life at a given moment. But does this experience even exist in real life? It seems like a sort of nirvana that is incredibly difficult to achieve given that most companies struggle with conquering the most basic customer service issues and are indeed a long way away from this realm of establishing a refined emotional relationship. But I am convinced that *not only is it possible to reach this "customer service nirvana"; it is absolutely crucial in today's atmosphere of people's heightened emotional expectations from brands.* A true Citizen Brand must establish this humanistic, emotionally sensitive relationship with people. In this chapter we will talk about some of the ways brands, such as Prada, Home Depot, and Lexus, are striving in various ways, with varying degrees of success, to reach this nirvana of an emotionalized relationship with people through great customer service.

The Stroke That Makes Real

As Lee Iacocca once put it, "If you take care of your customers, everything else will fall into place."[1] The reason great customer service is so important is simple: without it, everything else is hype. And an emotional relationship cannot be based on hype. Nor can a Citizen Brand afford to be accused of hype, even for a moment. This is the "stroke that makes real," the final test and the thing that often makes

In fact, the most recent Harris/Reputation Institute poll showed that "people are fed up with lousy customer service, and they let it show in their ratings of many of the world's best-known companies."

or breaks a brand in a customer's heart. A brand can have the most enticing advertising campaign, the most innovative product, the coolest Web site, the most original promotions, or fantastic-looking stores, but if the brand becomes a frustrating or negative experience at the customer service level everything else could go to waste. While it's true that as customer service levels in general have fallen so low that people's expectations have also lowered considerably, there are some very smart brands out there that have shown they understand the extra competitive edge spectacular service can give them. And when given a choice, people will always vote for the brands that make them feel loved! The question of tolerance is an interesting one from a business perspective. It is my feeling that there are many companies out there that haven't yet gotten this concept of creating an emotional relationship with the consumer, and they may be fine for the moment because the all-around standard in their business sector is very low, but smart consumers are beginning to understand the level of power and choice they do have in today's economy. In fact, the most recent Harris/Reputation Institute poll showed that "people are fed up with lousy customer service, and they let it show in their ratings of many of the world's best-known companies."[4] Harris' senior VP Joy Sever's comment on these results says it all: "When a company provides great service, its reputation benefits from a strong emotional connection with its customers."[2] As Kenneth Kannady, a corporate enablement manager in the CRM industry emphasizes, this emotional connection is built on empowerment: "'Empowerment' is the feeling that customers develop 'about themselves' as a result of interacting with a company through its people, products, processes or services. Empowerment is what differentiates a 'repeat' customer from a loyal customer."[5]

Brands that do not realize the value of this emotional connection from a loyalty standpoint are incredibly vulnerable to any new competition that may come along bringing a better service standard. One example of this was given to me by a friend who recently had cable installed with Time Warner. The overall experience was a bad one from practically every aspect—from missed appointments for installation to a botched installation job when the appointment was finally kept, to bills that were wrong that the company would not agree to correct to the impossibility of reaching anyone at the company who was able or willing to help straighten out the problems! Despite all of this, she so far has kept her service—because she really wants cable, and no other service is available at the present time in her location. But you can bet that once this monopoly situation changes and she can change services, she will not have one iota of brand loyalty to keep her from doing so. She said she would even spend more on another company with better customer service systems! What company can really afford to fail so miserably in the arena of brand loyalty?

People need to feel that their business and time are valued by a brand. They need convenient solutions and answers to their questions. Some of this can be tackled by the ingenious technological systems of our times, which certainly should be offered as a part of the solution, but there is another very interesting point to all of this, which is that *the technological revolution has made the personal touch even more valuable to people.* Think about it. How many of us are frustrated by never being able to reach a real person when we call a company with questions that are just too complex or important to leave to automation? Ironically enough, people expected the Web to automate many customer service functions, but it seems that technologies are only stimulating more contact between corporations and people and higher expectations from that contact. In fact, people expect more information today and while they may be happy with one level of questions being answered by a faceless technological interface, at some point they need and desire a human touch (or at least the option to press '0' and talk to a live agent when on the phone–and a phone number listing as an option when on a Web site!). Along these lines, there must be a way to make it unnecessary for people to re-explain their problem or question each time they are transferred to a new customer service agent who can better help them–what a feeling of a waste of time and speaking into an inhuman void . . . at least a computer would "remember" what was previously said through some data registry method! At least some companies, such as JetBlue, the airline company, have employed inventive ways of entertaining people when they are put on hold with cheeky, humorous on-hold messages.

There must be a way to make it unnecessary for people to re-explain their problem or question each time they are transferred to a new customer service agent.

But even when you do manage to get a "live" person–the right person for the situation–on the phone, how often is that person willing or able to help? As one *Brandweek* journalist put it, ". . . from Broadway to Baja, and countless points between, consumer cravings to connect with a company rep that can take care of business, troubleshoot, and talk in a reasonably lifelike manner go largely unmet."[5]

Some companies really invest in training their customer service agents and employees in the subtle skills of customer service through unique programs, emphasizing communication skills. Loyalty Factor, a New Hampshire company, trains employees to polish their people skills by, among other things, having them study the different personality types they may encounter, all of whom require a different interactive style. These four major personality types are derived from the Myers Briggs Type Indicator, a widely used psychological test, and can be detected through speech patterns and communication styles. Apparently, "Thinkers" have a monotone speaking style and need to win arguments, "Sensors" have melodic and variable speech patterns and need most of all to be presented with options and choices, "Intuitors" are types who talk profusely and quickly and need positive feedback, and "Feelers" who are "low talkers," most need someone to be agreeable with them (well, this last one I would say applies to all of us!).

Brands today could really win people's hearts by providing real, efficient, and caring human contact. Oldsmobile recently employed an interesting tactic along these lines to make the point to its consumers how much it cares. When Oldsmobile discontinued some of its namesake brand models it wanted to show people just how far Oldsmobile would go to stand by its brand and that it is committed to the car's five-year warranty and after-sales service. To do this, Oldsmobile gave out the direct phone numbers and e-mail addresses of four of its top executives in commercials so consumers could call them with their questions and talk about the brand. In one ad, CEO Martin Javier asked people to call him at 1-313-568-6100. The ad ended with the executive saying: "I believe in Oldsmobile that much." This kind of emotional commitment of a corporation to its customer's brand experience can be very powerful. In a similar, ongoing initiative, both JetBlue's CEO and President/COO often handle complaints personally as well as lend a hand checking in customers at JFK during high travel seasons. Another great example of this kind of total commitment to customer satisfaction is Diesel's free-jeans-wash policy that invites customers to bring their Diesel jeans to the store to have them washed for free for the entire lifetime of the product as a way of proving their strong belief in the quality of their jeans and the brand promise that they will never shrink or fall apart. Seemingly "little" touches such as this one really become part of the total brand experience in a very powerful way. This is part of the reason for the success of Starbuck's–their customer service is a unique, brand experience based on the intensive training programs they provide all of their employees to teach them the "Starbuck's way." They are so committed to this that when they open new stores in foreign markets, they even fly employees from around the world to Seattle to participate in an intensive training program!

Prada: A Brand That Doesn't Leave You Cold

Some brands have indeed mastered the art of moving from a "service standard," to creating the kind of emotional connection with people that means a genuine, long-lasting brand relationship.

I had my own "Tiffany's experience" when visiting the new Prada store discussed in chapter 3. Just like Audrey Hepburn, I had suspicions of snobbery before visiting Prada, the Italian fashion and beauty brand that seems to be only for the rich and famous. And just like her, I had a surprising experience of warmth and comfort. I discovered the reason for the brand's success and charisma–what really makes people excited about this brand, what makes it preferred. Prada's total personality permeates its business practices and engages people in discovering the richness of the brand's character in a very inviting manner.

It was one of those beautiful, cold New York winter days. As I entered through the first floor, I could sense that I was about to have a unique experience, but I was determined not to be charmed by the obvious sense of beauty the architecture delivered. I would be a shopper, I decided. A virtual shopper, since I felt I couldn't really afford those prices, but through fantasizing I would live the experience.

But there was one, seemingly unattainable item I had been seeking for ages. I had been searching for a special kind of warm winter overcoat that is so handy in the Northeast. I wanted something very specific: It had to be light (but warm), rainproof, three-quarters length, easy to wear over a jacket (and nice enough for business occasions) but flexible enough to wear in the springtime (i.e., a coat with an inside liner that could be taken out). Oh yes, and it had to have a hood and be either black or grey. In short, the impossible find.

I had looked almost everywhere—Banana Republic, The Gap, Brooks Brothers, numerous department stores, Roots, the Canadian store, and even some of the hip skateboard/roller-blade type stores on Broadway—with no luck.

I went down the stairs to the very busy and imaginatively designed shopping environment where most of the products are displayed and where the buying is happening. The crowd there was, as you can imagine, very young, beautiful, and hip, dressed "down" in outfits that cost thousands of dollars. How could those people afford this, I wondered! I was convinced that the salespeople would be off-putting. I saw an interesting coat, not exactly what I wanted, but what the heck, I decided to try it. I also realized that prices were 30 percent off; I started to dream. Hey, life is short anyway, I thought as I tried to brainwash myself into thinking that a bargain is a bargain at any level.

A friendly saleslady was passing by so I asked her to see if she had my size in the garment and in passing I explained to her the look of the coat I was seeking. I don't know if she thought I was a serious buyer, which I was not at this point, but she said she might find something to my liking and invited me to go to a large dressing room decorated in the most imaginative and cool fashion. Personalized service, I thought. Wow. Let's see what she will come up with. I was certain that she would not find the impossible dream. As a curious designer, I started to explore my fitting room and found that beyond the traditional mirrors, a camera was taking slow-motion pictures of me so that I could see how a specific garment fitted in a live three-way mirror. The camera shoots you from the back and projects your image on a screen next to the mirror you are looking at. As you make a 360-degree turn, you can watch yourself turning in delayed motion and, in this way, appreciate the complete look of the merchandise on you. Each garment has a hangtag with a chip that helps you get information about the product by swiping the hangtag card in a specific electronic monitor!

My help was back in a few short minutes with what I thought was "it." I tried "it" half hoping that it would not fit. It did. She had the exact coat I had been looking for—even better—lighter and warmer, with lots of great detail such as one very cool-looking, nonintrusive narrow label on the collar, which bore the Prada logo. I was pleased.

The sleeves were a bit long but a tailor on the premises came immediately, inspected the garment, discussed the alterations Prada would do free of charge, and arranged to have the work done. The saleswoman actually offered to drop the coat off at my office a few days later since it was on her way to work! I happily paid up!

In finding what seemed to me to be a perfect world of pleasurable shopping, I suddenly understood the success of Prada. I learned that the Prada brand is not about hype and snobbish Euro trends. I became a customer because of the real commitment to the experience the store tries so hard to deliver to their clients. In my case, the reason I was willing to pay more was purely emotional. Through a great effort to build a relationship with me, Prada delivered on a desire I had not been able to fulfill and made my frustration go away. Prada, I decided from this experience, is a brand that does not leave you cold.

Straighten Up and Fly Right!

How can an airline win people's hearts back? Simple. Improve service. Be nice. And communicate.

In a hilarious *New York Times* editorial, Joe Queenan offers airlines a few "helpful tips" that would accomplish this task. His tips show just how bad things really are, with advice such as: "Do something about the hideous cuisine: salmon with the texture of a rhino hide, crown cracking "fresh" rolls, carbon-dated lettuce . . ."; or "tell the air hosts and hostesses to stop acting like Mimi on her deathbed in *La Bohème* every time somebody asks them to brew a fresh pot of coffee"; or "Stop showing films that came out eleven years ago and pretending people should be pleased." He recommends taking out four rows of seats, because "anyone who stands taller than 5 foot 6 or weighs more than 165 pounds recognizes that flying is the most grueling experience known to man." On a totally serious note though, the crucial point Mr. Queenan makes in this editorial is that since taxpayers have essentially paid for the airline's $15 billion bailout, they have a right to expect better service.[6]

I recently had my own airline experience that elucidated what could be right about an airline and what is most often wrong. For a recent trip to Milwaukee, my travel agent booked me on an America West flight. We got there on time to meet with a client there. During the meeting, we talked a lot about emotional branding and, as is usual in these cases, people like to talk about their favorite brands in term of service and trust. I was surprised to hear all of them mention an airline, Midwest Express. I was interested in learning more about this brand. Apparently, it is recognized by Condé Nast *Traveler* and the Zagat survey as the best airline in the United States.

On my way back to New York, at the Milwaukee airport, I decided to take the opportunity to experience the brand firsthand. My America West flight was delayed fifteen minutes and there was a Midwest Express flight leaving just a little bit later, but arriving at an airport closer to my home. In order to change my ticket, I had to change my e-ticket into a paper ticket so that Midwest could issue me a new one so that I

Hey, I am not the type that jumps up and down when I feel abused, but I thought that the attitude of America West was particularly "noncitizen."

could be reimbursed for my fare. At America West, not only was I received with a cold shoulder, but I was also asked to cough up $10 in cash for them to perform this simple operation of issuing a ticket for me to take to Midwest. Hey, I am not the type that jumps up and down when I feel abused, but I thought that the attitude of America West was particularly "noncitizen." When I returned to Midwest, I asked what they would do if I had to change a ticket the same way with their organization; they almost laughed when they found out I paid money for what should be part of every normal consumer service policy . . . oh well! The rest of my travel experience that day, on Midwest Airlines, was great. I found the interior of the planes soothing and comfortable, with leather seating for all classes and I was treated to the best cookies I have ever tasted. Guess who will have my vote in the future? The way I felt in that moment with America West made me judge this airline in a completely new way.

My wife and I had another very bad airline experience, with Air Canada. One Saturday, my flight to Canada was delayed mostly because of bad weather, an understandable situation. But it turned out that the flight that was supposed to leave at 9:00 a.m. ended up leaving at 6:00 p.m. instead. I didn't blame the airline for this uncontrollable weather situation, but, nevertheless, I became very upset by the way the airlines handled information and communicated to the passengers. None of the screens were on to show delays or other destinations and the attendants did not seem to be communicating to us in a forthright manner about the real situation, leaving everyone guessing and making their wait even more uncomfortable. With better information, we could have gone back home to wait for the later flight without spending hours at the airport. But nobody would give us a straight answer; we were offered a flight to Toronto and then transfer, but this was not what we wanted because we were going to Montreal! The agenda seemed to be to keep people from leaving at all costs. Well, this attitude turned into a grab bag of criticism among the groups of travelers that bonded in bad-mouthing the airlines. One person said the name of Air Canada should really be "air can't nada!" and we all had a good time taking turns renaming this company for the worst. Those people will of course talk to other people about their "air can't nada" experience, making an association that could stick for years. In this case, the reputation of the airline was affected, not because of the inconvenience, but due to its lack of straightforward communication.

Roll Out the Welcome Mat

A great, old-fashioned and still very valid, customer service concept is to simply "make people feel at home." Lexus is one brand that has excelled in this endeavor. I met with Mike Wells, Lexus's vice president of marketing, and experienced the Lexus hospitality firsthand when, after our meeting, I was given the opportunity to drive one of their latest SC convertibles around Long Beach for the afternoon to enjoy the free time I had before flying back to New York.

Created in 1989 by Toyota from scratch, based on fifty years of Toyota engineering, Lexus launched its cars in the most competitive category: the luxury market dominated by giants like BMW and Mercedes. The company has been a huge success, with the Lexus LS 430 considered today by an independent automotive testing firm as the "Finest Luxury Sedan in America." Their 196 dealerships sell over 1,050 units per outlet per year and are beating the giants on the market, such as Ford and GM. "We wanted to own the dealership experience," is how Mike crystallized their innovative strategy. The focus on people is huge at Lexus. Their original, and still valid, mission statement reads in part, "We will treat customers as guests in our own home."

Lexus knew that they had invented and designed one of the best products in the market; the challenge was to create acceptance. They did this in part by creating a sense of welcome at Lexus dealerships that is truly personal and sincere. They will pick up your car at home if you have a problem and bring it back to you. Mike told me the story of how in Texas one of their customers was driving with his pregnant wife to the hospital and realized that he could not make it in time. He pulled into a Lexus dealership, trusting that they would be of help since they had been so great with him. They did everything they could to make the couple comfortable. The baby was delivered there, in the front seat of the SUV, and the couple named her Isabella Alexus.

When meeting with Mike Wells, I directly felt his pride and passion for the brand. When I asked him how it felt to work at Lexus, he said, "It feels elevating." This is a pretty good sign from someone who has been with the company since 1986! What is very clear to me from my visit there is that this "new kid on the luxury-car block" seems to have changed the entire paradigm of the traditional approach to servicing luxury customers. It has done so by building trust with people in a true Citizen Brand fashion and with a sincere commitment to their clients.

When meeting with Mike Wells, I directly felt his pride and passion for the brand. When I asked him how it felt to work at Lexus, he said, "It feels elevating."

In terms of the idea of making people feel at home, Home Depot has had a particular challenge with women. The brand certainly has that very approachable "meat-and-potatoes feel," and, as we saw in chapter 2, the stores work very hard to build a strong emotionally resonant spirit of partnership between employees and the community through community volunteer outreach programs. However, the brand realized it needed to put out more of a welcome mat for women, who, after all, make 90 percent of their kitchen purchases, in order to encourage them to feel comfortable to explore other parts of the store. In order to do this, *Home Depot had to understand the subtleties of women's relationship with the store. Home Depot understood that it was not about "feminizing" the brand, because women loved that "guy's guy" thing about the stores as long as they felt welcomed and that they could be part of the game too.* The feeling Home Depot wanted to create was about a couple building a house together with a feeling of partnership for both sexes. This involved the challenge of moving from a professional "carpenter/hard hat" culture to one that embraces new relationships, without losing touch with their core identity. They have answered this challenge in part by moving toward the "décor" side of the business. Home Depot created a concept called "EXPO: From inspiration to installation," a woman-friendly concept that offers dozens of showrooms under one roof, including lighting, carpeting, flooring, décor, and kitchen and bath products, all presented alongside complete design and installation materials and information.

Home Depot has had other challenges in the customer service arena, and it recently became aware of new problems when they dropped to nineteenth place from fourth place in the 2001 Harris/Reputation Institute's survey because of certain customer service issues–such as people not being able to find the products they need or someone to help them. Home Depot has responded swiftly to this issue by having salespeople unpack merchandise late at night instead of during store hours so that they can be more available to help customers during prime shopping times, and by putting more employees on the floor on the weekends.

Overall, Home Depot's reputation has been fairly solid for building emotional relationships with customers through good service. When I visited Home Depot, I was told that it had created initiatives such as on-premises workshops for customers, with lessons for kids in how to build birdhouses and toys. This kind of initiative is very valuable to people, both for its benefits to the children and to the parents who are then able to shop unhindered by their children.

And then there is a collection of stories that show how Home Depot tries very hard to go beyond the expected level of service from a pure business perspective to reach a more humanistic relationship level. One such story occurred when a Home Depot customer saw a mother duck crossing a highway at a peril to her life to fetch her chicks that had fallen into a sewer. The woman called the animal rescue league, the police, and the firemen, and then as a last resort, went to a nearby Home Depot for help knowing their reputation for good service. The store immediately sent some of its people over with pipes and gears to retrieve the little ducklings–and much to everyone's delight, they were successful!

The woman called the animal rescue league, the police, and the firemen, and then as a last resort, went to a nearby Home Depot for help knowing their reputation for good service.

Most crucial in this process of creating relationships with consumers at the customer service level is staying in touch with people by fostering personal experiences with the brand. Once you have feedback, as Home Depot did with the Harris/Reputation Institute survey, it is absolutely vital to jump into action immediately to make things better, because such results mean you have fallen out of touch. One very simple, straightforward way that Harley-Davidson stays in touch with its customers is to require that its employees–even the executives–go through a dealer when getting a Harley so that they can see what the customer's experience is like and understand the process of buying a bike from both a practical and an emotional perspective.

Passionate Employees As Brand Ambassadors

It is the employees who ultimately have to act on and embody the brand promise and live it in a meaningful way. As a senior executive told the Association of National Advertisers' Senior Marketers Roundtable, "I can do everything right in marketing–have the right messages, target the right customer, make the right promises–but it is all for naught if the $7-an-hour person at the case register is having a bad day. That is the last impression of my brand that the customer will have."[7] A big part of the problem is, of course, the $7-an-hour phenomenon. Wal-Mart was one of the first to approach this issue by binding employees to the brand through stock-purchase programs.

There are many other ways of motivating and training employees to become passionate about the brand and share that passion with customers. Encouraging or supporting volunteerism is one of the most potent motivators of all. Companies like Timberland have had enormous success in building loyalty and team spirit with their program that offers employees 40 paid hours per year to do volunteer work. Patagonia, the outdoor enthusiasts' company and a true pioneer in Citizen Brandship long before it became fashionable, has devised many ways of ensuring that their employees are just as committed to both their brand philosophy and their customers.

As I have mentioned previously, there is powerful evidence that employee involvement in corporate social causes really works in terms of creating a strong internal culture of pride.

Cole Haan has found some very interesting ways to inspire and involve its employees in the brand on a more intimate level. Cole

Haan's chairman & CEO Matthew Rubel told me, "The voice we need to create for the consumer needs to come from the heart, and it is our associates who carry this emotional message." One of their very successful initiatives for accomplishing this has been to organize internal fashion shows to ignite employee passion for the brand. The recent product innovations of Cole Haan require and deserve this kind of special attention and understanding from the sales associates. Recently, Cole Haan (which is owned by Nike) has integrated the Nike technology into its business shoes in a challenging mixture of the coolest youth brand and the most traditional men's shoes. Cole Haan's efforts to create excitement around the brand have worked. The business has experienced double-digit growth since Matthew joined the company several years ago. Matthew feels that the success came from Cole Haan's commitment to innovation, the change of the culture internally, and a commitment to the community. The company's commitment to the communities and causes it believes in is original in the way it is managed through the employees themselves who have direct ownership of the process. Instead of a corporate effort directed by the CEO and a small group of executives, Cole Haan created a committee inside the company that is representative of everyone's interests and run by someone who is elected every year to decide which initiatives will be taken. Seventy percent of the overall funds go directly to this committee, while 15 percent go to the store organization to support the communities in which stores operate and 15 percent is set aside to be used at the discretion of the CEO to support activities at the corporate level. The idea behind this is to create a platform for people to express themselves.

As I have mentioned previously, there is powerful evidence that employee involvement in corporate social causes really works in terms of creating a strong internal culture of pride, a desire to connect with the marketplace, and an overall commitment to build a relationship with clients that's better than any of its competition. Citizen branding is clearly the concept that is driving this company, creating a brand spirit that people want to be part of–a culture that is always searching for what's next. Matthew told me, "We wanted to create a party with the brand and make sure that everyone could come in by leaving all the doors to the brand wide open." This is a great concept on which to base customer service initiatives. Who wouldn't feel welcome at a good party and want to join in the fun?

A Final Note on Citizen Brandship

Overall, my principal aim in writing this book was to provide some insight into how to tear down the walls between brands and people and open the corporate doors so that a dialogue can take place. Establishing this dialogue can be a golden opportunity for answering one of the most urgent questions facing brands that would like to develop their "Citizen Brandship": how to inform people about the company's good deeds without seeming self-congratulatory and offending people in sensitive situations. No one seems to have yet found the answer to this question and companies are experimenting, many of them finding to their dismay that they are "damned if they do and damned if they don't." In this year's Reputation Institute/ Harris Interactive poll the public surveyed was split on this question, too: 50 percent felt that advertising and press releases concerning good deeds were appropriate, while 40 percent preferred "a less splashy message," and recommended that companies stick to talking about their good deeds in their annual reports and Web sites.

Well, it certainly does seem important for a company to communicate what they are doing as a good Citizen Brand. After all, of the twenty attributes in the Harris/Reputation Institute study, the question of whether a given company supported good causes brought the largest percentage of "not sure" responses. And sometimes companies can appear unfeeling or unresponsive to the public when in fact they are not. Take Procter & Gamble and Honda for example. They were harshly criticized by poll respondents for inaction in response to the World Trade disaster when in fact they both had made generous donations of money and products but had chosen not to advertise about it.

The fact is that brands must communicate who they are, and if they become true Citizen Brands, with aims of social responsibility as a core element of their corporate mission, then they must–very tactfully of course–communicate this point of view! There are many ways to do this. After September 11, Verizon chose to send its customers a letter explaining what they were doing to help instead of advertising. They also sent a notice to their customers in the Northeast that they were giving them and extra 200 minutes for the months of September and October in order to help them "find comfort in the support of friends and family in this difficult time." In many ways this is a more personal, more intimate approach than an advertisement. What is key here is that any ad of this nature should keep from promoting or trying to sell a particular product. I thought that a Merck ad announcing that the company will give free medication to the elderly worked because it was done under the banner of the parent company, not an individual Merck brand or product. In light of this, it is very important for brands to manage carefully their umbrella brand as an extremely valuable corporate asset–it is the only face to show in certain situations. This is why the GM 0% financing commercials worked, because in a very unusual move for GM, they did not show the products or promote any specific brands. When I met with GM's VP of North American communications, Tom Kowaleski, he explained how GM is currently emotionalizing their umbrella brand image through a GM branding program, which at this moment will not target consumers (since the divisional brands are the consumer face), but rather the media and business partners, financial community, and employment constituents. But, part of the benefit of having a strong umbrella brand is that GM will be ready to interface directly with consumers at a moment's notice if need be, as in the case of the 0 percent financing ads. The fact that it was able to execute this initiative so quickly and well shows the importance of sound management of the GM umbrella brand.

GM appears to be a culture of integrity built on respect for individuality. When I asked Tom about GM's social responsibility initiatives, he emphasized that the company does not attempt to weave this kind of message into all of its communications, but that it has been "living that way on a daily basis long before it became popular." Indeed, GM conducted their first report on environmental sustainability seven years ago, long before most of their competitors were thinking this way. Today on GM's Web site, Gmability.com, there is a section devoted entirely to environmental issues. There, people can find a well-presented, comprehensive compendium of everything GM is doing for the environment. Among other things, this listing contains information about a futuristic concept vehicle they have developed called AUTOnomy, which emits only water from the tailpipe and uses renewable energy!

Another way to let people know what your company is doing is to actually involve them in the process in the way we have been talking about all along—through dialogue. In other words, why not develop truly interactive campaigns, along the same lines as the BP ad I talked about in chapter 5, where BP asked people in the street for their thoughts and recommendations for how to become a better corporate citizen. A dialogue of this kind on a company's Web site would be so much more interesting than tons of information about all of a company's initiatives. Some companies do have programs that involve the general public and give people an opportunity to volunteer or participate in a cause through an event or program the company has organized. Taking the idea further, though, in the same way that people are now "voting" for certain new products to be developed or participating in designing ad campaigns, people could contribute their ideas for great programs to help humanity. Let's face it, many of us feel a real sense of helplessness in the face of the larger problems facing our society. Giving people an active role to play in helping lessen the world's ills could be a tremendous experience for people. Companies could tap into that frustration in a very positive way. What could be more exciting than helping corporations—which have more money and power to effect change than any mere individual (unless you happen to be a Bill Gates) can ever have—to use their influence and money in effective ways? The sense of empowerment and emotional connection with the brand could be huge!

> **Let's face it, many of us feel a real sense of helplessness in the face of the larger problems facing our society. Giving people an active role to play in helping lessen the world's ills could be a tremendous experience.**

But why would a company take such risks, breaking down the ivory tower and inviting customers into its world to find out what it's doing, and open itself to criticism? This takes courage and the willingness to be vulnerable, but I believe that the sincerity of effort and the "good faith" placed in people, which is so necessary for such an endeavor of this type, would be of inestimable value to people. This kind of "good faith," I believe, is what will ultimately create the kind of powerful emotional bond with consumers that makes for a brand's long-term success.

cul8r

notes

Introduction

1. "Pro-Logo: Why Brands are Good for You," *The Economist*, 8 September 2001.
2. Michel Lacroix, *Le Culte de l'Emotion* (Flammarion, Paris, 2001).
3. By Ethan Watters, 14 October 2001.
4. William Strauss and Neil Howe, *The Fourth Turning: An American Prophecy* (New York: Broadway Books, 1997).
5. Reed Abelson, "Consumers Look at Corporate Conduct," the *New York Times*, 13 November 2001.

Chapter 1

1. Geoffry Colvin, "What's Love Got to Do With It?" *Fortune*, 12 November 2001.
2. Gabrielle Mander, *Wan2tlk: LtlBk of Txt Msgs* (New York: St. Martin's Press, 2001).
3. Barbara Thau, "Kmart Goes Home for the Holidays," HFN, 12 November 2001.
4. Stan Gellers, "One Mo' Time with Feeling," DNR, 10 October 2001.
5. Dick Wimmer, ed., *The Extreme Game: An Extreme Sports Anthology* (Burford Books, 2001).
6. Vanessa O'Connell and Jon Hilsenrath, "Advertisers are Cautious as Household Makeup Shifts," *Wall Street Journal*, 15 May 2001.
7. Laurel Wentz, "Reverse English," *Advertising Age*, 19 November 2001.
8. Jeffrey Ball, "Chrysler's Latest Ads for Minivans Stress Multicultural Over Motherly," *Wall Street Journal*, 18 December 2001.
9. Cliff Rothman, "A Welcome Mat for Gay Customers," *New York Times*, 17 August 2001.

Chapter 2

1. Stephanie Armour, "Some Companies Choose No-Layoff Policy," *USA Today*, 17 December 2001.
2. Peter Drucker, "Survey: The Near Future (Part II)," *The Economist*, 9 November 2001.
3. Sue Shellenbarger, "Some Bosses, Fumbling in Crisis, Have Bruised Loyalty of Employees," *Wall Street Journal*, 17 October 2001.
4. Ibid.
5. Tom Chappell, *Managing Upside Down* (New York: William Morrow and Co, Inc., 1999).
6. Thomas Garvey May, "You Get What You Give," *New Product Review*, Spring 2000.
7. "On Second Thought, Don't Take this Job And Shove It," *Adweek*, 1 October 2001.
8. Kris Maher, "Some Companies Foster Creativity Despite Slowdown," *Wall Street Journal*, 22 May 2001.
9. Jane Bryant Quinn, "Cause Marketing Catches On," *Washington Post*, 10 December 2000.
10. 1999 Cone/Roper Cause Related Trends Report.
11. "Consumers Want Brands and Social Responsibility," *Sales & Marketing Management*, January 2000.
12. Don Tapscott and Anthony Williams, "What? Now We Have to Make a Profit and Be Ethical?" *www. Business2.com*, February 2002.
13. Becky Ebenkamp, "The National Trust," *Brandweek*, 8 April 2002.
14. "The Socially Correct Corporate," *Fortune*, 24 July 2000.
15. Jerry Useem, "Globalization: Can Governments, Companies, and Yes, the Protestors Ever Learn to Get Along?" *Fortune*, 26 November 2001.
16. Ibid.
17. Ibid.

18. Laurence Caramel, "Donnant-donnant: Le Nouveau Credo Nord-Sud," *Le Monde*, 19 March 2002.
19. Scott Malone, "Anti-Globalization Targets: Why Gap Is Number One," *Women's Wear Daily*, 27 February 2002.
20. Cara B. DiPasquale, "B&W Smoke Boasts Fewer Toxins," *Advertising Age*, 5 November 2001.
21. John Le Carré, *The Constant Gardner* (New York, Pocket Books, 2001).
22. Eleftheria Parpis, "Fear Factor: How Should We Feel About Mental-Health Drug Ads?" *Adweek*, 12 November 2001
23. Claire Rosenzweig, "Cause Related Trends," *Brand Marketing*, June 2000.
24. Myra Stark, "Brand Aid: Cause Effective," *Brandweek*, 22 February 1999.
25. Vanessa O'Connell and Jon Hilsenrath, "Advertisers Are Cautious As Household Makeup Shifts," *New York Times*, 15 May 2001.
26. "Brand Builders," *Brandweek*, 19 February 2001.
27. Serge Schememann, "Annan Cautions Business As Forum Ends," *New York Times*, 5 February 2002.

Chapter 3
1. *www.themills.com*, January 2002.
2. Alison Fass, "A Joint Venture Hopes to Tie the Product to the Entertainment and Create a Shopping Experience," *New York Times*, 1 June 2001.
3. Laura Klepacki, "The Second Coming of B&BW," *Women's Wear Daily*, 12 October 2001.
4. Barry Janoff, "This 'Roadie' Film Had the Right Elements: Snappy Images, No Rules," *Brandweek*, 19 November 2001.
5. Fara Warner, "Curb Your Enthusiasm," *Fast Company,* January 2002.
6. Stuart Elliot, "Leaving No Stone Unturned," *NYTimes.com*, 22 October 2001.
7. Ibid.

Chapter 4
1. Chris Taylor, *Time, www.apple.com.*
2. "Unfading Beauty: Best of East, West," *Forbes*, 7 January 2002.

Chapter 5
1. Scott Leith and Shella Poole, "Wendy's Founder Gained Fame in Homespun TV Commercials," *The Atlanta Journal-Constitution*, 9 January 2002.
2. *Forbes*, 7 January 2002.
3. Davide Dukcevich, "Wendy's Loses its Father," *www.Forbes.com*, 8 January 2002.
4. Courtney Kane, "Stonyfield Farm Tries to Change the World and Sell Some Yogurt," *New York Times*, 6 September 2000.
5. Mike Hoffman, *Inc Magazine*, December 2000.

Chapter 6
1. David Handelman, "A Rock 'n' Roll Art Director Moves to GQ," *New York Times*, 3 December 2001.
2. Paul Rand, *Design Form and Chaos* (New Haven: Yale University Press, 1993).

Chapter 7
1. "A to Z," *New York Times Magazine*, 2 December 2001.
2. Wendy Steiner, *Venus in Exile: The Rejection of Beauty in Twentieth-Century Art* (New York: The Free Press, 2001).
3. Danny Hakim, "An Artiste Invades Stodgy G.M.," *New York Times*, 19 October 2001.
4. William Hamilton, "With the World Redesigned, What Role for Designers?" *New York Times*, 25 October 2001.
5. The award winners were: Robert Mangurian, Mary-Ann Ray, Susan Kare, Stefan Sagmeister, Kathryn Gustafson, Daniel Rozin and Thom Mayne.
6. Gerry Khermouch, "Good Design–

And Good Business," *Business Week*, 5 November 2001.

7. Horacio Silva, "Too Cool for School," *Home Design*, August 2001.

8. Philip Nobel, "Dress Code," *House & Garden*, November 2001.

9. Ibid.

10. Lorenz Ackerman, "Solid Foundations," *Wallpaper*, November 2001.

11. Josh Quittner, "Apple's Latest Fruit," *Time.com*, 8 January 2002.

12. Danny Hakim, "An Artiste Invades Stodgy G.M.," *New York Times*, 19 October 2001.

13. Ibid.

14. Jessica Brinton, "Light Show," *Harpers Bazaar*, September 2001.

15. Ibid.

Chapter 8

1. Bob Garfield, "Patriot Games," *Advertising Age*, 15 October 2001.

2. "Living La Vida Barbie: Have Ads Aimed at Kids Hit a Highwater Mark?" *Adbusters* November/December 2001.

3. Shu Shin Luh, "Industry Struggles to Refine Promotions with Wireless SMS," *Asian Wall Street Journal*, 4 October 2001.

4. Hilary Cassidy, "Magic Feet," *Brand-week*, 15 October 2001.

5. Philip Weiss, "Big," the *New York Times Magazine*, 25 March 2001.

Chapter 9

1. Tobi Elkin, "iTV Applications Show Signs of Life," *Ad Age*, 17 December 2001.

2. "The Power of Ethnography," *Journal of the Market Research Society*, Vol. 41, No. 1, January 1999.

Chapter 10

1. *Fast Company*, 1 July 2001.

2. Ronald Alsop, "Reputations Rest on Good Service," *Wall Street Journal*, 14 January 2002.

3. Ibid.

4. Kenneth L. Kannady, "Being Satisfied is No Longer Satisfying," *www. crmforum.com*, 9 April 2002.

5. Laura Shanahan, "Designated Shopper," *Brandweek*, 8 October 2001.

6. Joe Queenan, "Some (Modest) Proposals to Reform Airlines, With a Special Emphasis on Those Movies," the *New York Times*, 17 December 2001.

7. Scott Davis, "Taking Control of Your Brand's Destiny," *Brandweek*, 15 October 2001.

index

228

Nikon, 95–96
Nissan, 169
noblese oblige, 110
Nokia, 103
not-for-profit organizations (NGO), 75,
    130–137, 161
Novartis, 66
Nucor, 49
nutrition, 60, 108, 109, 111, 112

O

Ogg, Steven, 168
Ogilvy & Mather, 178
Oldsmobile, 219
Olson, Eric, 136
Oprah (Winifrey), 116–119, 122, 149

P

Palm (Pilot), 102–103, 183
parent-child relationship, 16–17, 19–20
Patagonia, xi, 227
Peapod, 191, 192
Penn State, 34
people. *See also* demographic groups
    design for, 154–156
    imagination and, 155
    interactive relationships with, 198, 208
    love instead of fear for, 2–7
    mirror mood of, 177
    primary emotions for, 3–4
PepsiCo, 58–59, 109
personality
    brand with, 144
    of brands, ix–x, 114–120, 122–123, 132
    as character/charisma, 126
    color and, 148–149
    innovation and, 141–142
    logo and no, 142, 144
    to message, 143
    not perfection, but, 138–142
Pfizer, 64, 66, 108
pharmaceutical company, 205
    charitable endeavors of, 66–67
    consumer, emotional connections and,
        67–68
    exploitation of, 65, 67
    health condition information valuable
        from, 65–66
    new (Citizen Brand) steps for, 67–68, 108
    packaging design for, 169–171
    poor images of, 64
    research for, 64
Pharmacia, 66
Phillip Morris, 48, 63, 64, 209

Pier 1, 11
play, 14–15, 16, 23
population, 36
positive-engagement approach, 75, 77
poverty
    corporate/governmental concern for,
        60–61
    increase in, 61
    wealth v., xix
Power Bar, xxv, 108
Power DOT, 207
Prada, 91, 92–93, 170–171, 216, 220–222
    unique experience of, 220–222
preference, for sale, 79, 99
privacy, 190
Procter & Gamble (P&G), 12, 82–83, 229–230
product. *See also* creativity; innovation
    design, 165–169
    development, 53, 99–100, 110–111,
        122–123
    fulfilling needs with, 98
    innovate re-design of old, 105–112
    innovative design of new, 99–105
    less toxic, 63
    quality of, 79, 99
    voting for best, 140
product placement, 187, 189
profits, 50
promotion, xxv
protests, globalization, x, xi, xviii, 60–61
public spaces, 90–95

Q

Quaker Oats, 22, 107
QualiData Research, 211–212
Quicksilver, 70–71

R

Radio Shack, 109
Ralph Lauren, 142, 145, 177
Rand, Paul, 127
Rauschenberg, Robert, 94
reality check
    brands influence, 18–20
    plain truth desired in, 18, 20
    reality-based communication with, 18–19
    straight shooter approach in, 20
rebirth, xxx–xxxi
Red Bull, xxv, 192–193
Reebok, 30
Reef Check, 70
reputation
    from customer service, 217, 224, 226
    global, 60
    issues of, x

Books from Allworth Press

Emotional Branding: The New Paradigm for Connecting Brands to People
by Marc Gobé (hardcover, 6¼ × 9¼, 352 pages, $24.95)

Design Issues: How Graphic Design Informs Society
edited by DK Holland (paperback, 6¾ × 9⅞, 272 pages, $21.95)

Looking Closer 4: Critical Writings on Graphic Design
edited by Michael Bierut, William Drenttel, and Steven Heller
(paperback, 6¾ × 9⅞, 304 pages, 21.95)

Graphic Design Reader
by Steven Heller (paperback, 5½ × 8½, 320 pages, 19.95)

The Education of a Design Entrepreneur
edited by Steven Heller (paperback, 6¾ × 9⅞, 288 pages, $21.95)

Graphic Design History
edited by Steven Heller and Georgette Ballance
(paperback, 6¾ × 9⅞, 352 pages, $21.95)

Design Literacy: Understanding Graphic Design
by Steven Heller and Karen Pomeroy (paperback, 6¾ × 9⅞, 288 pages, $19.95)

Graphic Design and Reading: Explorations of an Uneasy Relationship
edited by Gunnar Swanson (paperback, 6¾ × 9⅞, 240 pages, $19.95)

AIGA Professional Practices in Graphic Design
edited by Tad Crawford (paperback, 6¾ × 9⅞, 320 pages, $24.95)

Business and Legal Forms for Graphic Designers
by Tad Crawford and Eva Doman Bruck
(paperback, 8½ × 11, 240 pages, includes CD-ROM, $24.95)

What Money Really Means
by Thomas M. Kostigen (paperback, 6 × 9, 240 pages, $19.95)

The Advertising Law Guide: A Friendly Guide for Everyone in Advertising
by Lee Wilson (paperback, 6 × 9, 208 pages, $19.95)

**The Trademark Guide: A Friendly Guide for Protecting and Profiting from
Trademarks** *by Lee Wilson* (paperback, 6 × 9, 192 pages, $18.95)

Turn Your Idea or Invention into Millions
by Don Kracke (paperback, 6 × 9, 224 pages, $18.95)

**The Entrepreneurial Age: Awakening the Spirit of Enterprise in People,
Communities, and Countries**
by Larry C. Farrell (hardcover, 6¾ × 9⅞, 352 pages, $24.95)

Please write to request our free catalog. To order by credit card, call 1-800-491-2808
or send a check or money order to Allworth Press, 10 East 23rd Street, Suite 510,
New York, NY 10010. Include $5 for shipping and handling for the first book ordered
and $1 for each additional book. Ten dollars plus $1 for each additional book if
ordering from Canada. New York State residents must add sales tax.

To see our complete catalog on the World Wide Web, or to order online, you can
find us at *www.allworth.com*.